D0786909

Marion Ledwig
Mixed Feelings
Emotional Phenomena, Rationality and Vagueness

Marion Ledwig

Mixed Feelings

Emotional Phenomena, Rationality and Vagueness

ontos
verlag

Frankfurt I Paris I Lancaster I New Brunswick

Bibliographic information published by Deutsche Nationalbibliothek
The Deutsche Nastionalbibliothek lists this publication in the Deutsche Nationalbibliographie; detailed bibliographic data is available in the Internet at http://dnb.ddb.de

North and South America by
Transaction Books
Rutgers University
Piscataway, NJ 08854-8042
trans@transactionpub.com

United Kingdom, Ire, Iceland, Turkey, Malta, Portugal by
Gazelle Books Services Limited
White Cross Mills
Hightown
LANCASTER, LA1 4XS
sales@gazellebooks.co.uk

Livraison pour la France et la Belgique:
Librairie Philosophique J.Vrin
6, place de la Sorbonne ; F-75005 PARIS
Tel. +33 (0)1 43 54 03 47 ; Fax +33 (0)1 43 54 48 18
www.vrin.fr

©2009 ontos verlag
P.O. Box 15 41, D-63133 Heusenstamm
www.ontosverlag.com

ISBN 978-3-86838-031-6

2009

Printed on acid-free paper
ISO-Norm 970-6
FSC-certified (Forest Stewardship Council)
This hardcover binding meets the International Library standard

Printed in Germany
by buch bücher dd ag

For Nicholas Rescher, Peter Machamer, Isaac Levi, Richard Otte, Christian Kanzian, and Gereon Wolters

Preface

This book opens up a new area of research by not only considering the rationality of such diverse phenomena as ordinary emotions, generalized anxiety disorder, social phobia, psychotic depression, major depressive disorder, and bipolar disorder, but also by evaluating the question whether the vagueness of these diverse disorders and emotions poses an obstacle to the rationality of these phenomena. As these emotional phenomena turn out to be vague on many different levels, an explanation is found for the millennia long dispute of which kind of phenomena fall under the emotions and whether such diverse phenomena as hope and alexithymia fall under the emotions. Since vagueness can be most easily identified in mixed feelings, the rationality of mixed feelings will also be dealt with. Finally, this book draws to a considerable extent on brain research in the neurosciences, psychology, and psychiatry to substantiate its position.

Marion Ledwig, Las Vegas, 01/14/2009

Acknowledgments

I would like to thank David Forman, Todd Jones, Matthew McAdam, Edward Slowik, John Sutton, and James Woodward and the colloquia at the University of Pittsburgh, James Madison University, and the University of Nevada at Las Vegas for very helpful discussions and constructive questions. This book was written during my visit at the University of Nevada, Las Vegas (2006-2009) and at the Loyola University of Chicago (summer 2008).

Table of Contents

Introduction

I. Aims and Background

In this book I seek to understand the connections between emotional phenomena, rationality, and vagueness. While the rationality of the emotions in its general form is no object of dispute any more, I have shown in my book *Emotions: Their Rationality and Consistency* (2006) in which different kinds of senses emotions and even moods can turn out to be rational, where rational in general is taken as being able to provide good reasons for one's emotions. Whilst my 2006 book advances the idea that the emotions, as a general category, can be termed rational, it does not investigate the question of whether there are arguments for the rationality of particular emotions, such as envy, fear, happiness, etc., which go beyond the arguments for the rationality of the emotions as a general category. Besides discussing whether emotional intelligence and emotional consistency are forms of emotional rationality, my account makes clear how far my view on the rationality of the emotions can be generalized: whether it can be generalized to computers having rational emotions and whether emotional responses to art can be considered to be rational.

At the end of the 2006 book I raised a hitherto unnoticed serious challenge for future research, namely that the emotions might turn out not to be rational after all, because the emotions are vague, where vagueness is taken to mean that there are borderline cases between the emotions, between the respective emotional phenomena, like moods, phobias, and affective disorders, and also between emotions and non-emotional phenomena, which might account for a long-lasting dispute about which phenomena fall under the emotions. In the case of mixed feelings, for instance, vagueness enters, because one might oscillate between being happy that one's friend has won the competition and being sad that one has lost the very same competition, and the question then is: where is the boundary between the different emotions? The reason why vagueness might make the emotions, moods, phobias, and affective disorders irrational is the following: how can anyone rationally base his or her choices on something like one's emotions if they are vague, meaning that in such a case one wouldn't base one's decisions on a solid basis, but on something slippery. That seems quite clearly irrational. In a similar vein Mahtani (2004) discusses the instability of vague terms. Changizi (1999), however, has already argued that as humans are computationally bound, avoiding vague concepts results in greater costs than adopting them, so that vague concepts are rational. Hence it still seems an open question whether emotional phenomena because of their vagueness are rational.

In accordance with this is that there are only a few remarks with regard to emotional phenomena and vagueness to be found in the literature: (1) Sloman (2002, p. 71) shortly states that the concept of emotion (and not only the respective phenomena) has vague boundaries. (2) Matthews et al. (2003, p. 516) consider the question whether emotional intelligence is a broad and vague concept. (3) Nussbaum (2001, p. 24, 133-135) distinguishes emotions, which have an object, even a vague or highly general or hidden one, from objectless moods. And (4) Carroll (2003, p. 533) highlights that a mood can be characterized only in very broad ways, such as up and down, thereby suggesting that moods are vague. In general, besides these very short remarks and a few others which we will encounter in the coming chapters, there is absolutely no single article or book on the connection between emotional phenomena, rationality, and vagueness in the whole psychological and philosophical literature up to now.

As a result of the last considerations, the following aims are proposed:

(1) determine which rationality concept is adequate for moods, phobias, and affective disorders. With regard to the emotions I advanced the following in Ledwig (2006): an emotion can be termed rational, if this particular emotion is reasonable, justified, warranted, and/or appropriate for a given situation. An emotion is reasonable, justified, etc. for a given situation, if the agent has good reasons for this particular emotion in the given situation. As the burden of explaining emotions lies with developmental processes, that is, with personal developmental and evolutionary processes, good reasons become those, which have been selected by means of developmental processes. Of course, I specified further what a good reason is in (2006); yet, listing this here would lead too far away. In (2006) I examined the following concepts of rationality coming from a decision-theoretic point of view and dismissed them as inadequate for the emotions: (1) one's emotions are rational if one follows

the principle of maximizing expected utility, which is a commonly used decision-theoretic principle; (2) Solomon's (1993, p. 222) view where every emotion maximizes one's personal dignity and self-esteem[1]; and (3) Kahneman et al.'s (1997) New Benthamism, where an emotion can be termed rational, if it maximizes the agent's total experienced utility of temporally extended outcomes. With regard to moods, phobias, and affective disorders, I will also consider all of the previously mentioned rationality concepts for their adequacy, if it is possible to apply them at all, but I will also apply the rationality concept of artificial intelligence to moods, phobias, and affective disorders, where

"reason could be mechanically explained as the operation of appropriate computational processes on symbols, where symbols are non-semantically indivisible items...and computational processes are mechanical, automatic processes that recognize, write and amend symbols in accordance with rules". (Clark 2003, p. 310)

However, if one takes this rationality concept of artificial intelligence seriously, then humans wouldn't turn out to be very rational because of all the reasoning mistakes they commit, as for instance the work of Tversky and Kahneman (1983) has shown.

Moods, phobias, and affective disorders are new and significant areas in relation to rationality, for no one in their wildest dreams would have considered these phenomena as in any way rational. In (2006) I have advanced that it is possible to justify a mood and even to reason about it, which might make moods rational. Yet, one might also want to look at which different kinds of functions moods, phobias, and affective disorders serve—do they have communicative, information selection, getting attention functions, etc.?—in order to determine their rationality.

(2) Determine which vagueness concept is adequate with regard to the emotions, moods, phobias, and affective disorders; Salmon (2007, p.

---

[1] Solomon (2007, p. 220), however, has revised his account of the rationality of the emotions in the mean time:

"Early in my work on emotions, I hazarded the very general empirical hypothesis that the ultimate strategy of all emotions was the maximization (or maintenance) of self-esteem....I have backed away from this overly bold hypothesis, which I now see as rendering all emotions overly self-interested and perhaps even narcissistic. I have also come to loathe the notion of 'self-esteem' because of its utter abuse by educators and pop-psych-gurus."

53), for instance, distinguishes between three different concepts of vagueness: vagueness in the sense of (1) the existence of borderline cases, in the sense of (2) "when several criteria exist for application of a term, with no specification of how many of the criteria have to be fulfilled or to what degree", and in the sense of (3) lack of specificity. It has to be pointed out that "vague" and "vagueness" are labels for real and common phenomena, for instance, whereas Bill Clinton is quite clearly not bald, Patrick Stewart (Captain Picard of *Star Trek*) is bald; yet, where is one supposed to draw the borderline between baldness and non-baldness? That seems difficult or even arbitrary. Moreover, there is a vast and highly technical and contentious philosophical literature surrounding the issue of vagueness.

(3) Determine whether the emotional phenomena are vague or their concepts. Up to now only Sloman (2002, p. 71) has noticed that one has to distinguish between the vagueness of emotional phenomena and their concepts, so this whole area is still untreated territory. If one, for instance, defined moods as persistent raw feelings, one could argue that this definition is vague; for what time-span does persistent amount to? Yet, one could also argue that the phenomenon is vague, because where is the border between being in a certain mood and not being in it any longer? That such a distinction between the vagueness of emotional phenomena and the vagueness of emotional concepts seems to be necessary becomes evident when one looks at Keefe's (2006, p. 15) statement that at least the possibility exists that there is a vague language in a non-vague world.

Similarly, Sorensen (2001, p. 121) points out that the vagueness of the term "cloud" cannot make the object cloud vague. In his epistemic account of vagueness, Williamson (1994, p. 6) also claims that the impossibility of knowing the boundaries of vague phenomena might be independent of the way in which the objects are represented. Yet, Williamson (1994, p. 257) in contradistinction to the foregoing states:

"To attribute vagueness to 'things themselves' just is to say that they have it irrespective of whether or how they are represented. But if vagueness is a matter of ignorance, it depends on whether or how things are represented to the supposedly unknowing subject. No representation: no distinction between vague and precise. Thus the epistemic view cannot consistently attribute vagueness to things themselves."

Sorensen (2001, p. 121) argues that an object language cannot be vague just because of the vagueness of a meta-language that is used to describe it. For some of the meta-languages which are used to describe algebraic chess notation are vague, such as the informal commentary in chess instruction booklets, whereas other meta-languages are precise, such as the various programming languages which are used in order to computerize chess. Likewise, Sorensen (2001, p. 122) claims that "An utterance can be a borderline case of a vague meta-linguistic term without having any vagueness of its own." Sorensen (2001, p. 122) gives the example of a half British/half American student who utters the sentence "The formula with Gödel number three billion is a logical truth.", where the student doesn't know what three billion really meant in order to illustrate such a borderline case.

(4) Determine whether the emotional phenomena are irrational, because they are vague. This issue is completely neglected in the literature so far, so this needs some especially thorough research. One could argue though that even if the boundaries between emotions, moods, etc. turn out to be vague, this does not have to have any consequences for the rationality of emotions, moods, etc., because these phenomena might still serve different rational functions.

II. Significance and Innovation

The **significance** of this project is to account for the following fundamental problem in emotion research thereby advancing the knowledge base of the discipline: there has been a dispute going on over the millennia concerning which phenomena fall into the category of the emotions, suggesting that the borderline between emotional phenomena and other phenomena such as desires and attitudes is rather vague. No one so far has yet tried to account for this ongoing problem by means of vagueness. Hence to account for this problem would resolve a long and serious conflict and above all would be a unique solution.

One might want to ask why nobody has accounted for this problem by means of vagueness? Braun and Sider (2007, p. 2) might have an answer to that:

12

"If semantic notions such as truth apply only to completely precise sentences, they do not apply to English or any other natural language. Thus, almost no English sentences are true (or false). We defend this seemingly radical and self-refuting conclusion by developing a theory of how vagueness is typically and harmlessly *ignored*."

That vagueness is typically ignored seems obvious, for who in their proper mind asks such questions as did the storm bring 1.5 inches of rain or did it actually bring 1.5000000000001 inches of rain, or is Timothy Williamson thin or is he really really thin, etc. and who besides philosophers and maybe even small children with their thirst of knowledge are interested in solving the sorites paradox all the time? Moreover, if we indulged in such questions all the time, we wouldn't get our everyday chores and work done and wouldn't be fit to manage our ordinary lives. So we not only ignore vagueness in fact in our everyday lives, but we also have to ignore it, otherwise our life would become an unbearable and unmanageable burden.

This project is **innovative** and **new**, because (1) it distinguishes between the vagueness of emotion terms and of emotional phenomena, (2) looks at the advantages and disadvantages of vagueness in these regards, (3) brings forth evidence for the vagueness of emotion terms and their corresponding phenomena, (4) determines which rationality concept is adequate for emotional phenomena, and (5) determines whether emotional phenomena despite their vagueness are rational.

Ordinary terms such as emotions are vague. Coates (1996, p. 3) has claimed that only ordinary concepts and not emotional phenomena are inherently vague and that the terms "emotion" and "mood" are such ordinary concepts. With regard to the latter, the position could be advanced that ordinary language is inherently vague, because its objects are inherently vague or the line between where an object or a phenomenon begins and ends cannot be drawn due to insufficient knowledge. With regard to the emotions, phobias, affective disorders, and moods, knowledge has increased over the last decades, with the advancement of neuroscience, cognitive science, etc., but is far from complete. Thus it is still an open question whether the emotions, phobias, affective disorders, and/or moods are vague, because the phenomena are vague or their concepts are vague or because enough knowledge has not been gathered yet to make that kind of a judgment.

Coates (1996, p. 167) suggests that ordinary language is inherently vague, because vague concepts, like "heap", are only used in contexts where a precise demarcation point would have little purpose. Whilst the terms "emotion", "phobia", "affective disorder", and "mood" are not as vague as "heap", precise demarcation points for these terms also do not seem to be needed in daily life, which might explain the vagueness of these concepts. The vagueness of these concepts might also be due to the fact that lots of different kinds of emotions, phobias, affective disorders, and moods fall under the respective terms, whereas one doesn't distinguish in ordinary language between different kinds of heaps. Moreover, with regard to certain phenomena, for instance, boredom or hope, it is an open question whether they belong to the emotions at all. So not only the distinction between the different emotional phenomena might suffer from vagueness, also the distinction to other not-emotional phenomena might turn out to be vague.

Ordinary phenomena such as emotions are vague. It might not only be the emotional concepts which are vague. Simons (1999) actually points out that many everyday objects are vague. Thus a corresponding vague ordinary language might actually capture the vagueness of its objects, which might be a good thing, in the sense that our language is not misleading, but rather represents the objects or phenomena as they really are. With regard to the emotions, vagueness enters in the cases where (1) either the feeling-tone of the respective emotion or the physiological response is rather weak, so that one cannot distinguish it clearly from cases where no emotion is given, or (2) where cases of mixed feelings are given, so that one has difficulty in stating which feeling is given.

With regard to the first point, if one for instance induced certain moods or emotions by music, which might not lead to big intensities of emotions, and then asked the respective person, do you feel any emotion at all or do you feel a certain desire or just a feeling, it would be interesting to see whether responses over large groups of experimental subjects were uniform or whether they were diverse. So, one could measure the intensity of emotions by means of verbal reports, but also by means of physiological responses, like for instance increase in neuronal activity, change in skin conductance, and the P300 component of evoked potentials, etc. With regard to the latter possibilities, it seems obvious, because these

14

components are measured on continuums, that it is very difficult to say when one has a significant increase in skin conductance, neuronal activity, and the P300 component of evoked potentials, and therefore even here vagueness in the sense of having trouble establishing clear borderlines enters into the picture. With regard to the former, verbal reports can be vague because of their possible lack of specificity, or they can be vague because the respective phenomena just differ from each other because they lie on continua where there are only quantitative and no qualitative distinctions to be found. Also if one advocates the view that emotions include judgments as an essential feature, some judgments because of their lack of specificity might be vague. Hence this might be another possibility for vagueness to arise. With regard to moods, it seems to be rather established that neurotransmitters have an effect on mood changes (cf. Griffiths 1997, chapter ten), and as neurotransmitters can be given in different degrees, so that even here a continuum is given, borderline cases might occur.

With regard to the second point mixed feelings have not been studied much in the philosophical literature yet (with the exception of Ledwig 2006 and Greenspan 1980) and it seems particularly puzzling to assume that mixed feelings, where the boundary between the respective feelings seems inherently vague or where one might not even experience any boundary at all because one experiences two feelings at the same time, might be rational to seek or have, so this needs to be explored further. In the case of mood-swings, as in the clinical case of bipolar disorder, where one goes from one extreme to the other extreme, the boundary between mania and depression seems to be vague, too, that is, how can one really establish that it is **this** point when one switches from mania to depression and/or vice versa. The latter seems to hold even more so for the weaker forms of bipolar disorder. Also if one is "moody", i. e. at one instance happy, at the next instance annoyed, at the third instance sad, etc. the boundary between these different instances is difficult to grasp clearly, like when exactly does the change happen from one instance to the next. Yet, philosophers might differ with regard to what they conceive moodiness to be. Damasio (1999, pp. 341-342, n. 10), for instance, writes:

"If people think that you are 'moody' it is because you have been sounding a prevailing emotional note (perhaps related to sadness or anxiety) consistently for a good part of the time or maybe you have changed your emotional tune unexpectedly and frequently....Because moods are dragged-out emotions along with the consequent feelings, moods carry over time the collections of responses that characterize emotions: endocrine changes, autonomic nervous system changes, musculoskeletal changes, and changes in the mode of processing of images....The term *affect* is often used as a synonym of 'mood' or 'emotion' although it is more general and can designate the whole subject matter we are discussing here: emotions, moods, feelings. Affect is the thing you display (emote) or experience (feel) toward an object or situation, any day of your life whether you are moody or not."

Yet, would we also call someone who is euphoric moody? I find that very difficult to accept. While moods in general range not only over negative prevailing emotional states, but also over positive prevailing emotion states, so that there is something like a euphoric mood, I doubt that there is something like euphoric moodiness. I admit, though, that one in fact calls persons moody who are in a negative prevailing emotional state. Yet, doesn't one also call someone moody, if one doesn't have the slightest clue why he or she is in such a state and that the arbitrariness of that state becomes most evident if one person changes from one emotional state to the next emotional state in rapid succession, so that the most prototypical case of moodiness seems to be the case of frequent change of emotional states?

Advantages and disadvantages of vagueness. According to Simons (1997), semantic vagueness concerns the meaning and reference of expressions. This might lead to interpretative indeterminacy. Is it a bad thing if ordinary language is inherently vague? From an evolutionary perspective this does not have to be the case as long as the species survives. In accordance with the latter, Greenspan (2001) points out that there might be good evolutionary reasons for depression, the emotional phenomenon. Also, if the aim is to motivate people, then a vague, general goal, such as "to preserve nature", might be very effective, whereas if the aim is definitely to reach that goal, then it has to be made more precise. Similarly, in philosophy, vague concepts might be a very good starting point for discussing philosophical concepts, but in order to reach an adequate analysis of a certain concept this would be insufficient and it would be necessary to be more precise. Also for a therapeutic intervention and especially for a successful diagnosis of affective disorders one needs a more precise analysis of the respective concepts and phenomena. That the diagnosis of mental disorders is still under constant revision and therefore has not reached a precise state yet can be seen by the fact that the American Psychiatric Association currently is working on the fifth edition of the Diagnostic and Statistical Manual of Mental Disorders DSM-V.

Coates (1996, p. 8) goes so far as to say: "sometimes a blurred picture may communicate more meaning than a sharp one." Yet identity conditions for vague concepts might be completely impossible, which might be a clear disadvantage. Furthermore, it might be questioned whether vague concepts can give the knowledge that philosophy actually wanted to deliver (cf. Coates 1996, p. 155). The law of excluded middle does not hold with regard to vague concepts, which might make logic more cumbersome, too. Hence, vagueness needs to be excluded from the concepts as much as possible. With regard to moods and their boundaries with the emotions, this might still be possible, because moods have not been studied that much in philosophy, let alone their relationships to other phenomena. With regard to the emotions, further research in neuroscience, cognitive science, and philosophy of mind and also attempts to synthesize emotions in computers is likely to reveal further insights into the emotions and might perhaps lead to a theory of the emotions that is not vague. Something similar might be possible for phobias and affective disorders. That one is able to synthesize emotions in computers might sound far-fetched, but actually there have been studies which developed software programs competing for space on the computer's hard disk employing Darwin's principles of evolution by natural selection, namely heredity, mutation, and differential selection, so that the better software programs survived, were able to reproduce themselves in different degrees, which included random errors (= mutation) in the reproduction process (cf. Evans 2001; Ledwig 2006). Perhaps if one just waited long enough, software programs with emotions might develop. This seems reasonable if one assumes that an intelligent being has to have emotions in order to survive.

Evidence for the vagueness of emotional phenomena. As many everyday objects, such as the sun or human beings, are vague (Simons

1999), it seems not impossible that phenomena like "emotions", "phobias", "affective disorders", and "moods" will turn out to be vague, too. Furthermore, evidence for the vagueness of emotions might arise from people's general inability to classify their own emotions. For example, on meeting a friend not seen for a very long time might generate feelings that are not mixed feelings as such, but rather feelings that are hard to put a label to. Mixed feelings are only insofar a case of vagueness, when feelings oscillate between two different feelings over a time-span and where the boundary between the two different feelings is difficult to locate. That is, mixed feelings are so called, because the different feelings experienced do not blend into each other, and not because they are so mixed that they produce another feeling, like in the case of mixed colors. In the case of mixed feelings one is still able to clearly identify which feelings are involved. It might be the case though that the respective feelings like the feelings involved in hate and love lie along a continuum and that in the case where the feelings oscillate between the different poles it might be hard to determine which feeling is given at a certain time, because the borderline between hate and love is not clearly defined. Also in the case where either one of the poles of the experienced feelings or even both lie in close proximity to the borderline of the two respective feelings as such, vagueness might be involved, for the simple reason that it seems difficult to identify a clear borderline. Also vagueness enters into the problem when feelings of two or more different people are involved. For feelings are a subjective thing unless one employs an objective measure, like for instance physiological responses, so that it is difficult to compare the intensity and quality of feelings of two persons with each other. Yet even with objective measures already problems appear, for Kendall et al. (2004, p. 336) report that parents of children diagnosed with generalized anxiety disorder don't agree in all the cases on the presence or absence of specific objective somatic symptoms experienced by the child with their children and that parents attribute significantly more somatic symptoms than their diagnosed children to their children.

Emotional phenomena, vagueness and rationality. While I have already dealt with the different ways emotions can turn out to be rational in Ledwig (2006), I have not looked at the connection between vagueness and the rationality of the emotions. Considering the function that moods serve,

Carroll (2003, p. 530) plausibly speculates that moods probably give the organism information about the agent's levels of energy and tension. It would be irrational for a depressed agent to go out and attempt to rescue the whole world, because he feels lacking in energy for that, or perhaps even anything right now, but if he is in a good mood, this would seem much more rational to try. Yet where is the boundary to be set between being in a good mood and being in a bad mood? Sloman (2002, p. 72) points out that some moods might be even rational or adaptive reactions to certain environments. For example, in an environment where partly risky actions fail most of the time, this might induce a cautious mood, to always take the less risky alternative, leading to more success in the long run. Yet, one can alternatively explain this fact by developing a cautious attitude and not by developing a cautious mood. But even here: it might be problematic to evaluate which the less risky alternative is, something might be less risky with regard to monetary issues, but more risky with regard to health. So saying that something is risky is very vague indeed.

With regard to phobias, that phobias are evolutionarily beneficial and therefore might be termed rational can be supported by the fact that the most frequently diagnosed phobias, such as phobias of insects, snakes, and heights, are directed at situations that reflect an evolutionary preparation to be sensitive to dangers that ancestral human populations encountered (cf. D'Arms and Jacobson 2003, p. 141). Yet one might want to ask why are humans not phobic with regard to ticks which look so similar to spiders and which are carriers of so many diseases and why aren't humans phobic to large predators, like lions or bears? Perhaps one needn't develop a phobia with regard to large predators, for the simple reason that the huge size of these animals was already sufficient to activate a fear response. With regard to ticks, one could say a phobia is also not needed, for according to Lorenz (1943) touch stimuli, given by an insect crawling on the skin, release the response of throwing it off with a quick movement of the hand. Moreover, being bitten by a tick does not lead to immediate death, although some of the tick-borne diseases actually can lead to death, so that at least immediate survival is not at stake. The latter might be at stake with regard to certain spiders and snakes, though. That the classification of phobias is open to the problem of vagueness might already derive from the fact that if one follows the DSM-IV classification of specific phobias, something can only be classified as a specific phobia if one exhibits persistent fear, where it seems unclear where exactly persistency starts and where it ends. What is of particular interest with regard to the rationality of phobias, the person who has a phobia recognizes that the phobia is excessive or unreasonable, while in children this feature may be absent according to the DSM-IV which might indicate the influence the person's environment has on the person classifying his phobia as irrational.

Another point of interest is that the majority of children with a specific phobia, like spider phobia, also suffer from another anxiety disorder (Ginsburg and Walkup 2004, p. 175) which might indicate that the boundary between the different anxiety disorders is a vague one. Similarly in a study of adolescents with a specific phobia Essau et al. (2000) discovered that this mental disorder goes together with another anxiety disorder in 47% of the cases followed by depressive disorders (36%) and somatoform disorders (33%). Moreover, ca. 80% of those with social anxiety disorder as young adults had an affective disorder or an anxiety disorder as adolescents (Newman et al. 1996). In contrast to that Perwien and Bernstein (2004, pp. 275-276) report that of the anxiety disorders examined, separation anxiety disorder had the highest rate of recovery with 95.7% and a very low rate with regard to the development of a new anxiety disorder (8.3%). Now just because one anxiety disorder goes together with other affective disorders does not necessarily mean that the boundary drawn between the different disorders is not adequate, after all, if someone has AIDS there are lots of different diseases going along with it, too, yet the possibility exists in the case of overlapping affective disorders that either the boundary is very vague or that the boundary established was not adequate for capturing the respective affective disorder. Yet in the case of AIDS the different diseases going along with it are of different kinds, such as diverse infections caused by bacteria, viruses, fungi, and parasites, and even various cancers, whereas in the case of different anxiety disorders, these at least have some features in common, such as persistent and excessive worry, sleeping problems, and clinically significant distress or impairment in social, occupational, or other important areas of functioning. Thus the boundary between different anxiety disorders may be very vague. With regard to the rationality of anxiety disorders, this might be possible.

For cognitive factors, especially the way people think and interpret stressful events, play a critical role in how anxiety is caused (Barlow et al., 1996). Hence it might be feasible to justify one's anxiety disorder and even to reason about it, which might make anxiety disorders rational.

Promoting and maintaining good health. If one can show that emotional phenomena despite their vagueness serve different rational functions, the public and the individual attitudes towards emotions as a burden would change making it easier for everybody to live with their emotions and even to **utilize** them for various purposes such as indicators that a certain piece of information is important, that something needs attention, that one wants to communicate something, that someone needs care, etc. thereby promoting and maintaining good health.

If one can demonstrate the rationality of emotional phenomena, this might lead to a different attitude towards these phenomena in the public, but also have an effect on therapeutic treatment of the different affective disorders seeing these disorders in a more positive light. If being in a certain mood leads to a focusing of attention on certain things (cf. Bach 1994), being in a depressed mood might lead to a focusing of attention on negative things. In accordance with this Wenzlaff et al. (2002, p. 544) report a failure of thought suppression among a depressive group. Also if emotional phenomena turn out to be rational, the emotionality of women might not be considered as so negative anymore—you are just being irrational—so that one form of discrimination against women might not appear so much so often anymore, which might lead to better health and productivity in women in the long run. Furthermore, men in opposition to women usually deny when they are depressed. If emotional phenomena turn out to be rational, men might find it easier to admit their depression leading to better possibilities for successful psychotherapeutic treatment and therefore for their own health and productivity over time. In this way also gender inequalities get reduced. Given the rationality of emotional phenomena, this implies that one can reason with the person about their emotional rationality which underscores the success of diverse cognitive psychotherapies, like for instance rational emotive behavior therapy. In this regard, my book is able to provide a theoretical basis for some of those cognitive therapies.

III. Approach and Methodology

The **conceptual framework, design, and methods of the project** are as follows: (1) having a psychologically realistic account of the different emotional phenomena by taking into account the psychological literature, (2) determining which rationality and vagueness concept is adequate for the different emotional phenomena by logic and scientific standards such as preciseness, and (3) evaluating whether the different emotional phenomena are vague and/or rational by analysis.

Philosophical and psychological literature. With regard to the philosophical literature, the topic of moods is still an unexplored subject with the exception of Carroll (2003), Griffiths (1997), Ledwig (2006), and Sizer (2000), and a few others. Also with regard to phobias and affective disorders one finds almost nothing in the philosophical literature (cf. Greenspan 1981 as an exception). In this regard it is absolutely necessary to have a look at the psychological literature, for (1) the different emotional phenomena have been studied to a considerable degree in psychology and (2) in one's account of the emotional phenomena it is of utmost importance that the account with which one comes up is **psychologically realistic**. The latter might be self-evident, but one finds enough philosophers who don't see the need to have a psychologically realistic account of the different emotional phenomena. Yet in my opinion this would amount to building castles in the air, which might be of interest for their fictional beauty, but otherwise worthless for clinical interventions in order to better an affective disorder like for instance depression. Hence I will take into account the newest results in neuroscience and cognitive science to have a psychologically realistic and empirically informed account of the diverse emotional phenomena.

Rationality and vagueness. With regard to rationality, one finds different accounts of rationality in philosophy, economics, and psychology, and I will look at all three different areas in order to determine which account of rationality is adequate with regard to the particular subject area under consideration. As my dissertation was in rational decision theory (Ledwig 2000), which ranges over philosophical, psychological, and economical accounts, I bring considerable expertise in evaluating diverse accounts of rationality with regard to their adequacy for the corresponding emotional phenomena. With regard to vagueness, I have explored the connection between vagueness, ordinary language, and common sense in 2007 and have hinted at the problem vagueness might cause for the rationality of emotions in 2006. Thus my present book builds on my work in 2006, but makes it more precise, elaborates on it and extends it by making clear how exactly vagueness can pose a problem for the rationality of the emotions and the rationality of the other emotional phenomena. In this regard, it is of utmost importance to determine which vagueness concept is adequate for the diverse emotional phenomena or whether each emotional phenomenon needs its own vagueness concept.

With regard to the adequacy of rationality concepts and vagueness concepts for emotional phenomena, certain concepts might rule themselves out, for the simple reason that they lead to absurd consequences; for example, it seems absurd to claim that one maximizes one's utility by crying when one is sad (Ledwig 2006). Other rationality and vagueness concepts might rule themselves out because counterexamples show that they are inadequate for the subject matter under consideration. Still others might rule themselves out, because they are not precise enough or cannot be given a coherent interpretation. Sorensen (1985) has, for instance, claimed that the concept "vagueness" is itself vague and here it might be of interest to see which vagueness concept he refers to and how one can distinguish vagueness from ambiguity and generality. In this regard it is also of interest to note that Varzi (2003) has demonstrated that Sorensen's argument involves circular reasoning and here it needs to be demonstrated whether the circle is a vicious one or not. Hence also logical considerations enter the subject matter under consideration.

As a result of the previous deliberations, the following chapters of this book are proposed: chapter one is on vagueness, where the different theories of vagueness are explored and made salient for the subject matter under investigation. Chapter two presents emotion theories as preparation for the subsequent discussion of the rational functions of the emotions in chapter four. Chapter three on the brain and the emotions points out the role the brain plays with regard to the emotions. Chapter five deals with hope and alexithymia—two phenomena where it is unclear whether they belong to the emotions. While chapter six explores vagueness and rationality in mixed feelings, chapter seven deals with vagueness and rationality in anxiety disorders. The last chapter investigates how and in which way vagueness and rationality figure into moods.

Chapter 1 Vagueness

The history of vagueness. Vagueness entered the philosophical debate with the sorites paradox (for an excellent review of the history of vagueness see Williamson 1994). According to Keefe and Smith (1999, p. 3) the sorites paradox[2]—sorites comes from the Greek word "soros" meaning heap—was first discovered by Eubolides. Rescher (2008, p. 1) states that "Eubolides of Megara (b. ca. 400 BC) was the most prominent and influential member of the Megarian school of dialecticians as whose head he succeeded its founder, Euclid of Megara, a pupil of Socrates."

Here is one example of the sorites paradox:

Base step: a collection of one billion grains of sand is a heap.

Induction step: if a collection of n grains of sand is a heap, then so is a collection of n-1 grains.

Conclusion: a collection of one grain of sand is a heap.[3]

The conclusion is quite clearly false and the base step seems quite clearly to be true, so there must be something wrong with the induction step or with the multiple combination of the base step and the induction step, namely **modus ponens**.[4] Yet, philosophers are reluctant to give up modus ponens and philosophers are reluctant to give up the **induction step**,

---

[2] Sorensen (2001, p. 122) points out with regard to the sorites paradox that while logicians were right in thinking that the sorites paradox arises because of vague predicates, they were wrong in thinking that the vague predicate must appear within the argument itself, for it is enough if one has vague predicates in the meta-language that describes the sorites argument. Yet, Williamson (1994, p. 298, n. 3) rightly emphasizes that a typical sorites argument is relevantly similar to the Heap and the Bald Man, that is to say, a typical sorites argument should be formulated without equivocation, the minor premise should be evident, the key expression should be vague, the difference between successive members of the series should be small enough, etc.

[3] Rescher (2008, p. 17, n. 2) points out that the paradox can not only be developed progressively starting from non-heapness, but can also be developed regressively starting from heapness. The regressive style of reasoning is called Galenic after Galen, while the progressive style Goclenic after Randolph Goclenius.

[4] Some philosophers try to rescue modus ponens by claiming that one can construe the sorites paradox also without modus ponens. Yet, if one is still able to construe the sorites paradox with modus ponens and if this is a sound construction, I don't see how the other construction can rescue modus ponens.

because for classical logic modus ponens is essential and because on the one hand the induction step resembles mathematical induction and on the other hand for any kind of logic one depends on the view that multiple applications of proof steps are admissible procedures for proofs (cf. also Keefe 2006, p. 20). As a result one has to believe in something **incoherent**, which is irrational.

Yet, Keefe (2006, p. 24) states: "Communication using vague language is overwhelmingly successful and we are never in practice driven to incoherence (a point stressed by Wright, e. g. 1987, p. 236)." Incoherence wouldn't be such a bad result, if one could isolate cases of vagueness. However, this seems to be not possible for the simple fact that vagueness seems to be a **ubiquitous** phenomenon. In this regard Dummett (1999, pp. 108-109) comes to the following conclusion:

"A satisfactory account of vagueness ought to explain two contrary feelings we have: that expressed by Frege that the presence of vague expressions in a language invests it with an intrinsic incoherence; and the opposite point of view contended for by Wittgenstein, that vagueness is an essential feature of language."

In a similar vein Keefe (2006, p. 46) points out that no theory of vagueness should imply that we don't understand vague languages and that we don't use vague languages successfully; moreover, a theory of vagueness shouldn't rule out the possibility of an explanation of how we manage to accomplish these tasks.

Sharp boundaries. Another way out of the sorites paradox is to claim that "heap" and predicates such as "bald" actually do have sharp boundaries, for four grains can suffice to make a heap and no one is bald unless they have absolutely no hair; yet, even if one accepts sharp boundaries in these cases, the same kind of solution cannot be given for most candidate vague predicates, such as "nearly bald", "tall", and "clever" (cf. Keefe and Smith 1999, p. 2, n. 2). However, a relatively similar approach has been defended by epistemicists, such as Sorensen (2001) and Williamson (1994), with the important **proviso** that these sharp boundaries are **hidden** to us, so that vagueness amounts to ignorance (cf. also Rescher 2008).

Yet, then a key question for the epistemic view is, how does it come that we are ignorant about where the boundaries of vague phenomena lie

(Keefe and Smith 1999, p. 7)? Keefe and Smith (1999, p. 7) report that "Cargile suggests that it is 'absurd to make an effort to find out' those facts (p. 96)." And one may add, if it is absurd or even meaningless to make an effort, then it is no wonder that we don't know. Similarly, Rescher (2008, p. 16) states that "greater detail is generally not needed in the relevant contexts of operation. (We do not need to know whether the approaching storm will bring 1 or 1.5 inches of rain for deciding whether or not to take an umbrella.)" Yet, while in cases such as "tall", "bald", etc. it indeed—under most circumstances—seems absurd, a waste of energy and time, and irrational to make an effort to find out where the boundary lies, there quite clearly seem to be cases where we are morally motivated and where it seems to be vital to find out where the boundary lies, such as in the case of when do we start to become persons to have legitimate answers for abortion cases or when are we really dead to have legitimate answers for organ donation cases. Yet, Rescher (2008, p. 16) points out that "The fact of it is that reality is so vastly complex in its mode of operation that a shortfall of detail in our description of it is an inevitable reality. In characterizing the real the indecisiveness of vagueness is not a failing but an inevitability." While I tentatively agree with the latter claim, one might also think that this hinges on whether we are able to find all the laws in the world and whether we are able to find the smallest particle in the world. So far there doesn't seem an end to finding the smallest particle and we are still far away from discovering all the laws which hold in our world. Besides, there is the fact that we are not able to describe far away worlds (such as other galaxies, stars, planets, etc.) in any way accurately. From an evolutionary perspective, as long as the species survives, there doesn't seem to be a need to find out the boundaries for vague phenomena even if we consider the abortion and organ donation cases. Similarly, Sorensen (2001, p. 134) explains our view to consider **vagueness as meaninglessness** by claiming that a statement is borderline when neither it nor its negation has a truthmaker.

Another criticism of the epistemic view is to point out that whereas there may be natural boundaries for natural kind terms, there are no such natural boundaries for vague expressions. (Keefe 2006, pp. 76-77). Yet, to argue like that is already to presuppose that there are no natural boundaries for vague expressions. That is to say, just because the boundaries in the

28

case of vague expressions don't show the same kinds of characteristics as in the case of natural kind terms, doesn't legitimate the conclusion that there are no boundaries at all. Yet, Williamson (1994, p. 269) admits that vagueness is one manifestation of the fact that our classifications are not determined by natural boundaries; in particular, he points out that the cause of our ignorance is indeed conceptual. Yet, does it have to be conceptual? Couldn't it also be that objects are vague? (For a discussion of this point, see later sections.)

Another line of criticism against the epistemic view is advanced by Cargile (1999, p. 97):

"this final disappearance of tadpoleness from Amphibius takes place at an instant is just as surprising, and the determination of this instant is just as mysterious, as in the case of the property of being a tadpole."

Yet, just because something is surprising, is no good reason for rejecting the possibility that such a boundary exists. After all, being surprised by things seems to be a common phenomenon. Just imagine yourself working on a bouldering problem, you have tried it so much and in lots of different ways and nothing worked. You just didn't get it done. Then after several weeks you try yourself on the same problem again and then out of a sudden it works. You have crossed the boundary. You are very surprised about yourself and mostly don't have the slightest clue what you did different or what kind of skill has improved in the mean time. And also here it is not obvious to you when you actually crossed the threshold of being able to solve that problem. Similar kinds of cases one can see in adolescent development where from one day to the next a change in attitude might be observed, a mature behavior which was not present before at all. Another case is where from one day to the next, out of a sudden, grief might be overcome or a depression might be left behind. Hence, it might be the case that such changes take place rather in an instant than over a period of time.

Keefe (2006, pp. 71-72, n. 6) points out another criticism against the epistemic view:

"Horwich 1997 notes the 'paralysis of judgement' typically witnessed in borderline cases and uses this to criticise and propose a replacement for Williamson's characterisation of vagueness in terms of ignorance. In reply (1997b) Williamson imagines an 'opinionated macho community' where there is no hesitation over assertions about borderline cases, but the pattern of use of the words shows them to be vague: he concludes that the paralysis of judgement is not necessary for vagueness."

After all these criticisms one might want to ask what speaks actually in favor of the epistemic view that we are ignorant of the boundaries with regard to vague phenomena? Sorensen (2001, pp. 1-2) motivates his account by comparing the sorites paradox with an argument which held prior to Albert Einstein's embedding the speed of light as a speed limit in the best theory of acceleration. Here is the argument which most physicists held to be true before Einstein's discovery (Sorensen 2001, p. 2):

"1. Any object can move at least 1 meter per second.
2. If an object can move at least n meters per second, then it can move at least $n+1$ meters per second.
3. Therefore, there is no upper bound on how fast an object can move....

Einstein showed that the second premise fails when $n = 299,792,458$ (the speed of light in a vacuum)."

Williamson (1994, p. 204) comes up with a similar scientific example to motivate his account; in particular, he claims with regard to Goldbach's Conjecture that state of the art knowledge considers it as a humanly unknowable, metaphysically necessary truth and that vague truths can be in that very same position. Moreover, he points out in that very same passage that metaphysically necessary claims, such as "Everyone with physical measurements m is thin", can be as unknowable as physically contingent claims, such as "Timothy Williamson is thin".

What these examples show is that at least with regard to certain phenomena boundaries exist which are unknowable or have been unknowable for us. Yet, these cases seem to be relatively remote from our paradigmatic vague predicates, such as "tall", "bald", etc., so that one might doubt whether these analogies are justified. Yet, perhaps there might be other kinds of phenomena which are unknowable for us and which are a little bit closer to our paradigmatic vague predicates.

In this regard, Rescher (2008, p. 5) comes up with a whole category of predicates which are unknowable for us; he calls them vagrant predicates: "F is a *vagrant* predicate iff $(\exists u)Fu$ is true while nevertheless

30

Fu_0 is false for each and every specifically identified u_0." Examples of such vagrant predicates are according to Rescher (2008, p. 4):
"- a thing whose identity will never be known.
- an idea that has never occurred to anybody.
- a person whom everyone had utterly forgotten.
- an occurrence that no-one ever mentioned.
- an integer that is never individually specified."
Moreover, Rescher (2008, p. 5) highlights with regard to vagrant predicates that they are referentially inaccessible; yet "to indicate them concretely and specifically as bearers of the predicate at issue is straightaway to unravel them as so-characterized items." Nevertheless it is a fact that such items exist, although we are not able to identify them, Rescher (2008, p. 5) maintains.

In my opinion Rescher's vagrant predicates are indeed closer to our paradigmatic vague predicates than Goldbach's conjecture and Einstein's speed of light. Yet, are all predicates which are unknowable for us vagrant? That doesn't seem so obvious. For other kinds of phenomena which are unknowable for us are, for example, what it feels like to hear like a bat, what it feels like to purr like a cat, what it feels like to be you, what it feels like to be of the opposite sex, what it feels like to live in another century, what it feels like to win eight gold medals in one Olympic game, or even what it feels like to climb a 5.15 which most of us will never be able to do in their life time, for only a few climbers in the world are able to do that. Yet, while these examples are unknowable for us now or in most of the given cases (eight Olympic medals in one Olympic game and the 5.15 climber), it is not obvious that in another time one is not able to know them. That is to say, nothing in these latter examples indicates that they are unknowable in principle. They might just be contingently unknowable. Whereas vagrant predicates are in principle unknowable, there are also other predicates which might be just contingently unknowable.

The question then becomes what holds with regard to vague predicates: (1) is the borderline in principle unknowable or (2) is it just contingently unknowable or (3) might there be certain cases where the borderline is in principle unknowable and certain other cases where the borderline is contingently unknowable? While Rescher (2008, p. 9) indeed holds that the boundary is vagrant and therefore is in principle undeterminable, I am not so sure whether this is really the case. For if one looks at such vague predicates as being tall or being intelligent nothing in how the predicates are paraphrased really indicates that the boundary is in principle unknowable, so on first impression one would have to conclude that such predicates appear more contingently unknowable than principally unknowable. Hence one would have to draw the conclusion that anyone who wants to claim that the boundary of vague predicates are principally unknowable would have to prove that, so that the burden of proof is on them and not on the one who maintains that they are contingently unknowable.

Rescher (2008, pp. 10-11) tries to support his position that the borderline with regard to vague predicates is principally unknowable by further examples

"that are real but unidentifiable. As regards the past, there is many a saying in circulation whose inaugurator nobody can by now identify. As regards the future, the person who will win the 2020 U.S. presidential election is for-sure currently alive and active among us, but cannot yet possibly be identified. And as regards abstractors there must exist an unprovable arithmetical theorem whose Gödel number is the lowest—but this too cannot be identified."

While on first sight all of these examples quite clearly appear as examples which are in principle unknowable, it is not obvious in which respect these examples are similar to vague predicates. As long as this is not established it could also be possible that the boundary in vague predicates is just contingently unknowable. Moreover, with regard to sayings in circulation where one doesn't know who inaugurated it, it might still be possible to find some such inaugurator—at least in principle nothing speaks against it. That is to say, in history, archaeology, paleontology, or even physics (what was there before the big bang?) one might still find out things about the past which one currently doesn't know. Also if the universe were deterministic and we knew all the initial conditions and laws holding in the universe, we should be able to identify the to be elect U.S. president of 2020.

With regard to examples of vague predicates, such as being tall, intelligent, etc. no borderline cases seem to be given—at least on first sight. Yet, according to Williamson (1994, p. 216) this doesn't have to be the case, for he assimilates ignorance in borderline cases to a wider phenomenon, namely a kind of ignorance which is given whenever our knowledge is inexact. As a consequence of this, Williamson's epistemic view of vagueness implies a form of realism, so that the truth about the boundaries of our concepts can outrun our capacity to know it; if one denies the epistemic view of vagueness, one imposes limits on realism, and if one asserts it, one endorses realism in a thorough-going form (Williamson 1994, p. 4). Yet, couldn't one likewise argue that the limits of realism depend on what we conceive realism to be? However, also Rescher (2008, p. 6) is of the opinion that "vagrant predicates mark a cognitive divide between reality and our knowledge of it."

Besides these unknowable phenomena with sharp boundaries, which other kinds of reasons could one have to postulate sharp boundaries for vague phenomena? Sorensen's (2001, p. 1) reasoning with regard to the sorites paradox leads him to reject the induction step which leads to the conclusion that there are sharp boundaries for vague phenomena:

"The first premise is obviously true. The conclusion is obviously false. Therefore my only recourse is to reject the induction step....If I reject the induction step, I thereby accept its negation. The negation is true only if there is a value for n such that n grains of sand is a heap and n-1 grains is not a heap. In other words, there must be a sharp threshold at which an eroding heap turns into a non-heap."

Besides the induction step, Sorensen (2001, p. 176) retains classical logic, though. Also Williamson's (1994, p. 3) account is in accordance with classical logic or semantics. Yet, does it have to be the case that if one rejects the induction step that one has to accept its negation? Isn't a third choice possible? If one wants to retain classical logic, this is not possible. Yet, if one doesn't mind giving up classical logic at least partially, this is possible. Moreover, couldn't one even argue that the induction step as it stands should be more qualified, such as if a collection of n grains of sand is a heap, then so is a collection of n-1 grains given that one doesn't go below a certain number which indicates the borderline between heaps and non-heaps and which reflects one's definition of heapness? This kind of reply might also be the reply of the ordinary person. In this regard, Braun and Sider (2007, p. 15) state:

"Press a non-philosopher on exactly when a non-heap turns into a heap, and she will invariably reply, 'It depends on what you mean by "heap". Confront her with the sorites, and she will say: 'Define your terms. Tell me what "heap" means, and I'll tell you which premise of the argument is false.'"

Williamson's (1994, p. xi) explanation for our ignorance of sharp boundaries with regard to vague phenomena is his margin for error principle. That is to say, vague knowledge demands a margin for error (1999, p. 279) and his margin for error principle is formulated thus (Williamson 1999, p. 278): "If x and y differ in physical measurements by less than c and x is known to be thin, y is thin.", where c is a small and non-zero constant.

From the above discussion one could get the impression that if one talks of hidden boundaries, these boundaries are absolute. Yet, Williamson and Sorensen seem to be of different opinions with regard to this problem. Whereas Sorensen (2001, p. 39) claims that only absolute borderline cases are cases of vagueness, Williamson (1999, p. 278) opts for relative borderline cases as we can see from the following passage: "On the epistemic view, the boundary of 'thin' is sharp but unstable. Suppose that I am on the 'thin' side of the boundary, but only just. If our use of 'thin' had been very slightly different, as it easily could have been, I would have been on the 'not thin' side." Yet, Sorensen (2001, p. 2) also admits that context counts, for "The threshold will vary from heap to heap and from mode of decomposition to mode of decomposition. Context counts!" To render Sorensen coherent and to see to the possibility that even Williamson turns out to be an absolutist one could advocate the view that with regard to particular contexts in the case of Sorensen or under particular language uses in the case of Williamson absolute borderlines are possible.

Slippery slope fallacy vs. mathematical induction. Another way out of the sorites paradox is to argue that the sorites paradox commits the slippery slope fallacy, but then any kind of mathematical induction seems to be such a fallacy. Yet, even if we commit the slippery slope fallacy here, there might be even advantages going together with vague languages. For Sainsbury (1999, p. 259) states: "vagueness offers freedom. It can be permissible to draw a line even where it is not mandatory to do so." In this regard, Sainsbury (1999, p. 264) particularly highlights the fact that only a pragmatic justification could be found for drawing a line with regard to vague phenomena. If one, for instance, considers the different driving ages in particular countries, in Germany one has to be 18 years old in order to apply for a driver's license, while it is 16 in the U.S.A. This makes practical sense with respect to the different countries, for in the U.S.A. the distances are very large, usually there is not a good public transport system available, and there is no German Autobahn with no speed limits, so that it is possible, better, and even not so dangerous that the children get their driving licenses earlier, while in Germany the distances are not as large and there is ample public transportation given and there is the Autobahn with no speed limits, so that it is not necessary to have a driver's license already at the age of 16; moreover, it might be even better in the case of Germany to not have a driver's license at the age of 16, because teenagers and their recklessness might lead to many driving accidents with high speed. So, with regard to vagueness, it might give you some freedom to set boundaries pragmatically which one might consider an advantage of vagueness.

Yet, there might be also disadvantages going together with vagueness. According to Williamson (1994, p. 46) Frege was of the opinion that we cannot reason reliably with a vague language. Moreover, Williamson (1994, p. 46) claims that it is commonly believed that successful inquiry involves a movement from vagueness towards precision. Yet, perhaps in some cases too much precision might not be comprehensible by a human being any longer and perhaps in some cases too much precision might be fatal in cases one needs an instantaneous decision and/or action. Also wouldn't one consider it reasonable to have as much precision as is necessary to accomplish a certain task? Yet, in certain cases to acquire and aim for more precision might be considered a waste of energy and/or time and therefore not very rational.

Phenomena which are vague. Keefe (2006, p. 3) points out that most of our language turns out to be vague. In particular, Keefe and Smith (1999, p. 5) highlight the fact that not only predicates are vague, but also adverbs like "quickly", quantifiers like "many", modifiers like "very", the singular term "the grandest mountain in Scotland", and also many terms with plural reference like "the high mountains of Scotland". Keefe (2006, p. 14) furthermore claims that there can be vague dyadic relational expressions, such as "is a friend of" which has pairs that are borderline cases; moreover, comparatives can be vague, particularly when they are related to a multi-dimensional positive, and superlatives.

Given that most of our language is vague, one might want to know why is this so. (1) One possibility is that most of our language is vague because most of the phenomena which our language denotes are vague. (2) Williamson (1994, p. 81) points out that on Hempel's view the vagueness of our language has to do with the fact that all words are learned from particular instances of their use. The latter seems to me a reasonable account of how the vagueness of our language could have arisen, for in order to use a word properly one analyses the different occasions when a word is used and then abstracts from that. As we humans are only finite creatures, such an analysis and abstraction can only be finite, leaving the possibility and even the inevitability for imprecision, that is vagueness. Even if proper language acquisition and use doesn't go by means of analysis and abstraction, but rather by means of association of words with particular situations or objects of which we might not even be aware, imprecision and therefore vagueness might result. For the associations might be erroneous, because human beings are imperfect. Moreover, as human beings are finite, they are also imperfect. (3) Another possibility of how we could have ended up with a vague language is that it is a blur of precise languages (cf. Keefe 2006, p. 141, with regard to Lewis's account of vagueness). Given that we have as a starting point that people had in the beginning precise languages, since children learn languages by the help of many people, the result would be that the children's language turned out to be a blur of these precise ones. Yet, is it reasonable to assume that people had in the beginning precise languages? That seems rather implausible to assume, for building up an adequate vocabulary might have taken quite some time. As a result coarse categories were probably the starting point of how the different languages evolved. Yet, the first two possibilities seem to me good contenders for why most of our language is vague.

Keefe (2006, p. 15) claims that while thoughts and beliefs show the central characteristics of vagueness, controversial cases might be perceptions. Williamson (1994, p. 93), for instance, states with regard to Waismann's account of vagueness that he argued for the view that since our visual impressions have vague content, one needs vague language to

36

report them. As some emotion theories defend the view that emotions are identical with or at least include judgments and as judgments are based on beliefs or even might be identical with beliefs, at least these emotion theories would have to deal with the issue that emotions are vague, given that beliefs turn out to be vague. As it seems very likely that most of our beliefs contain vague words, emotion theories which include judgments very likely will also have to deal with vague emotions. Moreover, since some of our emotions have visual perceptions as a triggering cause, such as seeing the fear arousing bear in front of me, and as one might even have perceptions with regard to one's own inner state, such as the sadness which one feels, it seems at least possible that in these cases our impressions might have vague content. Yet, I don't see why one needs vague language to report vague content. Shouldn't one be as precise as possible when one tries to report something and why shouldn't it be possible to describe vague content precisely? Perhaps vague language might be more appropriate for vague content than precise language, but then, if the language is vague, how can we be sure that we have captured the vague content precisely?

With regard to paradigmatically vague predicates, such as "tall", "bald", "red", "tadpole" and "child", Keefe and Smith (1999, pp. 2-3) mark out the following interrelated features:

"First, our sample predicates have *borderline cases*....Suppose Tek is borderline tall. It seems that the unclarity about whether he is tall is not merely epistemic....no amount of further information about his exact height...could help us decide whether he *is* tall....it is *indeterminate* whether Tek is tall. And arguably this indeterminacy amounts to the sentence 'Tek is tall' being neither true nor false, which violates the classical principle of bivalence. The law of excluded middle similarly comes into question: 'either Tek is tall or he is not' seems untrue....A second characteristic of vague predicates is that they apparently lack well-defined extensions. On a scale of heights, there is *no sharp boundary* between the tall people and the rest; nor is there an exact point at which our growing creature ceases to be a tadpole....Third, our vague predicates are *susceptible to sorites paradoxes*. Intuitively, a hundredth of an inch cannot make a difference to whether a man counts as tall. Such tiny variations, which cannot be discriminated by the naked eye or even by everyday measurements, are just too small to matter....So we have the principle [S₁] if X is tall, and Y is only a hundredth of an inch shorter than X, then Y is also tall. But imagine a line of men, starting with someone seven foot tall, and each of the rest a hundredth of an inch shorter than the man in front of him. Repeated applications of [S₁] as we move down the line imply that each man we encounter is tall, however far we continue. And this yields a conclusion which is clearly false, namely that a man less than five foot high, reached after three thousand steps along the line, still counts as tall."

Shapiro (2006, chapter 1) disagrees with the above classification, for on his view the presence of borderline cases is necessary for vagueness to arise, while being prone to sorites paradoxes is sufficient for vagueness. So according to Shapiro Keefe and Smith's second feature is not necessary for vagueness to arise. As we will see later on, the second feature is already captured in the third one. Hence Shapiro is right in this regard. Also Keefe and Smith don't point out how these three features are interrelated with each other, so saying that being prone to sorites paradoxes is sufficient for vagueness to arise, while the presence of borderline cases is necessary for vagueness, might just be considered a clarification of Keefe and Smith's view. Moreover, with regard to the sorites being sufficient for vagueness, this seems to be correct, for I don't know of any not-vague predicate that it is able to cause a sorites. Furthermore, with regard to the borderline cases also here Shapiro seems to be right, because there are not-vague predicates which do have borderline cases, such as being a brother of a particular person.

Shapiro (2006, p. 5) defines vague as follows: "A word is vague if it is relevantly similar to 'bald', 'heap', and 'red'." Yet, one might object to that definition that it is not sufficiently precise, because it is unclear to me what "relevantly similar" actually means. If it were to mean that in each such case sorites paradoxes could arise because sorites paradoxes are sufficient for vagueness to arise, then this could be considered an adequate definition, though. An alternative definition could be the one by Braun and Sider (2007, p. 2), who define vague in the following way: "An expression is vague if it can be unclear to a speaker informed of all relevant facts whether the expression correctly applies." With regard to this definition, it is not obvious to me what is meant by relevant facts. Also it is unclear to me why they state "it can be unclear" and not that they state "it is unclear".

Getting back to Shapiro, Shapiro's (2006, pp. 11-12) main claim is his open-texture thesis:

> "The open-texture thesis is that in some circumstances a competent speaker can...go either way without offending against the meaning of the terms, the non-linguistic facts, and the like....the open-texture thesis does not entail that he will always be conscious of the fact that he can go either way. Second, even if a is a borderline case of P, it is not true that the rules for language use allow a speaker to assert Pa in any situation whatsoever. For example, one is not free to assert Pa if one has just asserted...$\neg Pa$. This would offend against logic....Similarly,...one is not normally free to assert Pa if one has just asserted...$\neg Pa'$, where a' is only marginally different from a. That would offend against tolerance."

Shapiro (2006, p. 11) also points out that open-texture is mostly an empirical claim about the proper use of vague terms. Yet, if one takes the stance that meaning is use and if we want to stay as close as possible to the natural language English, then we wouldn't represent the meaning of "bald" correctly by stating that such borderline cases can either be called bald or not bald (cf. Ledwig 2008). For consider the following case: if person C were to describe the respective borderline person, person A, to a third person B and this third person were supposed to identify A given this description, then B would have problems identifying A and would probably accuse person C of having given a misleading description. The reason for that contention would be that one would have expected a different looking person given that description. For a short critique of Shapiro's theory see Ledwig (2008).

Let's return to Keefe and Smith's characterization of vague predicates: with regard to the first point of Keefe and Smith that vague predicates have borderline cases, Fine (1999, p. 120) makes that even more precise by distinguishing between **extensionally vague** and **intensionally vague** predicates: "A predicate is extensionally vague if it has borderline cases, intensionally vague if it could have borderline cases. Thus 'bald' is extensionally vague...and remains intensionally vague in a world of hairy or hairless men." Another kind of distinction which one could make with regard to vagueness, is to distinguish between **objective vs. subjective vagueness**. When Williamson (1994, pp. 74-75) describes and discusses Black's account of vagueness, he points out that on Black's view vagueness is rather an objective matter, for the willingness of a speaker to assert "*x* is *L*" with regard to vague languages depends on what the object *x* is, not just on who is making the assertion; Black admits, though, that given a borderline case, there will be variation between different speakers at the same time and in the same speaker at different times, and additionally there will be statistical regularities in the variation. Williamson (1994, p. 82) highlights the fact that Black modified his views on vagueness in 1963, though.

With regard to these degrees of change which are too small to make any difference whether a predicate applies or not, Wright uses the term "tolerant" to describe such predicates (Keefe and Smith 1999, p. 4). Moreover, Keefe and Smith (1999, p. 4) point out that tolerant predicates, such as "tall", lack sharp boundaries. For if *F* has sharp boundaries, then a minute boundary-crossing change will make a difference whether *F* applies. As a result actually Keefe and Smith's second feature of vague predicates becomes obsolete, because it is already captured in the third. Yet, are emotional phenomena and/or their concepts relevantly similar to these paradigmatic vague predicates, so that these three features also apply to them? At least with regard to multi-dimensional accounts and/or multi-component accounts for the emotions this doesn't seem to be the case.

Keefe (2006, pp. 11-12), however, has a remedy for this problem, for she states:

"many vague predicates are *multi-dimensional*: several different dimensions of variation are involved in determining their applicability. The applicability of 'big', used to describe people, depends on both height and volume; and even whether something counts as a 'heap' depends not only on the number of grains but also on their arrangement....The three central features of vague predicates are shared by multi-dimensional ones. There are, for example, borderline nice people: indeed, some are borderline *because* of the multi-dimensionality of 'nice', by scoring well in some relevant respects but not in others. Next consider whether multi-dimensional predicates may lack sharp boundaries....for a sharply bounded two-dimensional predicate the candidates would be more perspicuously set out in a two-dimensional space in which a boundary could be drawn, where the two-dimensional region enclosed by the boundary contains all and only instances of the predicate. With a *vague* two-dimensional predicate no such sharp boundary can be drawn. Similarly, for a sharply bounded predicate with a clear-cut set of *n* dimensions, the boundary would enclose an *n*-dimensional region containing all of its instances; and vague predicates will lack such a sharp boundary....When there is no clear-cut set of dimensions—for 'nice', for example—this model of boundary-drawing is not so easily applied: it is then not possible to construct a suitable arrangement of candidates on which to try to draw a boundary of the required sort....'Nice' is so vague that it cannot even be associated with a neat array of candidate dimensions, let alone pick out a precise area of such an array. Finally, multi-dimensional vague predicates are susceptible to sorites paradoxes."

Yet, in the introduction of this book, Salmon (2007, p. 53) distinguished between three different concepts of vagueness: vagueness in the sense of (1) the existence of borderline cases, in the sense of (2) "when several criteria exist for application of a term, with no specification of how many of the criteria have to be fulfilled or to what degree", and in the sense of (3) lack of specificity. In the above characterizations, however, only the first concept is used by the authors—unless one equates several dimensions with several criteria—, so that one may ask oneself, is Salmon's distinction which she uses in a critical thinking book found in the literature on vagueness?

Roughly with the exception of (1) supervaluationism, (2) Frege, (3) Copilowish, (4) Machina, and (5) Peirce, current accounts of vagueness distinguish vagueness from prototypicality (where several dimensions or criteria might be involved), ambiguity, lack of specificity/generality, context-dependence, and incompleteness of definition. (1) Supervaluationism considers vagueness as a form of ambiguity, that is to say, "tall", for example, has a range of senses, each corresponding to a precisification of that predicate (Keefe 2006, p. 156). (2) Frege puts vagueness together with ambiguity and partiality into one category of which according to Williamson (1994, p. 43) coherent accounts can be given, that is to say, if a mathematician uses the name "10" ambiguously for two different objects, one has no problems in coherently determining what they are (Williamson 1994, p. 43). (3) Copilowish tries to show that borderline cases involve a conflict of semantic rules, which amounts to ambiguity (Williamson 1994, p. 285, n. 6). (4) Machina (1999, p. 192) distinguishes three different kinds of vagueness from each other of which the first one as in Copilowish involves a conflict of semantic rules which—although Machina doesn't say so—could amount to ambiguity:

"We can name these types of vagueness with suitably descriptive phrases: (a) Conflict Vagueness, (b) Gap Vagueness, and (c) Weighting Vagueness. Briefly, Conflict Vagueness occurs when a single predicate is used in such a way that the semantical rules governing its application on the occasion in question conflict with one another. Gap Vagueness occurs when the semantical rules for a predicate fail to say anything at all about whether certain sorts of possible objects are to be included in the extension of the predicate. And Weighting Vagueness occurs when the natural semantics governing the use of the predicate provides that some one property or some combination of properties of a given object count to only a certain limited extent toward placing the object into the extension of the predicate, even though these properties are the only ones which are at all relevant in deciding the applicability of the predicate to the object. All the well-worked examples of vagueness occurring in the literature are of this latter sort."

(5) Williamson (1994, p. 47) shows that for Peirce all unspecificity is a kind of vagueness:

"The certainty of many vague beliefs lies in their unspecificity. Now there are different ways of lacking specificity. If I believe that you are between 11 mm and 9,437 mm in height, my belief is unspecific because a wide range of heights would make it clearly true. If I believe that you are of average height, my belief is unspecific because a wide range of heights would make it neither clearly true nor clearly false, even though only a narrow range would make it clearly true. The former belief draws a sharp line around a wide area; the latter draws a blurred line around a small one. What the beliefs have in common is that a wide range of heights make them not clearly false.

42

Of the two, most contemporary philosophers would classify only the belief that you are of average height as particularly vague....Peirce, in contrast, would have counted both beliefs as vague".

Vagueness vs. prototypicality. Prototypicality roughly corresponds to Salmon's second concept of vagueness. For an eagle is a prototypical bird, because it fulfills several criteria for being a bird to a high degree, whereas a penguin who cannot fly is not a prototypical bird, because it doesn't fulfill a prototypical criterion for being a bird, namely being able to fly, although it fulfills all of the other criteria. Yet, Sainsbury (1999) argues against the identification of vagueness and prototypicality, for he (Sainsbury 1999, pp. 262-263) states:

"Eleanor Rosch...has suggested that the notion of a prototype helps us understand vagueness since prototypicality is a property of degree, and vague predicates are associated with such properties. However, it turns out that prototypicality, in this sense, is orthogonal to vagueness, as demonstrated by the fact that an absolutely definite case may have low prototypicality (as penguins do relative to their classification as birds)."

Yet, in my opinion it is not so obvious that penguins are really absolutely definite cases with regard to their classification as birds. One might think that such a judgment depends on one's knowledge with regard to birds and penguins and one's definition of birdhood. On twin Earth it also doesn't seem so obvious whether their water which looks and tastes the same as Earth water is H_2O or not. Moreover, with regard to the definition or classification of birdhood, this depends to at least some considerable extent on how birds evolved and whether there might have been some parallel co-evolution leading to the same body-structure, etc. That is to say, if penguins had co-evolved with birds and birds and penguins shared the same essential characteristics, then one would have reason to say that they shouldn't be classified as birds. The knowledge of the evolution of birds, however, depends on which fossils survived and eventually are found, leaving always the possibility of gaps in our knowledge of evolution. Thus, I would be hesitant to call a penguin an absolutely definite case of a bird; it seems very likely that this is so, but I wouldn't ascribe a probability of one to it.

Vagueness vs. ambiguity vs. lack of specificity/generality. In order to bring out the distinctions between these three different terms, let's take a look at Fine's (1999, p. 120) characterization:

"Suppose that the meanings of the natural number predicates 'nice$_1$', 'nice$_2$', and 'nice$_3$' are given by the following clauses:

(1) (a) n is nice$_1$ if $n > 15$

(b) n is not nice$_1$ if $n < 13$

(2) (a) n is nice$_2$ if and only if $n > 15$

(b) n is nice$_2$ if and only if $n > 14$

(3) n is nice$_3$ if and only if $n > 15$

…'nice$_1$' is vague, its meaning is under-determined; 'nice$_2$' is ambiguous, its meaning is over-determined; and 'nice$_3$' is highly general or unspecific."

If we analyze Fine's distinction, then it seems clear that being under-determined as in the case of "nice$_1$" seems to go together with borderline cases being present, in the sense that with regard to the number 14, for example, it is unclear whether n is nice$_1$ or not, whereas in the other two cases such borderline cases are missing.

Fine was not the only one who distinguished vagueness from generality and ambiguity, although in the end he as a supervaluationist wants to close the gap between vagueness and ambiguity (cf. Keefe and Smith 1999, p. 6).[5] According to Williamson (1994, p. 73) also Black makes the distinction between vagueness, generality, and ambiguity:

"Vagueness consists in 'the existence of objects concerning which it is intrinsically impossible to say either that the symbol in question does, or does not, apply'.…Black means that neither thing can be said because neither is true, not just because neither can be known. If vagueness is blurring of boundaries, generality is breadth in the area enclosed.…Ambiguity is another phenomenon again; one can resolve it, as one cannot resolve vagueness, by supplying an alternative word."

Keefe and Smith (1999, p. 6) motivate the conflation between ambiguity and vagueness, for there are certain terms which are ambiguous

---

[5] Besides wanting to close the gap between vagueness and ambiguity—a form of reductionism—Fine (1999, pp. 121-122) also considers the possibility of reducing vague names and vague quantifiers to vague predicates.

and vague; for instance "bank" has two different main senses, such as financial institutions and sloping river edges, yet both of these senses are vague. Yet, the latter example then also makes clear why one has to make that distinction according to them.

Another theorist who advocates the distinction between vagueness and ambiguity is Mehlberg (1999); in particular, Mehlberg (1999, pp. 86-87, n. 1) points out the effect context has on ambiguity in contradistinction to vagueness—an effect which was not obvious in the case of Fine's distinction:

"A proper name is vague if it can be interpreted as applying to any individual of a number of overlapping individuals. A proper name is ambiguous if its correct interpretation depends upon its context. The name 'Toronto' is vague. It is also ambiguous because there are several non-overlapping localities denoted by it. The expression 'Toronto, Ontario' is no longer ambiguous but it is still vague. To remove the ambiguity of a word, it suffices to place it in a suitable context. A vague term, however, cannot cease to be vague unless it acquires another meaning and thus becomes another term."

Besides context also the intention of the speaker seems to have an effect on whether a term is vague or ambiguous, for consider the following example from Sorensen (2001, pp. 111-112):

"Suppose an instructor in sentence logic asks the class for a sample sentence so that she can display its logical form. Mr Vague volunteers (A) If it is both the case that either 1=1 or not, and 2=2 or not, then it is not the case that either 1=1 or not, or 2=2 or not. Under the exclusive reading of 'or', (A) is a tautology. Under the inclusive reading of 'or', (A) is a contradiction....The instructor asks Mr Vague whether he meant the inclusive or exclusive reading of (A). She makes the question clear with the help of truth tables....Mr Vague confesses that at the time, he did not clearly intend one meaning rather then the other. The absence of a clear intention makes his utterance vague rather than ambiguous. If Mr Vague's utterance were merely ambiguous, then Mr Vague would know which reading he intended."

Yet, this is not the only reason why one must distinguish ambiguity from vagueness according to Sorensen, for he (Sorensen 2001, pp. 121-122) emphasizes another difference between ambiguity and vagueness, namely that propositions can be vague, but they never can be ambiguous, for the role of propositions is to disambiguate. Yet, the latter is not so obvious to me. Doesn't the role of propositions hinge on who uses the propositions for which purpose? Hence with regard to certain purposes, such as for instance to confuse or distract the intended audience, the role of propositions should be to ambiguate, whereas with regard to certain other purposes, such as helping the intended audience to understand a difficult problem, the role of propositions should be to disambiguate.

After having dealt with vagueness and ambiguity, I will now proceed to the pair vagueness and lack of specificity/generality. There might be two reasons why one might conflate vagueness with lack of specificity/generality. (1) Williamson (1994, pp. 4-5) points out that lack of specificity is a term to which the term "vagueness" is also applied in everyday usage. In this regard, Keefe and Smith (1999, p. 5) highlight that the utterance "Someone said something" would naturally be described as vague; also "X is an integer greater than thirty" would often be considered a vague hint about the value of X. Yet, according to Keefe and Smith (1999, p. 5) vagueness taken in this way is underspecificity, a matter of being less than adequately informative for what one wants to accomplish. Moreover, according to the authors these cases have nothing to do with borderline cases or with the lack of sharp boundaries. (2) Williamson (1994, p. 283, n. 57) points out that there are many words which are both vague and general. Williamson (1994, pp. 281-282, n. 29) also emphasizes the fact that a sentence can be vague with respect to one component and general with respect to another component in the sentence, as is the case in "Someone loves everyone".

Although Williamson (1994, p. 47) shows that for Peirce all unspecificity is a kind of vagueness, Peirce distinguishes between vagueness, generality, and determinacy (Williamson 1994, p. 48). Williamson (1994, p. 49) emphasizes that in Peirce's view conjunctions are general and disjunctions are vague. Another thing which distinguishes vagueness from generality in Peirce are their truth conditions according to Williamson (1994, p. 50): "A vague utterance is true if some way of determining it results in a truth (hence the certainty of vague common sense). A general utterance is true only if every way of determining it results in a truth." Yet, what happens if the utterance is both vague and general, as is the case with regard to "Someone loves everyone"? That doesn't seem so obvious to me. If one advances the point of view, though, that utterances can either be vague or general, the problem disappears. Yet, then one would have to explain what utterances such as "someone loves everyone" are instances of. In my opinion utterances such as "Someone loves everyone" are true, if one—in this case—finds one person to which it applies with regard to every conceivable person.

Williamson (1994, p. 51) points out that Peirce gives a second characterization of vagueness and generality, which Peirce considered to be more scientific than his first pair, namely "'anything is *general* in so far as the principle of excluded middle does not apply to it and is *vague* in so far as the principle of contradiction does not apply to it'." Moreover, according to Williamson (1994, p. 51) in Peirce's view a proposition satisfies the principle of excluded middle given that the proposition is either true or false, and the proposition satisfies the principle of contradiction provided that the proposition is not both true and false.

Williamson (1994, pp. 52-68) points out the following with regard to Russell's account of vagueness: although Russell distinguishes between vagueness and generality in his 1923 paper, his theorizing unmade it again, because he treats both generality and vagueness as the contradictory of precision.[6] In particular, Russell uses the term "generality" more widely than Peirce, namely for unspecificity. In Russell's view only representations are vague and vagueness is a natural phenomenon because representation is a natural phenomenon. Due to the view that only representations are vague, vagueness is not confined to language, although all language is vague, but vagueness can also be found in thoughts and images. Russell denies the validity of the law of excluded middle for vague languages and uses this failure as a diagnosis of the sorites paradox that there must have been a sharp boundary. Moreover, Russell is not explicit about whether the law of excluded middle is the only law of classical logic which is invalidated by vagueness. Additionally, for Russell there is higher-order vagueness.

---

[6] Williamson (1994, p. 284, n. 70) points out, though, that in 1948 Russell does not confuse vagueness and generality any longer.

Vagueness vs. context-dependence. Keefe and Smith (1999, p. 6) point out why one could conflate vagueness with context-dependence, in the sense of having a different extension in different contexts, namely that many terms have both features, such as in the case of "tall". For instance, I am as a woman considered to be of average height in Germany, but in the U.S.A. I am very tall for a woman. Yet, the authors make clear that they are not open to that conflation. Similarly, for the possibility of conflating vagueness with context-dependence speaks that Braun and Sider (2007, p. 3) state: "unlike ambiguity, vagueness is rarely (if ever) totally eliminated in context". In this regard, Williamson (1994, p. 215) emphasizes that while in principle a vague word might exhibit no context dependence, in practice the lack of boundaries for vague words makes context dependence difficult to avoid.

Vagueness vs. incompleteness of definition. According to Williamson (1994, p. 38) Frege tended to put vagueness and incompleteness of definition into one category. Yet, according to Keefe (2006, p. 191) Sainsbury finds a counterexample to that identity, namely the example of "pearl" when discussing "incompleteness" in predicates, that is to say, one cannot answer the question whether a pearl-shaped piece of pearl-material that has been synthesized outside of an oyster should be called a pearl; moreover, to find an answer to that problem is not a matter of vagueness. Yet, why is one not able to answer that question? After all, we also call human beings which are in vitro fertilized human beings. Moreover, also human beings which are born several weeks early are also called human beings. Furthermore, categorization problems because of incomplete knowledge and/or definitions might explain that there are boundary areas where it is not obvious in which category a particular instance falls.

Frege seems not to be the only one who doesn't distinguish between vagueness and incompleteness. For Sorensen (2001, p. 35) finds something similar in Charles Sanders Peirce's entry for "vague" in the 1902 *Dictionary of Philosophy and Psychology*:

"A proposition is vague when there are possible states of things concerning which it is *intrinsically uncertain* whether, had they been contemplated by the speaker, he would have regarded them as excluded or allowed by the proposition. By intrinsically uncertain we mean not uncertain in consequence of any ignorance of the interpreter, but because the speaker's habits of language were indeterminate." (Peirce 1902, p. 748)

In particular, Sorensen (2001, p. 35) points out with regard to this passage that "Relative borderline cases arise from incompleteness in the available resources for answering the question. Absolute borderline cases arise from incompleteness in the question."

Borderline cases vs. boundarilessness. Keefe and Smith (1999, p. 16) entertain the possibility that the lack of any sharp boundary would be a better criterion of vagueness than borderline cases and point out that Sainsbury defends that possibility, in the sense that he maintains that there is no unsharp boundary, so that the defining feature of vagueness is "boundarylessness". In particular, Sainsbury (1999, p. 257) argues:

"A vague concept is boundaryless in that no boundary marks the things which fall under it from the things which do not, and no boundary marks the things which definitely fall under it from those which do not definitely do so; and so on....To characterize a vague concept as boundaryless is an improvement on characterizing it as one which permits borderline cases, since a non-vague concept may admit borderline cases. If 'child*' is defined as true of just those people whose hearts have beaten less than a million times, false of those whose hearts have beaten more than a million and fifty times, and borderline with respect to the remaining people, it has borderline cases but behaves quite unlike our paradigms of vagueness."

I agree with Sainsbury that boundarylessness seems to be a more appropriate characterization of vague phenomena. Yet, boundarylessness has to be qualified by normal conditions, because humans can quite clearly set boundaries for vague phenomena in a pragmatic or even in an arbitrary manner.

Vague objects. Besides vague perceptions another controversial area is whether there are vague objects. Yet, Williamson (1994, p. 248) argues that since words are objects and since there are vague words, there are vague objects. Nevertheless this conception of objects might at least not coincide with a common sense notion of what an object is. According to Keefe and Smith (1999, p. 17) also Tye believes that there are vague objects, including such things as mountains, clouds, and sets. Yet, do we really say that a mountain is vague? Don't we rather say it is vague whether the mountain starts here or over there? So it is rather properties which the mountain has which are vague and not the mountain itself at least if one follows ordinary language. As the emotions are mental phenomena and since nothing really hinges on an answer to the question whether emotional phenomena or their concepts constitute vague objects for the topic at hand, I will not delve into this subject matter any further here. That is to say, the question of interest is whether emotional phenomena are vague and/or their concepts are vague and not the question whether the emotional phenomena and/or their objects constitute vague objects.

However, just for the sake of the argument, if one takes words to be objects, why shouldn't it be possible to equally claim that emotional phenomena are objects? Here a clarification is necessary what one considers an object to be. One's emotions can be objects of reflection and critical judgment, as is the case when one questions oneself whether an emotion is appropriate in particular circumstances. So despite the fact that emotions are changing and are not stable over time, they might nevertheless be objects. Also everyday objects change all the time, such as is the case when one repairs a defect instrument and exchanges the defect part with a new functioning part. Perhaps even abstract things might be considered to be objects, such as when I say "Freedom is the object of discussion". Yet wouldn't one rather say in this case "Freedom is the topic of discussion"? Here perhaps looking at different languages might also reveal different facts, for in German one can quite clearly say "Freedom is the object of discussion". So, perhaps language use is not decisive when it comes to determining what kind of things objects are. As determining what an object is doesn't constitute the main purpose of this chapter and book and as it is not necessary to answer the question what an object is for the purpose of this project, I will not delve into this topic any further.

Truth-values of vague predicates. If one considers vague predicates, such as "tall", "clever", "old", etc., then it is obvious that such predicates always have a counterpart, such as "short" in the case of "tall", "stupid" in the case of "clever", "young" in the case of "old", etc., so that one could represent these predicates on the opposites of continua. Now as one approaches the borderline cases with regard to these vague predicates, the question comes up what kind of truth-value should one assign to sentences including such a borderline vague predicate. According to Keefe and Smith (1999, p. 7) the following possibilities exists: (1) predications in borderline cases lack a truth-value, that is to say, there is a truth-value gap; (2) predications in borderline cases have a third value, such as "neutral", "indeterminate", or "indefinite" leading to a three-valued logic; (3) predications in borderline cases get degrees of truth assigned ranging from 0 (complete falsity) to 1 (complete truth). A fourth option is a truth-value glut which according to Keefe and Smith (1999, p. 7) is endorsed by Black, that is to say, predications in borderline cases are both true and false. According to Williamson (1994, pp. 74-75) Black is also a proponent of the degrees of truth view, so that it is possible to entertain more than one possibility with regard to these cases.

With regard to (1) Williamson (1994, p. 46) points out that Frege was later inclined to deny both sense and truth-value to sentences involving vague expressions. Yet that would have as a consequence that many sentences lack a truth value which would be undesirable. For how can one make decent predictions and explanations if one doesn't know whether the facts and laws turn out to be true or not? Yet, even if it is undesirable, it might turn out to be true. According to Keefe and Smith (1999, p. 8) Wright claims that one can avoid a gap between truth and falsity by inserting an operator which expresses definiteness or determinacy. For then one can assert that there is a gap between definite truth and definite falsity without having to deal with a gap between truth and falsity. With regard to (3), Keefe and Smith (1999, p. 47) object that it seems inappropriate to associate the vague predicate "red" or any other such predicate with any particular exact function from objects to degrees of truth. But perhaps one could associate "red" with a range of functions from objects to degrees of truth. With regard to (1) and (4) Keefe and Smith (1999, p. 7, n. 7) highlight the fact that according to Fine truth on the gap view could just be truth-and-the-absence-of-falsity on the glut view. Hence one could reduce one view to the other.

Yet, how is this relevant for the current project on emotional phenomena? Truth values for emotional phenomena can be assigned if one for instance asks a person "Is it true that you at this very moment experience an emotion and not a desire?" Depending on how one analyzes the different emotional phenomena, different kinds of truth values seem to be adequate. So, to a certain extent we have to await the coming chapters in order to justify which truth value is adequate for the phenomenon at issue. However, in my opinion whenever a continuum is involved with regard to the respective components of emotional phenomena, I think the representation which most closely resembles that continuum is degrees of truth. Moreover, I think that instead of assigning predications in borderline cases degrees of truth ranging from zero to one, one should assign degrees of truth ranging from zero to one to the whole continuum, because in that way one evades the problem of having to clarify whether a particular case is already a borderline case or not.

Higher-order vagueness. Any adequate account of vagueness, besides providing for a logic or semantic for vagueness, solving the sorites paradox, and providing solutions for all the other problems mentioned at the beginning of this chapter, has to find an effective way of dealing with cases of higher-order vagueness given that one acknowledges it as a phenomenon. Yet, what is higher-order vagueness? Williamson (1994, pp. 2-3) gives an excellent characterization of it:

"The difficulties presented by the question 'When did Rembrandt become old?' are also presented by the question 'When did Rembrandt become clearly old?'....The same difficulties are presented by the question 'When did Rembrandt become clearly clearly old?'; the point reiterates *ad infinitum*. This is the phenomenon of higher-order vagueness. It means that the meta-language in which we describe the vagueness of a vague language will itself be vague."

Moreover, Williamson (1994, p. 3) points out with regard to his own account of vagueness that it doesn't pose a problem for him, because higher-order vagueness is nothing but ignorance about ignorance. Thus, because it is just an epistemic phenomenon, one doesn't have to provide a logic for it, whereas non-epistemic views do have to come up with a logic for it, which yields a clear economical advantage of epistemic theories.

Now with regard to emotional phenomena, there might be something comparable, namely when one asks oneself or others "Have I emoted?", "Have I really emoted?", "Have I really really emoted?", etc. As this parallel exists, one has to become clear about whether an epistemic account of vagueness turns out to be the right solution to the myriad of problems vagueness causes. While on the one side I find it very plausible to assume that with regard to many things we are ignorant not only contingently, but even in principle, one might want to ask oneself: is there any reason to assume that a boundary in fact exists with regard to emotional phenomena? Or do we have better reason to believe that there is no such boundary? As we in fact don't have any kind of proof that such a boundary exists, I find it more plausible to assume from the very outset that boundarilessness is given, especially since Sainsbury in one of the previous sections has given a convincing argument to prefer boundarilessness to borderline cases.

   The vagueness of "vague". Sorensen (1985) has argued for the vagueness of "vague". Yet, Varzi (2003) has criticized his argument, if it is used in Hyde's (1994) argument for the view that vague predicates must suffer from higher-order vagueness. In particular Varzi (2003, p. 297) points out that in Hyde's (1994) argument one cannot rely on Sorensen's argument to motivate the fact that the predicate "vague" is vague; for Sorensen's argument "*presupposes* the existence of border border cases. Specifically, it presupposes the existence of border border cases for 'small'." Varzi (2003, p. 298) later on elaborates on that: "Of course, this is no objection to Sorensen's argument, because Sorensen is perfectly entitled to assume that 'small' has border border cases....But in the context of Hyde's argument we are not entitled to that assumption, on pain of circularity."

   Here is Varzi's (2003, pp. 295-296) reconstruction of Sorensen's argument:

   "First, vague predicates give rise to the sorites paradox....

   (1a) 1 is small.

   (1b) For every integer n: if n is small, then so is $n+1$.

   (1c) Therefore, 10^{10} is small.

   Now, for every integer n, let 'n-small' be a numerical predicate defined by the following condition:

   (2) k is n-small iff k is either small or less than n.

   Clearly, '1-small' is just as vague as 'small': both apply to 0 and apply exactly in the same way to all other integers. By contrast, when n is clearly not small, say $n=10^{10}$, then the extension of the predicate 'n-small' is determined exclusively by the 'less than n' clause, and is therefore perfectly sharp: every integer less than 10^{10} is 10^{10}-small, every other integer is not. Since there is no clear value of n which marks the difference between predicates of the first sort (with border cases) and predicates of the second sort (without border cases), one can now construct a soritical argument for 'vague' that parallels (1a)-(1c):

(3a) '1-small' is vague.
(3b) For every integer n: if 'n-small' is vague, then so is '$n+1$-small'.
(3c) Therefore, '10^{10}-small' is vague.
Consequently, 'vague' is vague."

Yet, as Varzi's critique was not directed at Sorensen's argument per se, so that no circularity is involved in that argument, we don't have to deal with the question whether Sorensen's argument involves a vicious circle. That "vague" is vague is actually not something new in the literature, for according to Williamson (1994, p. 71) already Austin pointed that out.

If the term "vague" is vague, then does this have any consequences for our analysis of whether emotional phenomena and/or their concepts are vague? This seems to be the case, for if "vague" is vague, then one should also be able to construct sorites paradoxes in this regard and also boundarilessness should be given in these cases. However, by clarifying that vague goes together with boundarilessness and by distinguishing vagueness from ambiguity, prototypicality, context-dependence, etc. as we have already done it in the previous sections, eliminates the vagueness of vagueness at least to a certain extent.

Conclusion

I agree with Sainsbury that one should characterize vagueness by means of boundarilessness. While I acknowledge that there are many phenomena which are hidden to us not only in principle but also contingently, it is not obvious whether this applies to emotional phenomena and their vagueness. While I am very sympathetic to epistemic accounts of vagueness, I still think the burden of proof is on them to show that emotional phenomena admit of borderline cases where the respective boundaries are hidden to us.

Chapter 2 Emotion Theories

Vagueness and the emotions. Ortony, Norman, and Revelle (2005, p. 177) point out that "emotions...do not comprise a discrete category with easily identifiable boundaries. Rather, they vary in their typicality, with some cases being better examples than others." If one considers this quote in detail one gets the impression that emotions are vague on the authors' account and that vagueness amounts to prototypicality. It is not so obvious whether they consider emotions to be phenomena with boundaries or not, for to say that emotions don't have easily identifiable boundaries could suggest that either there are borderline cases which are difficult to make out or that emotions in fact exhibit boundarilessness.

Yet, the claim that emotions range in their prototypicality already depends on which kind of phenomena fall under the emotions according to the authors' account and which kind of phenomena fall under the emotions hinges on how emotions are defined. If one, for instance, defines emotions in such a way that it is an essential criterion for an emotion to be short-lived, then it might not be so obvious whether love falls under the emotions—unless one characterizes love as an accumulation of many short-lived episodes of love—and indeed there are researchers who take that stance (cf. Ledwig 2006, pp. 10-11); yet, in common opinion love quite clearly is considered to be an emotion. Something similar might hold with regard to phenomena such as surprise and fear. For it is usually argued that the onset of surprise is so fast that it cannot be an emotion; yet, the same would then also have to hold for fear with its very fast onset reaction time and where nobody doubts that fear is an emotion.

Besides coming up with necessary and sufficient conditions for the emotions, one could alternatively advocate a family resemblance or prototypicality definition for the emotions à la Wittgenstein. With regard to Ortony et al. in the quote above one also gets the impression that they advocate a prototypicality definition for the emotions. They might not be the only ones to entertain such an account of the emotions, for according to Sloman, Chrisley, and Scheutz (2005, p. 209) it is pointless to argue what emotions really are, because "emotion" is a cluster concept having some clear instances, such as violent anger, some clear non-instances, such as remembering a mathematical formula, and a lot of indeterminate cases where people cannot easily reach an agreement over. Yet, settling for a prototypicality account of the emotions would only be justified, if it really resembled the phenomena in question; otherwise one would rather think that trying not for necessary and sufficient conditions would amount to defeat at the very beginning of inquiry. Whether a prototypicality definition for emotions would be a vague definition might depend on the particular definition at issue. For whereas prototypicality at least according to Sainsbury (see the previous chapter) doesn't amount to vagueness, the definition itself could use words or refer to phenomena or their features which are quite clearly considered to be vague. The latter will become clearer when we discuss which phenomena in the brain, for instance, are involved with regard to the emotions.

That vagueness might really cause a problem for the study of the emotions is acknowledged by Fellous and LeDoux (2005, pp. 84-85) who point out the following: that the limbic system still survives is partially due to the fact that the anatomical concept and its alleged emotional function were defined so vaguely that they were irrefutable. The authors in particular highlight the fact that in most discussions on the mediation of emotion by the limbic system the meaning of the term "emotion" is used similar to the common English-language use of the term, namely "feelings"; yet, in actuality the term "emotion" is a rich and complex concept with many nonintuitive aspects, which are therefore inconsistent with the common use of the term, because the common English use of the term "emotion" is only a poor theoretical notion. In my opinion the reason why such behavior occurs has to do with the fact that psychologists mostly don't define, but rather operationalize their definitions. They have not acquired the carefulness in defining things as philosophers have been taught from early on. The same might hold for psychiatrists and neuroscientists given that they have not had any philosophical training.

That vagueness might really cause a problem for the study of the emotions is also emphasized by Damasio (2000, p. 12); in particular, he points out that neuroscience and cognitive science have neglected the study of the emotions until recently because of its being too subjective, elusive, and vague—being too much at the opposite end of reason and therefore being probably irrational to study. Moreover, Damasio (2000, p. 14) continues in the same vein by claiming that

"The alleged vagueness of emotions and feelings is the most frequent excuse offered to justify the difficulty of studying these undesirable phenomena. A commonplace statement, from neuroscientists and cognitive scientists alike, is that somehow the representation of emotion, cognitively and neurally speaking, is of a nature different from that of other representations and that feelings are indescribable with any degree of precision."

While it certainly seems difficult to describe one's feelings with any degree of precision, nevertheless there might be ways of trying to make the description of one's feelings more precise by considering different dimensions feelings have, such as intensity, variation in intensity, duration, positive (negative) valence, variation in positive (negative) valence, familiarity[7], etc. With regard to these dimensions with the exception of duration one could employ a 10-point scale ranging from 1=very low to 10=very high or equivalent terms to grasp the subjective experiences of the experimental subjects better. Although with such scales it still seems impossible to compare the subjective feelings of different people with each other, after all a "10" in intensity for one experimental subject might objectively correspond to a "5" for another experimental subject, and although one would like to have more precision than just whole numbers, this might nevertheless be a good starting point.

Besides this difficulty with feelings that they are hard to describe with any degree of precision, there might be other problems going together with feelings which might be even more detrimental to the evaluation of emotional phenomena. Clore and Ortony (2000, p. 50) report a particular challenge for the cognitive view of emotions, namely the fact that people are very bad at describing and explaining their feelings and that people are often wrong about what caused their feelings. Additionally, there is a whole class of people who have problems emotionalizing, that is to say the ease by which one experiences an emotional feeling or becomes

---

[7] With regard to familiarity, some people might find it strange to evaluate feelings as familiar. Yet, for instance I am not very familiar with the feelings of jealousy or Schadenfreude, because I rarely experience them, whereas there are definitely others who experience such feelings much more often and are therefore familiar with them.

emotionally aroused, fantasizing, identifying emotions, verbalizing emotions, and thinking about or analyzing emotions, namely people who are diagnosed with alexithymia (cf. Bermond, Vorst, and Moormann 2006, p. 333). And if one advocates the view that emotions are identical with feelings, people with alexithymia will also have corresponding problems with regard to their feelings. Yet, I will devote a whole chapter to alexithymia, so I will not discuss these cases here right now.

Yet, what about these people who are wrong about the causes of their emotions, who give inadequate explanations of their emotions, and who are unable to describe their emotions properly? Solomon (2007, p. 121) rightly distinguishes between two different cases in this regard:

"Animals and infants have emotions for reasons, perhaps (a dog gets angry *because* his territory has been violated, a baby cries in fear *because* she does not know the person who is holding her), but we adult humans can articulate these reasons and, if called on to explain ourselves, spell out our emotional reactions to other people....a dog or a baby might err in their emotions (if there is no trespasser, if the baby-holder is a loving friend of the family), but we adult humans can be mistaken about our emotions in a very different way. We can misidentify our emotion and we can misdescribe or get quite wrong our reasons for having the emotion. Once there is a gap between having an emotion and naming that emotion, there is room for a very special kind of error. In reflection, we can be mistaken *about* our emotion as well as in our emotional response. But in reflection, we can also contrast our emotion with what we think we should or would rather be feeling, and by means of such reflection we can take steps to modify, modulate, or alter our emotional states, or, perhaps, decide that what we do feel is correct and what we think we 'ought' to feel is mistaken."

However, also adults can be mistaken about their emotions in the same way dogs and babies can be. For an adult might err in his or her emotion, too, such as when the trespasser of the property was in fact a friend, but couldn't be recognized as such because it was too dark. Solomon instead of speaking of causes of emotions speaks of reasons for emotions. There might not be a difference between these, if one identifies reasons with causes. As discussing this issue leads us too far away from the topic of this chapter and book, I will not deal with the question whether reasons are causes when it comes to emotional phenomena.

Solomon (2007, p. 156) raises another important issue:

"What of the fact that we do know our own emotions (even if we can be wrong about them) in a way that is different from the way that anyone else—a friend, a voyeur, a psychiatrist, a neuroscientist— knows of our emotions? Don't we have some sort of 'privileged access' to our own emotions, thoughts, and feelings? That is, we typically do know what we are thinking or feeling without having to look at our facial expressions or watch our behaviour or listen to what we say (much less look at our brains), as we do when we try to read the thoughts and feelings of other people, even those with whom we are most intimate."

I think that Solomon is right here that a first person perspective gives a privileged access to one's emotions. Yet, just because human beings have in principle this privileged access, doesn't mean that they in fact permit themselves to have that privileged access all the time. After all, sometimes it is better not to know everything there is to know about oneself. Sometimes it might be even better to forget what one knows or remembers, because knowledge or memory of it might lead to self-realizations which could be quite hurtful. Also a first person perspective might not allow for too much objectivity. After all, it might at times be very difficult to distance oneself from oneself to take other perspectives into account and to get a more balanced and well-rounded version of oneself. Hence although one has privileged access to oneself in principle, doesn't mean that one is able and willing to retrieve the necessary information all the time.

Similarly to Solomon I would like to argue: that people are very bad at describing their feelings in general, this might constitute a real problem, for who is to verify what feelings and in which variety and intensity they have them if not the people themselves? There are three ways out here: (1) to provide them with enough descriptions to choose from in the form of adjectives or short phrases, so that at least the basic material for a proper description is given, (2) to find out the reasons why they are bad in describing their feelings and if possible to remove those reasons, (3) if it is impossible to remove those reasons to get an adequate description of their feelings by means of trained professionals and objective measures, and/or

(4) to train them in describing their feelings better. The latter might take some time and might also be problematical, for the simple reason that the training might be done in such a way that it just corresponds to the emotional world of the trainer and not resemble a more objective account. Yet, if several trainers agree independently on the description of particular feelings, then a greater amount of objectivity is reached.

Multi-component theories of emotions. While I have already evaluated Ben-Ze'ev's (2000) multi-component theory of the emotions in Ledwig (2006, chapter one) and also made some comments with regard to Panksepp's (1998) account of the emotions, there are many more multi-component theories of the emotions out there which need to be evaluated. In particular, we have to remember here what Keefe said in the last chapter on the multi-dimensionality of vague predicates, for if the emotions are comprised of many different components, then some emotions could be high, medium, or low with regard to some dimensions respectively components, whereas other emotions could be high, medium, or low with regard to some other dimensions respectively components. While Damasio's definition of (2000, p. 15) emotions seems to me too general to admit of a proper evaluation in terms of vagueness, for he claims that "emotions are specific and consistent collections of physiological responses triggered by certain brain systems when the organism represents certain objects or situations"[8], there are others who have been more explicit about what they consider emotions to really be.

Clore and Ortony (2000, pp. 24-25), for instance, claim the following:

"Emotions in humans are normally characterized by the presence of four major components: a cognitive component, a motivational-behavioral component, a somatic component, and a subjective-experiential component. The cognitive component is the

---

[8] Damasio's (1999, p. 282) earlier definition of emotion and also feeling seem to me too general, too: "To the simple definition of emotion as a specifically caused transient change of the organism state corresponds a simple definition for feeling an emotion: It is the representation of that transient change in organism state in terms of neural patterns and ensuing images." Here one would like to know which neural patterns and images is he talking about and how do they particularly look like. Also one would like to know which kind of causes does he have in mind.

representation of the emotional meaning or personal significance of some emotionally relevant aspect(s) of the person's perceived world. These representations may be conscious or nonconscious. The motivational-behavioral component is concerned with inclinations to act on the construals of the world that these representations represent, and with their relation to what is actually done. The somatic component involves the activation of the autonomic and central nervous systems with their visceral and musculoskeletal effects....Finally, the subjective-experiential component is the total 'subjective feeling' part of an emotion."

Starting with the cognitive component, representations are at least according to Russell vague (see previous chapter). Yet, in the case of nonconscious representations we are not even able to evaluate whether they are vague or not unless one found a method to make these nonconscious representations conscious or in any other way accessible. With regard to the motivational-behavioral component, inclinations to act might be captured by means of degrees where "one" stands for "I definitely want to do this" and "zero" stands for "I definitely don't want to do this". In this regard, one might want to argue because a continuum exists, boundarylessness is present where people are undecided whether they want to act on their emotions or not. Hence, provided that one can construe a sorites paradox vagueness seems to be given with regard to that particular aspect. With regard to the somatic component, the activation of the autonomic and central nervous systems can also be a matter of degree. Yet, here one would have to be much more explicit what this all involves or even can involve. We will get to that in the chapter on the brain and the emotions.

With regard to the subjective-experiential component, feelings might be analyzed on several dimensions, such as intensity, variation in intensity, duration, positive (negative) valence, variation in positive (negative) valence, familiarity, etc. and also here with regard to each dimension a continuum exists, so that boundarylessness with regard to each dimension could be given making way for vagueness to appear in case one can construe a sorites paradox. As there is multi-dimensionality involved with regard to feelings, vagueness might also develop on other levels, for the intensity of a feeling might be moderately high, but the duration might be very very short, so it is not so obvious whether a feeling is actually given or not.

Because one could defend the view that the emotions, as Clore and Ortony (2000) portray them, constitute a multi-dimensional enterprise, for one could view every component as a separate dimension, whether an emotion is given or not might hinge on to what degree each component is present. As there is variation in degree possible with regard to each single component, so that one could construe a sorites paradox with regard to each single component, quite clearly emotions turn out to be vague on Clore and Ortony's account.

Aleman, Medford, and David (2006, p. 194) report that

"Emotion can best be thought as a multicomponent process (Scherer, 2004). That is, emotion involves several components, each of which fulfils a specific function in the adaptation to the situation that has triggered the emotion process (cf. Frijda, 1986). Scherer (2004) proposed that three hypothetical types of central representation can be distinguished in the emotion process: (1) unconscious reflection and regulation (involving cognitive appraisal, physiological symptoms, motor expression and action tendencies); (2) conscious representation and regulation (involving feelings); and (3) verbalisation and communication of emotional experience."

In Scherer's process view of the emotions the first component involves the unconscious, so that as in the case of Clore and Ortony an evaluation of this component with regard to its vagueness is impossible unless one could somehow get an access to the unconscious or make the unconscious conscious. With regard to the second component, as before if Russell is right that all representation is vague, then we have already found a point where Scherer's account turns out to have vagueness involved in its account of the emotion process. As before, feelings can be analyzed on several dimensions, so provided that a sorites paradox can be construed vagueness enters Scherer's account on another level. With regard to the third component, verbalization and communication can in many respects be vague, so that even here vagueness might be justifiedly inferred. Moreover, with regard to this component, although one might verbalize one's emotion and communicate it to others, one can also abstain from doing so or even verbalize and communicate emotions which one actually doesn't have, so that verbalization and communication of emotions shouldn't be considered as constitutive components of the emotions.

Some similar kind of critique as in the previous two cases can be applied to Bradley and Lang's (2000, p. 270) conception of what emotions really are; the authors come up with the following analysis of emotions:

"We propose that emotions are better understood as behavioral complexes, organizations of responses that include three broad output systems, including (1) overt acts....(2) emotional language, which includes both expressive and evaluative responses; and (3) physiological reactions, including changes in the brain and in the somatic and visceral systems that are conceived to be the logistic support of intended action and affective display. The resulting emotional response patterns that are observed across systems have two major determinants: the practical dictates of the specific local context and the consistent emotional strategy of appetite or defense."

While overt acts and emotional language can be suppressed or even faked, physiological reactions are harder to control or fake, so the latter can be used to detect emotions and seem proper part of the emotions. Yet, to evaluate physiological reactions for their vagueness one would have to be more precise what changes in the brain and in the somatic and visceral systems all amount to with regard to the emotions according to the authors' opinion. Unless the authors provide us with these precisifications, their account cannot be evaluated properly with regard to its being open to vagueness.

Heilman's (2000, p. 328) account of the emotions is not an improvement to the previous accounts: for according to Heilman emotions have at least two major components, namely (1) emotional behaviors and (2) emotional feelings or experiences. Emotional behaviors can be overt and covert in Heilman's account and both of them make up the adaptive aspect of the emotions. Under the overt behaviors fall emotional faces, gestures, and words, under the covert behaviors fall changes in the viscera and autonomic system. With regard to the second component, feelings or experiences, in Heilman's view these are subjective and are one of the major factors that motivate avoidance and approach behaviors.

With regard to Heilman's account, it is for instance not so obvious why feelings or experiences shouldn't be classified as covert, too, after all they are not directly accessible to other people. Moreover, if feelings or experiences are the ones which motivate approach and avoidance behaviors, I don't see why this is not an adaptive feature of the emotions, too. For if you see a fearful image, such as your mother in law approaching your house, then not to show any kind of adaptive reaction to it would appear not very rational. Also to state that emotions have at least two major components is not very precise. This would fall under Fine's third classification (see previous chapter), namely a highly general or unspecific classification of phenomena. As before, overt behavior can be suppressed or faked, so these kinds of phenomena cannot count as proper criteria for identifying emotions; likewise with regard to covert behavior, such as for instance cramps of the intestines, they can be suppressed to a certain extent by means of auto suggestion and/or diverse breathing techniques or even faked. Moreover, the covert behaviors which are stated in that passage are much too unspecific.

Besides these multi-component theories of the emotions, there are also emotion theories which just employ one criterion and we will deal with an example of this kind in the next section. There is, however, another approach to the emotions which is in some sense also a multi-component one, namely a classification of emotional experiences along several dimensions. Yet, such kind of approaches only consider emotional experiences in the form of emotional judgments and therefore wouldn't yield a comprehensive account of the emotions as will be argued for later on. They might, however, still yield some insights into how humans structure their emotions.

Heilman (2000, pp. 332-333) reports the following with regard to these dimensional accounts: Wundt maintained that emotional experiences show variance in three dimensions, namely quality, activity, and excitement; furthermore, factor analyses on verbal assessments of emotional judgments by Osgood and colleagues found that the variance could be accounted for by three major dimensions, namely valence, arousal, and control, which were partially supported by psychophysiological studies by Greenwald and colleagues. Yet, according to Heilman (2000, pp. 332-333) these three dimensions couldn't discriminate between anger and fear, for both are unpleasant or negative, show high arousal, and are out of control. Frijda then proposed "action readiness" as an important dimension when exploring the cognitive structure of emotion, Heilman (2000, pp. 332-333) observed. As control in the discussion of Osgood and colleagues and Greenwald and colleagues can be closely linked to valence and motor activation, Frijda's action readiness may be the third dimension, Heilman (2000, pp. 332-333) contends.

Yet, if one thinks about it, also action readiness might be very closely related to at least arousal. For if one is not aroused at all, then why should one show any kind of action readiness? Couldn't one equally say that if the emotion is highly negative or unpleasant, then one might have a big incentive to do something about it, whereas in the case of a positive emotion, action readiness doesn't seem to be necessary at all? Hence both arousal and valence might be connected to action readiness, so this is no reason to prefer the combination valence, arousal, and control over the combination valence, arousal, and action readiness.

Be that as it may, if we take the dimensions valence, arousal, and action readiness as the valid dimensions for the judgments of human emotions, then how does vagueness figure into this evaluation of human emotions? As these three dimensions lay on continua, boundarylessness might be given in each such case, so that the emotions turn out to be vague provided one is able to at least construe one sorites paradox out of any of these dimensions. As a result we would not always be able to judge adequately which emotion is given, which would actually be in accordance with the data in the literature, namely that humans are not very good at describing their feelings even misdescribing them at times (here we assume for the sake of the argument that feelings and emotions are synonymous). One could alternatively argue as humans are not very good at describing their feelings and as feelings are part of the emotions, they are a fortiori also not very good at describing their emotions.

Appraisal theories, such as the ones by Lazarus (1991) and Prinz (2004), assume that the complexity of emotions is reflected in the grammar of emotion ascriptions. Although it might be problematic to infer a mental state's psychological structure solely from the grammar of its ascription, such grammar can provide a starting point for a first conceptual analysis, which in turn can provide at least some guidelines for psychological investigation. If one, for instance, considers the self-ascription, "I feel angry *about* your being late for the date", "about" marks a relation between a state that has sensational dimensions—I feel angry—and a representation of an event (your being late for the date) that seems to lack such dimensions. As appraisal theorists are committed to have publicly confirmable theories, they don't individuate emotion types by their sensational or phenomenal quality. Nevertheless they are still able to acknowledge the central role of feeling in the emotions in different ways, such as by viewing the sensational or phenomenal aspects of emotions as subjective manifestations of emotion components that are either directly or indirectly publicly observable by means of physiological conditions and/or motivational states when they are manifested behaviorally.

Many appraisal theories agree on how an emotion like my anger about your being late for the date is produced. First, I mentally represent the event of your being late for the date. This representation then gets evaluated on several dimensions of personal significance. The result is an affective state directed at its represented cause, namely your being late for the date. As representations according to Russell are vague (see the previous chapter), vagueness seems to be an essential part of many appraisal theories at least if one follows Russell's view.

On Lazarus's view, anger about P is a result of P's content having been evaluated along several dimensions, such as goal-relevance, goal-congruence, and agent accountability. As these are dimensions with continua and as the appraisals can vary on these dimensions in matters of degree, vagueness enters the picture in two ways: first, as being boundaryless on each dimension provided that one can construe a sorites paradox, so that we have one-dimensionality vagueness, and second, because the evaluation depends on the applicability of several dimensions some of which might not be as expressive as others, as showing multi-dimensionality vagueness. As an instantiation of anger's "core relational theme", for it is a demeaning offense against me or mine, such an appraisal causes an "emotional response configuration" including physiological reactions, feelings, and action tendencies. Additionally, according to Lazarus the emotion includes the cognition that was its triggering cause, for Lazarus (1991, pp. 173-174) states:

"[E]motion is a superordinate concept that includes cognition in a part-whole relationship, but the reverse is not true. The cognitive activity, A—namely, blaming someone for an offense—combines in an emotion with the physiological reactions and action tendencies, B, to form an organized configuration, AB. The blame causes the emotion, anger, and is also a continuing part of it. To say that anger (AB)—which includes thoughts of blaming someone for an offense (A)—is the cause of the angry reaction (AB) makes no sense unless we realize that a component of the configuration, A, can produce another subsequent AB, of which A is an essential part."

As the "emotional response configuration" consists of three features vagueness might not only be given at the appraisal level but also at the emotional response configuration level, for some of these features might not be as expressive as others. However, as the term "physiological reactions" is too unspecific for a proper evaluation with regard to its vagueness and as one also would have to be more precise what constitutes an action tendency, only the feeling component is left for such an evaluation. As I have already maintained before, feelings might be analyzed along several dimensions and as these dimensions all have continua, which might be open to a sorites paradox, it seems reasonable to suppose that vagueness is given with regard to this component. One might want to object to evaluating emotions on such dimensions as valence, intensity, etc. by stating that none of these features is essential for feelings and that what is of particular relevance with regard to evaluating the vagueness of feelings are the necessary and sufficient conditions for something being a feeling. Although this very much sounds correct, one might reply that these dimensions actually are necessary and sufficient conditions for something being a feeling. Yet this would have to be proven first. We will come back to this question, when encountering some definitions for feelings later on.

In order to get a better grasp of Lazarus's account please take a look at the following figure:

68

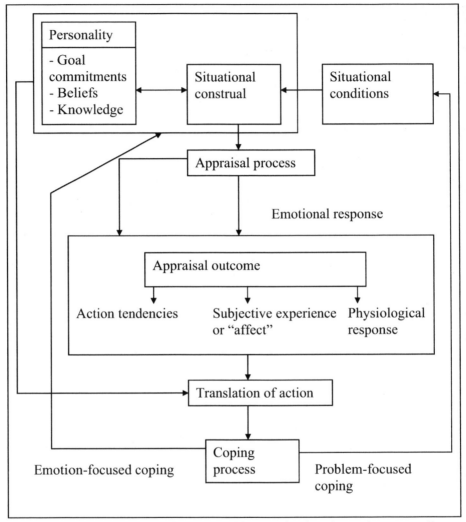

Figure 1. Lazarus's model of "the cognitive-motivational-emotive system", adapted from Lazarus (1991, p. 210).

According to Lazarus (1991) this figure not only illustrates the emotion-causation process, but also emotion's motivational function, namely coping. The subject's personality, which involves her goals, beliefs, and knowledge, together with situational construals which are influenced by both her personality and current situational conditions, belong to the appraisal process's background conditions. If one looks at these three different features, namely goals, beliefs, and knowledge, then it seems obvious that at least the person's beliefs can be vague because of the terms which might be involved in them—something which is in accordance with Keefe as we saw it in the last chapter.

With regard to knowledge, to say that it is vague sounds like a contradiction. Yet, this might also depend on how one defines knowledge. If one defines it in the traditional way as justified true belief, then vagueness in the form of belief might enter. Tucker (2004, p. 25; cf. also Ledwig 2007, p. 139), however, points out that one can define knowledge not only as justified true belief; there are at least two further options, namely one can define knowledge as (1) true belief that was got by a reliable process, or (2) as belief caused or sustained by information (Dretske 1981, p. 86). Yet, in both of these alternative definitions also belief enters and therefore vagueness might be given, too. Now, if there exists a definition of knowledge which is not given in terms of belief, then it might be the case that no vagueness is involved with regard to such a conception of knowledge.

With regard to goals, whether goals can be vague might depend on how one expresses one's goals. If one uses vague language, as in "Safe nature!", then also goals turn out to be vague. How about the situational construal? Could this turn out to be vague? As the person's goals, beliefs, and knowledge influence the situational construal of the person, and as at least the person's beliefs could turn out to be vague, also the situational construal of the person could end up being vague. Moreover, if one takes the stance that even objects are vague, the situational conditions which influence the situational construal are vague resulting in the situational construal to be vague, too. Yet, here it has to be made more precise what the situational conditions all include. Do we also include the cases where other people are trying to influence us with regard to how we should view the situation and what we are supposed to do? If this is the case, then the other persons' beliefs, knowledge, and goals also would have an influence on us via the situational construal, and as at least another person's belief might turn out to be vague, also the situational condition might turn out to be vague. If one considers the multiple possibilities for vagueness to arise, one might think that it amounts to a miracle that we make up our minds to finally draw consequences from our deliberations, emote, and act on our beliefs, knowledge, goals, etc.

Back to Lazarus' theory itself: the appraisal process causes an emotion which is labeled as an emotional response configuration that includes an "appraisal outcome", that is to say, an evaluation, that immediately causes physiological responses, felt affect, and action tendencies. This response configuration is then "translated further into coping processes"; the results of those processes "feed back to the appraisal process to produce a reappraisal", which is not shown in the figure (Lazarus 1991, p. 210). As the appraisal itself was already infested with vagueness, the same problem will occur with the reappraisal.

One-component theories of the emotions. While Lazarus' theory quite clearly falls under the multi-component theories of emotion, Nussbaum's (2001) theory opts just for one component, namely that emotions are judgments. In this regard Ben-Ze'ev (2004, pp. 451-452) points out the following:

> "In Nussbaum's view, emotions can be defined in terms of the cognitive-evaluative component alone (64). Emotions are judgments of value, which include cognitive aspects. She sees such judgments as not merely necessary constituent elements in the emotions, but also as sufficient elements—that is, if the emotion is not there, the judgments themselves are not fully...there (44). If emotions are identified with judgments, then no other component is necessary or sufficient for emotions. Feelings and motivations (desires) in her view are intimately connected with emotions, but are not essential to them....Nussbaum argues that if feelings and desires were missing from a certain emotion, we would not withdraw our ascription of that state as an emotion."

While Nussbaum's view on first sight sounds absolutely implausible, there is some evidence for her view. In this regard Arbib (2005, pp. 336-337) states: "One can have emotion without feeling the emotion—as in 'I didn't know I was angry until I over-reacted like that'—and one can certainly have feelings—as in 'I feel that the color does not suit you'—that do not seem emotional."

Yet with regard to the first case, just because one doesn't know that one was angry, doesn't make it the case that one wasn't angry, unless one wants to defend the view that one is conscious of every emotion which one has and that consciousness and therefore knowledge and/or memory is necessary for having an emotion. We will come to the significance of the consciousness of an emotion later on. With regard to the second case, the question arises whether this is a proper case of feelings or if it is just an odd and not falsifiable way to express one's opinion. For if one were to say "I think that the color doesn't suit you", then one's opinion can be questioned, whereas if one says "I feel that the color doesn't suit you", no such questioning seems possible, for the simple reason that unless you know the relevant psychological literature nobody would consider it possible that from a third person perspective there is someone who can doubt one's feelings. That is to say, who are you to doubt my feelings? After all it is "I" who has these feelings and not "you", and I have privileged access to my feelings. Yet as I mentioned earlier, people are not very good at describing their feelings. With regard to this case, I find it rather odd to say "I feel that the color doesn't suit you". How is the suitability of color connected to one's feelings? That seems to be hard to determine. One can imagine a scenario, though, where one is surrounded by lots of New Age people and where it seems important to always to connect and to refer to one's feelings. Yet, then the questions come up is this just using a certain language code—a jargon—or does a real connection exist between the suitability of color and one's feelings?

Perhaps one just has to look for a better example to determine the emotionality of such feeling statements. What about "I feel that Lord Voldemort is coming"? Perhaps this might not be such a good example either, because if one imagined oneself to be Harry Potter, then a certain emotion might go together with this feeling, because Harry Potter is afraid of Lord Voldemort—the other complication being that this is a case of fiction and not reality. But what about "I feel that there will be a thunderstorm coming", where one neither is a particular thunderstorm lover nor is afraid of thunderstorms, but rather has a neutral attitude towards thunderstorms? In my opinion this example goes through. That is to say, one can attain such a feeling and nevertheless not feel any emotion. Yet, wouldn't we rather say that although it is possible to have a feeling without having an emotion, it isn't possible to have an emotion without a feeling? That is to say, to have a feeling seems to be a necessary and not a sufficient condition for having an emotion. It is not a sufficient condition for having an emotion, because at least in the case of higher cognitive emotions also a judgment is necessary for an emotion to arise, that is, one can only feel guilt, if one has judged oneself to have done something wrong. With regard to feeling being a necessary component for having an emotion I refer the reader to a later section on the consciousness of emotions, where this issue becomes evident and will hopefully be resolved.

A related case to the "I feel that there will be a thunderstorm coming" are cases of **affective inertia** where an emotional feeling displays such inertia when it still lingers after the directed emotion in which it originated ceases, as when someone reports of himself: "I was still fuming, even though I was no longer angry at Peter after learning that he was not responsible for the theft". In cases of affective inertia, the physiological arousal underlying the feeling might give an explanation as to why the feeling lingers (de Sousa, 1987, pp. 237 ff.). What characterizes affective inertia then is that emotional feelings are separable components of directed emotions. Yet this doesn't speak against the fact that feelings are necessary but not sufficient conditions for the emotions. Cases of affective inertia rather indicate the influence cognition has on the emotions, because a value judgment that Peter was not responsible in the above example makes the emotion disappear, while the feeling is still given.

How does vagueness enter the picture in cases of affective inertia and similar cases such as "I feel that there will be a thunderstorm coming"? In case the emotion disappears because of a value judgment, while the feeling still lingers, the value judgment might include vague concepts or be about vague objects. In case there is no emotion, but just a feeling, vagueness might enter along the dimensions which one uses to analyze feelings be it of the one-dimensional kind or multi-dimensional vagueness, or vagueness might be due to the fact that the necessary and sufficient conditions for feelings display characteristics of vagueness and/or in their combination show such characteristics of vagueness.

In the case of "I didn't know I was angry until I over-reacted like that" where an emotion is given, but no feeling, one would have to analyze further what an emotion then really is. Yet with regard to this example, one could also defend the view that actually a feeling is given, for an over-reaction only refers to something external, whereas at least in common understanding a feeling is something subjective and internal. So just from the fact that an over-reaction is given, one cannot conclude that no feeling is given. How this feeling then manifests or expresses itself is another matter, whether it manifests itself in an over-reaction, in avoidance behavior, etc. Moreover, there might be some people who probably would like to maintain, when one says that "I am angry" instead of saying "I feel anger", the emotion which one expresses by "I am angry" also includes a feeling. That is to say, on what kind of basis could one actually conclude that "I am angry" doesn't say anything about a feeling which one has? In my opinion "I am angry" is an expression of an emotion state which might include a feeling component. It would be a very efficient way of using one's resources, if one just had to say "I am angry", where that statement made clear that one has an emotion and a feeling going together with it at the same time. But why does one then have two words "feeling" and "emotion" to denote one state? Quite simply because there are certain kinds of feelings which are not accompanied by emotions, such as pain, which is not an emotion, but only a feeling. One's pain can be accompanied by an emotion, though, such as when I am angry about the pain I feel.

Cognition and emotion. From the foregoing one already gets an impression how cognition and emotion are interrelated and connected to each other. In this section we are going to explore that connection further. In this regard, Lane, Nadel, Allen, and Kaszniak (2000, p. 6) make the following plausible thesis: "It is not likely that one can identify a structure or region of the brain that is exclusively devoted to cognition or emotion and has no interaction with the other process." Yet, whether this is really the case, will be discussed in the chapter on the brain and the emotions. For it could also be the case that the brain is organized in a modular way and that there is functional segregation in the brain. In this regard, patients and animals with brain lesions will give us important information which claim turns out to be true, but also neuro-imaging studies and positron emission tomography (PET) studies on healthy humans will be looked at. The reason why studies on healthy humans are of vital importance has to do with the fact that lesions in humans—especially if they come from accidents, wars, or crimes—are not very precise; moreover, in the case of brain lesions of accident, war or crime victims one lesion probably differs from another lesion in some way. Furthermore, also brain lesions of patients who are neither accident nor war nor crime victims probably also differ from each other unless the operation was always done by the same physician using always the same technique. As a consequence the comparable samples of patients with brain lesions are most of the time really small, so that the results cannot be generalized to the overall population.

Heilman (2000, p. 331) reports some interesting observations which might throw some light on the cognition-emotion debate clarifying to some extent where cognition appears in the emotion process:

"in the clinic one can see patients who have strong emotions (such as fear) associated with medial temporal lobe or amygdala seizures. Sometimes patients become aware that they are beginning to have a seizure and the fear of having a seizure may lead to a fearful cognitive set. Autonomic and visceral changes may be associated with these partial seizures, and the patients may be aware of these changes and therefore experience fear. However, in many epileptic patients the emotional experience is often the first symptom. Therefore, in these patients the cognitive set comes after the experience rather than before the experience. The Schachter and Singer attribution theory cannot account for these observations."

The Schachter and Singer (1962) study confirmed that the cognitive set comes before the experience. However, the study by Schachter and Singer was not uncontroversial and received some criticism (cf. Cotton 1981; Mezzacappa, Katkin, and Palmer 1999; Plutchik and Ax 1967; Stricker 1967; Truax 1984). Yet, if one looks at Heilman's subjects, these are patients with epilepsy. One could assume or suspect that in patients with epilepsy the functioning of the brain might be different from healthy subjects. Also with regard to people with brain lesions the functioning of the brain might be totally different, for the simple reason that it might be possible that the body respectively the brain adapts to the lesion, so that healthy parts take over the work of the damaged parts. It could also be possible at least in principle that the brain gets completely rewired in the case of a significant lesion. Hence results from patients with epilepsy or brain-lesioned patients might not be of significance for the healthy population. Therefore, although the Heilman results are interesting, it is still an open question whether cognition comes before or after the emotional experience. Yet, that cognition quite clearly has an effect on one's emotions was demonstrated for the case of affective inertia. Perhaps future research will show more clearly that different cases have to be distinguished with regard to where, in which way, and how many times cognition enters the emotion process.

Prinz (2007, p. 57) summarizes in a very convincing way the different results found so far with regard to the cognition-emotion debate:

"Zajonc (1984) cites…evidence against cognitive theories.…Studies on facial feedback show that changing one's facial expression can unwittingly trigger the corresponding affective state (Strack et al., 1988). Studies of opponent-processing suggest that intense positive emotions cause a negative emotional after-affect, as in drug withdrawal, and conversely (Solomon, 1980).…LeDoux (1996) has shown that a visual stimulus can trigger an emotional response before the involvement of the neocortex. There is a subcortical pathway from the eyes into the amygdala, mediated by the thalamus.…When the amygdala triggers a bodily change, that change is experienced as an emotion.…Thalamic representations of visual stimuli are relatively unprocessed but they are sufficient for identifying certain emotionally salient objects. LeDoux gives the example of a coiled snake. This…can trigger a fear reaction before the cortex has time to allow for a perceptual judgment. Morris et al. (1999) present evidence that the thalamo-amygdala pathway also underwrites emotional responses to rapidly presented facial expressions. This pathway even allows for emotional responses to faces in blindsight.…[Individuals with blindsight] react emotionally to faces presented in their blind field even though they have no visual experience of those faces (de Gelder et al., 1999). It would be totally untenable to claim that the thalamus or the amygdala harbour concepts.…These findings strongly suggest that emotions can arise without judgments, thoughts, or other cognitive mediators."

Yet, just because emotions can arise without judgments, etc. this doesn't have to mean that they in fact in all the cases arise without judgments, etc.

Moreover, this doesn't have to mean that later on in the emotion process judgments might have no effect on the emotions.

Consciousness and emotions. I said with regard to the case "I didn't know I was angry until I over-reacted like that", where one can have an emotion without feeling the emotion, that in this case it is presupposed that one has to be conscious of one's emotions in order to have an emotion. Yet, we also ascribe emotions to animals such as cats, dogs, etc. where one might want to argue that their level of consciousness is not as high as ours with a declining amount of consciousness the farer away the evolutionary chain is from us humans, which seems then to suggest that the above case is an impossibility in extreme cases. As a preliminary result one would then have to conclude that emotions can be unconscious and conscious; the latter being obvious from our every day experience.[9] Something similar along these lines has been claimed by Damasio (2000, p. 15):

> "I will simply say that the term 'feeling' should be reserved for the private, mental experience of an emotion. The term 'emotion' should be used to designate all the responses whose perception we call feeling....Feeling and knowing that you feel are separable processes. It is conceivable that some animals have emotions and feelings but are not conscious of having them. Although I believe many nonhuman species are indeed conscious of their feelings."

Damasio's definition of feeling is also of significance with regard to the case "I didn't know I was angry until I over-reacted like that"; for Damasio seems to share my understanding expressed earlier that an over-reaction is not really a feeling, but rather an expression of a feeling, for he talks of all the responses whose perception we call feeling.

Later on Damasio (2004, p. 5) revises his definition of feeling quite a bit:

> "Feeling consists of the *joint perception* of (a) the causative object; (b) the ensuing *emotional state*, and (c) the cognitive mode and related thoughts that may follow. Thus the intentionality of the emotions...arises early in this physiological cycle with the perceptual definition of the emotionally competent stimulus, and is completed in

---

[9] I will discuss evidence for unconscious emotions later on in this section.

the feeling stage whose unfolding remains pointed to the emotionally-competent stimulus."

The only way to make these two different definitions compatible with each other is by maintaining that the private, mental experience of an emotion is equivalent to the joint perception in the just given definition. Yet, it seems odd to equate an experience with a perception, for one can say "I perceive the white wall in front of me", but it sounds a bit strange to say "I experience the white wall in front of me". That is to say, experiencing something seems to have at least in some cases some more active connotation than perceiving something. Also with regard to Damasio's last text passage, one could come up with the following counterexample to what a feeling is: I have pain, because I have a headache, but I don't have the slightest clue what caused the headache. Thus according to Damasio's definition I would have to conclude that I don't feel the pain of the headache which of course seems ridiculous unless one were to come up with a whole new term for cases where one has a feeling, but is not able to give the cause of that feeling.

With regard to the question of vagueness of feelings, if we consider the first definition for feeling given by Damasio, namely that it is a private, mental experience of an emotion, then one could at least maintain with regard to the term "private" that it has an opposite namely "public", so that these terms could be at the opposite ends of a continuum where boundarylessness might be given. Yet, could one also construct a sorites paradox out of these opposites? Yes, this could be possible, for consider the following case: a person lives in an apartment which has windows that are publicly accessible by everyone. At the beginning of the experiment the windows are not covered by anything, so that the person's life appears totally accessible to the public, but every five minutes there is paint sprayed on his windows which makes the windows less transparent each time, where the difference to the previous paint job is barely visible with the eye. Yet after five days or so, one is not able to see through the windows at all, so that the person's life becomes totally private. Hence, with regard to the term "private" quite clearly a case of vagueness is given.

With regard to Damasio's second definition of feeling that it is the joint perception of the causative object, the ensuing emotional state, and the cognitive mode and related thoughts that may follow, the following can be said: to start with the obvious, the term "related" is a very general term, and therefore would need some more specification in order to be able to obtain a proper evaluation of its vagueness. Yet, taken at face value, the term "related" is opposite to the term "unrelated" which at least with regard to certain subject areas could turn out to lie on a continuum, such as in the case of different, though related literature categories, where the distinctions between mystery thriller, romantic novel, etc. might just be a matter of degree and where each instance of one category could turn gradually with small insignificant steps into an instance of any of the other categories, so that boundarylessness exists and a sorites paradox can be construed. If one, however, considers other subject areas, such as related parallel evolutionary developments, which took part completely independently of each other, then there wouldn't be a continuum between "related" and "unrelated" and no sorites paradox could be construed. In this latter case "related", however, refers more to certain features shared in common, whereas in the literature case "related" refers more to how one can get from one category to the next.

With regard to the terms "causative object", at least the term "causative" is still underspecified, for there are many different explications of the term "causation" possible where there is up to now no agreement what the best explication is. Hence, it is very difficult to determine the vagueness of the term "causative". Also the term "object" is problematic with regard to evaluating it for its vagueness, for the simple reason that researchers are still undecided whether abstract objects exist or not; that is to say, there is no agreement yet what entities fall under the term. Also the terms "cognitive mode" and "emotional state" are not specified enough for being evaluated with regard to their vagueness. It is also unclear with regard to the terms "joint perception" how these different things—cognitive mode, emotional state, etc.—are connected with each other making it impossible to evaluate the terms "joint perception" for its vagueness. Hence, Damasio's second definition still leaves many questions unanswered.

But we should be getting back to the connection between consciousness and the emotions—the topic of this section. There are several questions to ask: (1) is the relation between consciousness and the emotions of relevance for an adequate analysis of the emotions? (2) What are the advantages and disadvantages of conscious respectively unconscious emotions? (3) Is unconscious emotion a coherent notion? (4) Is there evidence for unconscious emotions?

With regard to the first point, we first have to clarify how the evidence for unconscious emotions might look like, before we can answer the question whether the relation between consciousness and the emotions is of relevance for an adequate analysis of the emotions. In this regard Neu (2000, pp. 212-213) has advanced the view that evidence of the unconscious has to be indirect and cannot be direct, for the crude demand for confirmation by direct observation with regard to the unconscious is as misplaced as a demand to be shown electrons which we can see only by means of electron-microscopes. Yet, we will see later on some evidence for unconscious emotions by means of subliminal phenomena which seems pretty direct evidence for unconscious emotions.

Damasio (1999, pp. 252-253) points out that there is a connection between consciousness and the emotions, if one takes brain research into account:

"The divider between the part of reticular formation whose damage alters consciousness...is fairly clear. You can see it well when you imagine a plane sectioning the brain stem in an orientation perpendicular to its long axis. The level for setting the plane is about the level at which the trigeminal nerve...happens to enter the brain stem....a number of nuclei involved in high-order control of homeostasis, including the control of emotion, are located above this plane....Likewise for the monoamine nuclei concerned with delivery of norepinephrine and dopamine, and for the acetylcholine nuclei. They begin to appear precisely at this level and creep upward along this region. Serotonin nuclei are also located above this area (although...serotonin nuclei also occur at lower levels...)."

The fact that serotonin nuclei also appear below the level of consciousness in the brain and not only above speaks in favor of the possibility of unconscious emotions. However, at the same time the location of norepinephrine, dopamine, and acetylcholine nuclei is evidence for conscious emotions.

In favor of unconscious emotions speaks that Lane (2000, p. 362) reports the fact that decorticate cats can show fear and pleasure reactions.

Yet, Panksepp (1998, p. 57) highlights the finding that complete separation of the viscera from the brain by spinal cord lesions leads to a reduction of the intensity of emotions. Similarly, Damasio (1999, p. 289) states that the higher the placement of damage in the spinal cord, the more impaired the subject's feeling is. While in the first case no consciousness is given, in the second case consciousness is given, but the intensity of emotions is reduced by spinal cord lesions, because the brain doesn't get any input of these paralyzed areas, so that a reduction in the intensity of emotions is to be expected in the second case.

Damasio (1999, p. 96) points towards other evidence for the connection between consciousness and the emotions, for in the case of absence seizures not only consciousness but also emotion, attention, and appropriate behavior is momentarily suspended. Moreover, Damasio (1999, pp. 99-100) highlights the fact that one finds the suspension of emotion also in absence automatism and in akinetic mutisms, which leads him to believe that the absence of emotion is reliably correlated with a defective core consciousness; furthermore, Damasio thinks it is no coincidence that deep sleep is not accompanied by emotional expressions, whereas in dream sleep when consciousness returns one can easily find emotional expressions in humans and in animals.

Yet, if one has a nightmare with fearful experiences or an erotic dream with joyful experiences is one then really fully conscious? Or is more of a semi-consciousness given, for one mostly cannot remember the respective dream the next morning? Another example is where you get a complete anesthesia and are about to drift off into sleep when someone annoys you by banging the doors. In this case consciousness is also not fully given. Or consider the case where you are about to wake up and you get scared because of feeling something crawling on your arm. Also here full consciousness is not present. Yet, with regard to this question, whether one has to be conscious in order to have an emotion one might have problems answering it completely and correctly as it stands unless one made an effort to define consciousness properly. Observe, however, with regard to the presented cases so far, no appeal was made to repressed or suppressed emotions to defend the view that emotions don't have to be conscious. Thus the evidence so far seems already to support the view that emotions don't have to be conscious.

Even if there is so much evidence for a connection between consciousness and the emotions, does one have to take it seriously? In this regard Lane (2000, p. 345) reports:

"Some investigators (Bradley & Lang, this volume; LeDoux, 1996) have argued that the conscious experience of emotion is a red herring....These investigators tend to focus on the biological...substrates of emotion in laboratory animals or on the biological similarity between lower animals and people. Other investigators (Clore, 1994; Damasio, 1994; Heilman, 1997) consider the conscious experience of emotion to be a core component of the emotion construct....these investigators tend to study the behavior of human beings including their self-reports."

In my opinion, even if consciousness were not a peripheral but a central component of the emotions, it would be a mistake to study just human subjects with regard to the emotions, for that would amount to denying where we are coming from. From emotions' predecessors in other animals we could also learn something about why we do have emotions; moreover, predecessors of emotions might also reveal the components of emotions more clearly than our emotions in fact do. That is to say, in my opinion the history of a phenomenon might also reveal something interesting and valuable about the phenomenon.

With regard to the second point, namely the advantages and disadvantages of conscious respectively unconscious emotions, Lane (2000, p. 346) reports the following deliberations by Damasio:

"Damasio (1994) points out that the advantage of conscious awareness of emotion is that it allows emotional information to be integrated with cognitive processes. If emotions were always unconscious, it would not be possible to voluntarily control emotional responses and expressions....If emotions are conscious, it is possible to think ahead, avoid, plan, and generalize to similar but unfamiliar situations. Planning ahead requires drawing on past experiences as reference points. Thus, consciousness extends time from the present into both the past and future. Conscious awareness therefore offers flexibility of response in the moment based on the particular history of an individual's unique interactions with his or her environment. This flexibility includes the capacity for emotional control. Thus, it may be that the capacity to be consciously aware of emotions is not an epiphenomenon but in fact has evolved through natural selection because it contributes to adaptational success, including survival."

In this quote Damasio, as reported by Lane, supposes that emotions are under our voluntary control and that actions are connected to the emotions in that the emotions help us planning our life. Yet, the former point has been a bone of contention for millennia. However, Damasio (1999, p. 50) reports some anecdotal evidence for it which was got by means of an experiment with the pianist Maria João while she was listening to music: in the condition "emotion allowed" she showed a skin conductance record full of peaks and valleys, while in the condition "emotion reduced" her skin conductance record was flattened and the movement of the head and facial musculature was reduced. In my opinion, already the capacity of actors to fake and suppress their emotions quite clearly speaks in favor of us humans being able to control our emotions to at least some extent (for more on this issue see Ledwig (2006, chapter one)). Also if emotions are most of the time conscious, they can help us solve the frame problem (cf. Ledwig 2006, p. 50 ff.) and draw our attention to the relevant information in ourselves or our environment and make our lives therefore more manageable.

After having dealt with the advantages of conscious emotions, now to the question what could unconscious emotions be good for? Perhaps sometimes it is better that certain bad emotionally laden memories are repressed, because it would offset our normal functioning in such a way that we would completely lose control over ourselves which wouldn't be very good with regard to an optimal adaptation to the situation and therefore bad for our overall survival. Another possibility for the goodness of unconscious emotions is the following: perhaps our unconscious emotions are faster than our conscious emotions, so that we could act faster on the basis of an unconscious emotion instead of a conscious one, which could be good for our survival. As fear reactions are so fast, why cannot there be other kinds of emotions which are also that fast? At least in principle nothing speaks against that possibility. Perhaps it could also be the case, if our unconscious emotions were also conscious, our system would have too much information to deal with at the same time—too much input so to speak—, so that it is better for us that they are unconscious.

Another speculative idea is that unconscious emotions are the extra gram which might make the scale tip to the other side in cases of conflict between different courses of action.

With regard to the third point, namely the coherence of unconscious emotions, Öhman, Flykt, and Lundqvist (2000, p. 298) observe the following:

"Unconscious emotion becomes a serious problem only if one claims that feeling is the necessary condition of emotion, because then it implies a contradiction in terms (Clore, 1994)."

But why can't there be unconscious feelings? After all, we sometimes do perceive things without perceiving them really as in the case of change blindness. If one in a picture, for instance, changes an insignificant detail, people mostly don't perceive the difference between the two different pictures if they are presented sequentially. Hence, cases like this one might make it appear possible that emotion theories with unconscious feelings could turn out to be true.

With regard to Öhman, Flykt, and Lundqvist's (2000, p. 298) claim that it is the common sense view that all causally important psychological events appear in consciousness before they, for example, lead to actions, I would like to know why this is considered to be a common sense view, for I was not aware of this view (common sense should be known to everyone—otherwise it wouldn't be common). That common sense doesn't believe in hocus pocus or ghosts appearing in a séance seems obvious, but that doesn't mean that common sense doesn't believe in things which are not for everyone else to see or perceive. For instance, everyone knows the phenomenon that one knows a word, it doesn't come to one's mind, but it lies so to speak on the tip of one's tongue. Here quite clearly we have a phenomenon which is unconscious but which everyone is aware of, so that there are unconscious phenomena possible in the common sense view. Of course, Öhman and colleagues could reply that the tip of the tongue phenomenon is not of causal importance; yet it is not obvious to me why one can't construe a case where the tip of the tongue phenomenon might be causally important and where despite its unconsciousness the phenomenon might lead to actions.

With regard to the fourth point, namely evidence of unconscious emotions, Damasio (1999, pp. 43-46) reports the following findings of the so-called good-guy/bad-guy experiment conducted with David, one of his patients, who cannot learn anything new due to extensive damage to both temporal lobes including the hippocampus, which is necessary for creating memories of new facts, and including damages to the amygdala: David was involved in three different kinds of human interaction over the period of a week. One type of interaction was with a good guy, who was always extremely pleasant, welcoming, and rewarding. Another type of interaction was with a neutral guy, who was emotionally neutral and who engaged David in activities that were neither rewarding nor punishing. A third type of interaction was with a bad guy, who was unpleasant and not welcoming, and who engaged David in an extremely boring task. These kinds of interaction were spread over five consecutive days for specified time intervals arranged in random order. When this part of the experiment was over, David participated in two different tasks. In the first task David looked at sets of four photographs which included the face of one of the three collaborators in the experiment, that is, the good guy, the neutral guy, or the bad guy, and David was asked to whom he would go for help in case he needed it and who in this group he thought was his friend. When the good guy was in the set, David chose the good guy in over 80% over the cases which clearly suggests non-randomness. When the neutral guy was in the set, he was chosen with a probability not greater than chance. When the bad guy was in the set, he was almost never chosen. In the second task, David was asked to look at the faces of the three collaborators in the experiment and asked what he knew about them. Nothing came to his mind. However, when he was asked, who among the three his friend was, he consistently chose the good guy. Damasio explains David's nonconscious preferences for the good guy over the others by the emotions that arose during the experiment and by the nonconscious reinduction of some part of the emotions at the time David was being tested.

Despite the fact that in this case we just have evidence of nonconscious emotions indirectly, namely by means of David's preference for the good guy over the others, despite the fact that nothing was said about the emotions experienced during the initial setup of the experiment, and despite the fact that just one experimental subject participated in the experiment, it seems very difficult to interpret Damasio's findings differently. However, I still find it problematic to generalize from just one instance to the overall human population. Yet, one finds also other kinds of evidence for unconscious emotions as pointed out by Lane (2000, p. 360):

"Zajonc and colleagues (Kunst-Wilson & Zajonc, 1980) have demonstrated that people develop preferences for stimuli to which they have been subliminally exposed but have not consciously perceived....Murphy and Zajonc (1993) have shown that subjects can accurately make crude positive or negative judgments about stimuli that are not consciously perceived, but more refined evaluations of the stimuli, such as the type of emotion depicted, are not possible in the absence of conscious awareness....Ladavas (Ladavas et al., 1993) has shown that the presence or absence of emotional content can be accurately detected in subliminally presented pictures."

LeDoux (2000, p. 142) distinguishes between implicit and explicit emotional memories, their connection to consciousness, and relates them to different parts of the brain:

"Implicit emotional memories are automatically elicited in the presence of trigger stimuli and do not require conscious retrieval or recall, whereas explicit memories of emotion are retrieved consciously. In humans, damage to the amygdala interferes with implicit emotional memories but not explicit memories about emotions, whereas damage to the medial temporal lobe memory system interferes with explicit memories about emotions but not with implicit emotional memories (Bechera et al., 1995; LaBar et al., 1995)."

With regard to these results, it is unclear to me whether the evidence refers to episodic memory or not. What becomes obvious from these results is that it might be difficult to part emotions from other phenomena such as memories or perceptions, so that it might be difficult to say which brain parts are really necessary for the emotions to arise. What becomes evident when one looks at these results is that one has to distinguish between unconscious and conscious emotions on the one hand and unconscious and unconscious retrieval of emotional memories on the other hand. Taken all the facts together, it seems pretty much proven that besides conscious emotions there are also unconscious emotions.

That were is a close connection between emotions and memory in humans and in animals is supported by the following findings (Damasio

86

1999, pp. 294-295): if you are told two stories which are comparable in the number of facts given with one of them differing from the other because it has high emotional content, you will remember much more from the emotional story than from the other one. Rats react similarly when they are placed in an equivalent situation. However, if the vagus nerves of the rats are severed, emotion no longer helps the rats in their performance, for they don't have the necessary visceral input to the brain any longer.

As it is generally assumed that animals don't have such high levels of consciousness as humans do, these latter findings also support the hypothesis that emotions cannot only be conscious, but also unconscious, I conclude.

Vagueness, consciousness, and emotions. With regard to the following cases one could argue for a continuum between consciousness and unconsciousness, so that even here boundarilessness is given and a sorites paradox can be construed: drifting into sleep due to complete anesthesia or due to natural tiredness, dream sleep, and waking up from an ordinary sleep or after an operation. Moreover, because one could argue that the level of consciousness ranging from plants over animals to humans changes quantitatively and not qualitatively—one just has to look at cases where plants direct themselves towards the sun or where amoeba avoid certain chemicals as very primitive forms of consciousness—, also in this regard vagueness might enter the picture.

Conclusion

Many emotion theories turn out to be relatively vaguely formulated. As a consequence one has problems to evaluate the phenomena behind them for their vagueness. However, both multi-component theories of the emotions and one-component theories of the emotions reveal the vagueness of their components due to the presence of continua. With regard to the cognition-emotion debate it is not settled yet in which different kind of ways cognition may enter the emotion process. With regard to the consciousness of emotions, there is ample evidence for the view that emotions cannot only be conscious but can also be unconscious. Moreover, it seems reasonable to assume that vagueness also pertains to the conscious-unconscious dimension.

Chapter 3 The Brain and the Emotions

How the brain works. In this book I don't want to deal with the question whether a dualism or monism holds with regard to the mind and the brain or whether mind-states can be reduced to brain-states or vice versa. However, with advances in the neurosciences, it seems to be inevitable that one deals with the results found in brain research as it relates to the emotions. In order to do that one first has to get an idea how the brain works. In this regard, Dolan and Morris (2000, pp. 225-226) point out the following two hypotheses of how the brain functions:

"functional segregation, emphasizes that processing in discrete modules may be anatomically localized. A contrasting view is that higher brain functions are emergent properties of interactions between functionally specialized brain regions. Evidence of functional segregation within the human brain is now overwhelming....the integrationist model derives its appeal from the likelihood that the function of even highly segregated brain regions are coordinated during normal perception and action (Roelfsema et al., 1997)....segregation and integration are amenable to a unifying framework (Tononi et al., 1994)."

At the end of this chapter, we will hopefully be in a better position to evaluate whether functional segregation or integration of the brain is a more appropriate model with regard to the emotions or whether even a combination of the two seems best to fit the data. Perhaps it might be even possible that emotions differ with regard to whether functional segregation or integration or a combination of the two holds, for higher cognitive emotions might involve more different structures in the brain than basic emotions. One finds the distinction between higher cognitive emotions and basic emotions in Griffiths (1997, pp. 14, 77-99, 100-122). Damasio (1994, pp. 131-134) similarly distinguishes between primary and secondary emotions drawing on James (1967). For a historic account of basic emotions see Goldie (2000, p. 87).

Brainstem. With regard to the brainstem, there have not been so many connections to the emotions made yet. However, as the brainstem belongs to the oldest parts of the brain, it is not to be expected that higher cognitive emotions, which are supposed to come later in evolutionary development, might be completely driven by it. One could rather expect that there is a connection between basic emotions, which are supposed to come earlier in evolutionary development, and the brainstem. In this regard, Damasio (1999, pp. 48-49) points out that already in *Descartes' Error* he drew attention to the fact that spontaneous smiles that are caused by genuine delight or spontaneous sobbing that comes from grief are produced by structures in the brainstem over which we have no direct voluntary control. As smiles and sobbing are expressions of emotions and as happiness and sadness belong to the basic emotions, there is a connection established between basic emotions and the brainstem.

In 1999 Damasio (pp. 258-259) makes the connection between certain emotions and the brainstem more specific; for he points out the following findings: in a positron emission tomography study with healthy subjects, brainstem structures within the upper reticular formation become maximally active with sadness and anger, but only little active with happiness. Also here we just have a connection between certain basic emotions and the brainstem and no connection between higher cognitive emotions, such as envy, guilt, jealousy, etc., and the brainstem.

Further evidence for a connection between emotions and the brainstem we have from patients who suffer from locked-in syndrome, Damasio (1999, p. 243) reports; for locked-in syndrome only occurs when the damage is located in the front part of the brain stem and patients who suffer from locked-in syndrome show a profound defect of motor control which leads to a reduction of emotional reactivity producing an inward calm state. Hence, one could derive the hypothesis that there is a connection between the brainstem and the intensity of emotions, because the visceral and behavioral in- and output has to pass the brainstem, when emotions are elicited. This hypothesis would have to be proven with healthy subjects, however, in order to be advocated without question.

Hemispheres. As there has been ample evidence that certain parts of the hemispheres of the human brain have specific tasks, such as Broca's area and Wernicke's area in the case of language, something similar might also hold with regard to emotional phenomena. In this regard Damasio (1999, pp. 38-39) reports that Darwin, James, and Freud were vague about the brain aspect of the emotions, but their contemporary, Hughlings

Jackson, hypothesized that the right hemisphere was probably dominant with regard to the emotions. Yet at least some current evidence speaks in favor of a differentiation with regard to the emotions. For Prinz (2007, p. 75) reports findings which associate approach emotions with the right hemisphere, whereas withdrawal emotions are more associated with the left hemisphere. That the different hemispheres get associated with different emotions has historic predecessors, for Kolb and Taylor (2000, p. 79) highlight the following facts:

"The idea that the two hemispheres might have different roles in the control of emotion goes back at least to Goldstein (1939), who suggested that left hemisphere lesions produce 'catastrophic' reactions characterized by fearfulness and depression, whereas right hemisphere lesions produce 'indifference.' The first systematic study of these contrasting behavioural effects was done by Gainotti in 1969, who showed that catastrophic reactions occurred in 62% of his left hemisphere sample, compared with only 10% of his right hemisphere cases. In contrast, indifference was more common in the right hemisphere patients, occurring in 38%, as compared with only 11% of the left hemisphere cases."

As the experimental subjects were patients, the results have to be taken cum granum salis and further evidence from imagining studies and PET scans should verify these results for normal subjects who don't have any brain damage or diseases which involve at least parts of the brain before any generalizations are made.

Heilman (2000, p. 332) also just reports evidence from patients:

"Ross et al. (1994) observed that some patients undergoing selective hemispheric anesthesia…changed their emotional response to events that they previously recalled and that the emotional response appeared to be dependent on the hemisphere that was anesthetized. For example, in the absence of hemispheric anesthesia, one of their subjects told of an incident where he was very frightened. However, when his right hemisphere was anesthetized and he was asked to recall this incident, he stated that he felt embarrassed. Based on observations such as these, Ross et al. posited that whereas the right hemisphere is important for primary emotions such as fear, the left is important for social emotions such as embarrassment."

Notwithstanding the fact that only patients were involved in the last two groups of studies, if we compare the results of those studies, another problem arises. For Ross et al. claim that the right hemisphere is important for primary emotions such as fear, whereas Goldstein and Gainotti associate the left hemisphere with catastrophic reactions such as fearfulness and depression. Alternatively, one could advance the view that these results don't exclude each other, so that both hemispheres are involved with regard to different emotional phenomena, such as primary emotions and catastrophic reactions, but I take it that these researchers actually made such exclusivity claims.

Different ways to make these results coherent are the following: perhaps Goldstein and Gainotti take fearfulness to be anxiety and not fear, so that no problem of incoherence with Ross et al. results. Another way out is to look for restrictions such as in the case of emotional reactions the left hemisphere is involved, whereas with regard to the sustaining of an emotion, the control of an emotion, etc. the right hemisphere is involved in order to render their results coherent. Another possibility is to check for what kind of lesions, diseases, or damages to the brain the different patients had in order to explain their different reactions in these different studies. The fact that decorticate cats can show fear (cf. Lane 2000, p. 362) might, however, speak against just only a particular hemisphere being involved with regard to the primary emotions such as fear, given that the analogy between cats and human beings is justified in this case. The upcoming sections will give us more clarity with regard to which sections of the brain are involved with regard to which emotions.

Frontal lobe. Although Heilman (2000) also emphasizes the importance of the different hemispheres, Heilman (2000, pp. 339-340) focuses more on the frontal lobes and comes up with explanations why certain emotions might be connected to certain sides of the frontal lobes; in particular he points out the following in this regard:

"Whereas the right frontal lobe appears to be important in the mediation of emotions with negative valence, the left frontal lobe may be important in the mediation of emotions with positive valence. Depending on the nature of the stimulus, some positive and some negative emotions are associated with high arousal (e. g., joy and fear) and others with low arousal (e. g., satisfaction and sadness). Whereas the right parietal lobe appears to be important in mediating arousal response, the left hemisphere appears to inhibit the arousal response. Some positive and negative emotions are associated with motor activation (e. g., anger, fear, and joy) and others are not (e. g., sadness). The frontal lobes, especially the right, appear to be important in motor activation. The motor activation associated with emotions may be either toward the eliciting stimulus (approach) or away from the stimulus (avoidance). Whereas approach behaviors may be mediated, in part, by the parietal lobes, avoidance behaviors may be mediated by the frontal lobes."

In comparison to the foregoing studies where Ross et al. maintained that primary emotions such as fear are related to the right hemisphere and social emotions such as embarrassment are connected to the left hemisphere, Heilman partially agrees and partially disagrees with this statement. For according to Heilman negative emotions are connected to the right frontal lobe, whereas positive emotions are related to the left frontal lobe. One could assume that both fear and embarrassment would be connected to the right hemisphere according to Heilman, because they are both considered as negative, and not to the left hemisphere as was postulated for embarrassment in the case of Ross et al. One way to make these two different standpoints compatible with each other would be that Heilman doesn't consider embarrassment to be an emotion. And I am sure there are researchers who take that position. Another possibility could be that Heilman takes the stance that embarrassment is in fact a positive emotion, because it motivates the person to show better behavior, performance, etc. in the future. Although Heilman distinguishes between different functions in the brain with regard to the emotions, such as motor activation, and therefore shows a considerable improvement to the previous studies, taken by itself, the evidence which has been accumulated so far doesn't seem to be entirely convincing, but still rather contradictory. Perhaps one has to make further distinctions with regard to the brain and/or one has to conduct metastudies to obtain significant overall results with regard to the emotions.

Kolb and Taylor (2000, p. 68) add further to the already existing confusion because they point out the following:

"There is a general impression in the literature (e. g., Benson & Blumer, 1975; Kolb & Whishaw, 1996) that right frontal and left frontal lobe patients have distinctly different changes in emotional behavior. Left frontal lobe patients tend to be very quiet and display little affect, whereas right frontal lobe patients tend to be more talkative and, at times, can appear almost psychopathic in their interpersonal behaviors."

These results go quite clearly against the suggestions by Goldstein and the results by Gainotti, for patients with right hemisphere damage were characterized by indifference in Gainotti, whereas patients with left hemisphere damage showed catastrophic reactions in Gainotti. Yet, it might be problematic and difficult to characterize a psychopathic and talkative patient as indifferent unless one takes talkativeness as chattiness and psychopathy as emotional flatness. While I have already made some suggestions what could be responsible for the discrepancy in the results in the previous section, another possibility is that certain experimental effects might be responsible for the diverging results. That is, in case there have not been any double blind studies done, one cannot be absolutely sure that the experimenter consciously or unconsciously tried to influence the reactions of the experimental subjects and/or one cannot exclude the possibility that the experimental subjects just wanted to be good experimental subjects and tried to fulfill the experimenter's wishes by conforming to the experimenter's implicit or explicit suggestions. Looking at the results of this and the last section, the results are not very encouraging for drawing any general conclusions so far.

Prefrontal activation. That the prefrontal cortex is involved with regard to emotion regulation has been supported by neuroimaging studies, for Phillips (2006, p. 237) points out the following results: "in healthy individuals, findings from neuroimaging studies have indicated that dorsal and ventromedial prefrontal cortical regions may be implicated in the regulation of emotional responses and behaviour, both during suppression and reappraisal processes." Also Davidson (2000) seems to make up for the up to now not very promising studies and inconclusive results, because Davidson (2000, pp. 376-377) states:

"In both infants (Davidson & Fox, 1989) and adults (Davidson & Tomarken, 1989), we noticed that there were large individual differences in baseline electrophysiological measures of prefrontal activation and that such individual variation was associated with differences in aspects of affective reactivity. In infants, Davidson and Fox (1989) reported that 10-month-old babies who cried in response to maternal separation were more likely to have less left-side and greater right-side prefrontal activation during a preceding resting baseline compared with those infants who did not cry in response to this challenge. In adults, we first noted that the phasic influence of positive and negative emotion elicitors (e. g., film clips) on measures of prefrontal activation asymmetry appeared to be superimposed upon more tonic individual differences in the direction and absolute magnitude of asymmetry (Davidson & Tomarken, 1989)."

When considering these results, one could hypothesize that in the previous cases, where hemispheric differences were reported which were inconsistent with each other, one possible explanation of these facts is that in these studies individual differences might account for these effects, too. For differences in affective reactivity might not also be due to separation as is the case here, but might also result from other manipulations during the experiment which might explain the incompatible results in the previous studies. That is to say, certain stimuli might have led to high affective reactivity in certain experimental subjects, whereas other stimuli might have caused low affective reactivity in certain other experimental subjects. Thus the present results are helpful in interpreting and illuminating the previous evidence.

With regard to the Davidson studies, the following can be said: to take crying as a sign of affective reactivity in infants might be justified as infants probably don't know yet how to fake and/or suppress affective reactions. In adults this might be considered much more problematical and cannot be taken as completely granted. The bigger individual differences in the case of adults might be due to the faking and/or suppressing of emotional tendencies in certain adults, whereas certain other adults might not have faked and/or suppressed their emotions. The bigger individual differences in the case of adults might, however, also be due to the fact that adults might differ in their evaluation of what they are exposed to and how they conceive of it from infants.

Elaborating further Davidson (2000, p. 378) points out the following particular results of his study:

"We found that individual differences in prefrontal asymmetry predicted the emotional response to the films even after measures of baseline mood were statistically removed. Those individuals with more left-sided prefrontal activation at baseline reported more positive affect to the positive film clips, and those with more right-sided prefrontal activation reported more negative affect to the negative film clips. These findings support the idea that individual differences in electrophysiological measures of prefrontal activation asymmetry mark some aspect of vulnerability to positive and negative emotion elicitors."

These results could quite clearly help explain the conflicting results in the previous studies and would go together with Heilman's findings, so that positive affect was connected to individuals with more left-sided prefrontal activation and negative affect was related to individuals with more right-sided prefrontal activation. Thus individual differences might account for the incompatible effects.

When one considers the previous study by Davidson one might wonder what accounts for the huge individual differences in the sidedness of prefrontal activation. In another study, where Davidson (2000, p. 380) investigates the emotional behavior of other primates, Davidson suggests a preliminary explanation:

"we obtained measures of brain electrical activity from a large sample of rhesus monkeys (n = 50) (Kalin et al., 1998)....A subsample of 15 of these monkeys were tested on 2 occasions 4 months apart. We found that the test-retest correlation for measures of prefrontal asymmetry was .62, suggesting similar stability of this metric in monkeys and humans. In the group of 50 animals, we also obtained measures of plasma cortisol....We hypothesized that if individual differences in prefrontal asymmetry were associated with dispositional affective style, such differences should be correlated with cortisol because individual differences in baseline cortisol have been related to various aspects of trait-related stressful behavior and psychopathology (see, e. g., Gold et al., 1988). We found that animals with right-side prefrontal activation had higher levels of baseline cortisol than their left-frontally activated counterparts....Moreover, when blood samples were collected 2 years after our initial testing, animals classified as showing extreme right-sided prefrontal activation at age one year had significantly higher baseline cortisol levels when they were three years of age compared with animals who were classified at age one year as displaying extreme left-side prefrontal activation."

While 15 is a very small subsample which is actually too small to base a generalization on and also 50 is not particularly high besides the fact that we deal with rhesus monkeys and not with humans, the discovery of a connection between the baseline cortisol level and the different sides of prefrontal activation seems to be of significance especially as it seems to be rather stable over time. While stressful behavior and psychopathology might be connected to the emotions as one for instance can see in the case of depression (cf. the chapter on moods in this book), one would like to have a more explicit connection between levels of cortisol and the different emotions stated—otherwise it seems rather difficult to explain and predict different emotional behavior of different people. Yet, we will come back to the role of cortisol in later sections and chapters elucidating with regard to which emotions it might be of utmost importance, at which location cortisol interferes in the brain, and whether cortisol not only has a function for rhesus monkeys, but also for humans.

Insular cortex. Bermond, Vorst, and Moormann (2006, p. 345) report that a number of studies have shown that the insular cortex is involved in the regulation of negative emotional experiences, such as pain, distress, hunger, thirst, fear, anger, sadness, and disgust, emotional decision making, and the production of facial emotional expressions. Yet, ordinarily one wouldn't consider pain, distress, hunger, and thirst to be emotions; they might lead to certain emotions, however. Pain, for instance, might lead to anger directed at the cause of the pain. Also as I already said before, facial emotional expressions can be suppressed and/or faked, so they might not be a good indicator that a certain emotion is present.

That the insular cortex is implicated with regard to certain emotions is interesting. Yet, one would like to know in which way, and is it vital that the insular cortex is involved? The evidence presented so far doesn't yield enough information in order to evaluate the importance of the insular cortex in the emotion process. That differs widely from what we know

96

about the amygdala. Its central role with regard to the emotions has been widely demonstrated. Hence we turn now to the amygdala and its function and/or particular involvement with regard to the emotions. In the following section, however, it will also become more obvious in which way the insular cortex is involved with regard to the emotions.

Amygdala and connections to other structures in the brain. Heilman (2000, p. 330) makes clear in a very detailed and informative way how the amygdala is connected to other structures in the brain, such as the insula, and points out the significance of the amygdala and the insula with regard to visceral feedback, such as heartbeat, etc.; as a result it becomes more obvious how the amygdala and the insula are involved with regard to the emotions and whether there is more segregation or integration of the brain given with regard to the emotions: according to Heilman one needs efferent and afferent systems in order to receive visceral feedback. Moreover, the autonomous nervous system consists of two components, namely the sympathetic and the parasympathetic. While the descending sympathetic neurons receive input from the hypothalamus, and the hypothalamus receives input from many limbic and paralimbic areas which includes the amygdala, the most important parasympathetic nerve is the vagus. The vagus originates in the dorsal motor nucleus which is located in the brainstem and which projects to visceral organs, such as the heart. According to Heilman the amygdala projects information to the hypothalamus and sends information directly to the nucleus of the solitary tract and to the dorsal motor sympathetic system. Heilman states that the amygdala not only projects information, but also receives neocortical input. Heilman reports that besides the fact that the amygdala might be the most important part of the limbic system to influence the autonomic nervous system and viscera, the insula and orbitofrontal cortex can also induce autonomic and visceral changes. The insula and orbitofrontal cortex also receive information from the neocortex. The vagus nerve is the major nerve that carries visceral afferent information back to the brain. These afferents have their end point in the nucleus of the solitary tract which sends information to the central nucleus of the amygdala. The central nucleus of the amygdala sends information to other amygdala nuclei and the insula. The amygdala and insula send information to the temporal, parietal, and frontal lobes.

From Heilman's description one gets the general impression that there is more integration than segregation within the brain with regard to the emotions. For Heilman just mainly states how the different areas in the brain are connected to each other functionally. Yet, later on in this chapter it will become obvious that the amygdala is very much involved in the emotion of fear, which might separate the amygdala from other regions in the brain with regard to the emotion of fear. That is to say, it is not obvious from Heilman's account whether with regard particular emotions, such as love, envy, anxiety, fear, etc., there is more integration than segregation within the brain or whether emotions might differ from each other with regard to integration and segregation within the brain. Heilman's account also leaves unclear whether there is insofar segregation between the amygdala, the insula, and the orbitofrontal cortex in that the amygdala may be responsible for certain autonomic and visceral changes, whereas the insula and orbitofrontal cortex are connected to certain other kind of autonomic and visceral changes, which is unfortunate because we are then not able to evaluate whether these areas are more segregated than integrated with each other.

Also the following passage by Tranel et al. (2006, p. 228) is too unspecific in order to evaluate properly whether there is more segregation than integration of different brain regions with regard to the emotions given; yet, Tranel et al. point to regions of the brain which have not been implicated in other studies of the emotions so far which is illuminating in itself:

"Another important point is that several structures other than the amygdala have been implicated in mediating various aspects of emotional experience: for instance, somatosensory cortices in the right hemisphere, the insula (Craig, 2002), the substantia nigra (Dejjani et al., 1999), a number of pontine and brainstem nuclei involved in control of and representation of interoceptive information (Damasio et al., 2000), anterior cingulated cortex (Lane et al., 1998), and even regions of the spinal cord (Hohmann, 1966)."

As the data so far seems to be inconclusive with regard to the question of integration or segregation of different brain areas with regard to the emotions, we still have to await further evidence which will be presented in the following sections to come to a decisive conclusion.

Amygdala, fear, and other emotions. Yet, to further dampen our high spirits Reddy (2008, p. 84) goes so far as to claim the following:

"As with intentions or perceptions, we have evidence of emotions in others only indirectly. Psychologists can measure slowed reaction times, misperceptions and slips, endocrine system states, arousal levels, even blood flows through the amygdala or neurotransmitters in the nucleus accumbens—but these are not emotions. Despite long effort, no one-to-one correspondence has been found between specific emotions and specific arousal states."

With these critical remarks, Reddy draws our attention to important questions, though. For what kind of status do findings with regard to the brain actually have? Do they show that certain features of the brain are essential for eliciting, sustaining, and/or changing emotions? Especially with regard to neuroimaging studies one might wonder in which way the results found in rather artificial situations carry over to the real life. For a very critical but also very illuminating study of neuroimaging see Huesing (2008). Yet, perhaps in the future these new measurement instruments become more patient friendly, so that one, for instance, doesn't have to worry about whether the experimental subjects become claustrophobic and whether emotions were really elicited and one can hope that the results also carry over to normal conditions.

Against Reddy's dreadful diagnosis, one can, however, quite clearly show a one-to-one correspondence between the feeling of trust and amygdala damage according to Damasio (1999, pp. 66-67): in this experiment 100 human faces which had been previously rated by 46 normal individuals as showing different degrees of trustworthiness and approachability were to be judged by different kinds of experimental groups. One group included 3 patients with bilateral damage to the amygdala; another group included 7 patients with damage to either the left or the right amygdala. A third group consisted of 3 patients with damage to the hippocampus and an inability to learn new facts. And finally, a fourth group which included 10 patients had damages outside the amygdala and outside the hippocampus, but within the brain. With regard to trustworthy faces, patients with bilateral amygdala damage evaluated them as trustworthy; however, suspicious faces were evaluated by this group as equally trustworthy separating patients with bilateral amygdala damage from all the other groups and healthy persons.

While this study has too few participants, so that one has to be careful with regard to generalizing the results, it nevertheless shows a quite clear one-to-one correspondence. However, one might want to criticize this study on the grounds that the feeling of trustworthiness is not really an emotion. Also as previously already pointed out, we have here brain damaged patients as experimental subjects, where it is not obvious whether what holds with regard to them also holds with regard to healthy people. Hence overall Reddy's criticism is not completely off the table yet.

Yet, Damasio (1999, pp. 61-62) comes up with further evidence for the view that there is a one-to-one correspondence between certain emotions and certain brain regions: he for instance has shown that sadness consistently leads to an activation of the ventromedial prefrontal cortex, hypothalamus, and brain stem, whereas anger and fear don't activate the prefrontal cortex and the hypothalamus. However, all three emotions lead to brain stem activation. Moreover, Damasio has demonstrated in a series of studies that the amygdala is necessary for recognizing fear in facial expressions, to being conditioned to fear, and to expressing fear. Damasio has however also pointed out that the amygdala is not involved in recognizing or learning about disgust or happiness. This should cast considerable doubt on Reddy's claim and actually bolster the view that there is in fact a one-to-one correspondence between different emotions and different regions in the brain.

That there is a clear connection between fear and the amygdala has been shown in many other studies involving both humans and animals besides the ones already mentioned. In order to consolidate Damasio's findings with regard to fear and the amygdala further and to cast further doubt on Reddy's position, studies on humans with regard to fear and the amygdala are presented and discussed first; then animal studies, in particular studies on rats and cats which are relatively distant to us humans evolutionary-wise, are presented. These animal studies might yield interesting and illuminating comparisons and insights and might point towards a generalizability of the results to all mammals, if the results are not only found within one species of mammals but hold with regard to all or most of the mammals studied.

Before getting into more detail, it seems however of interest to see how the amygdala develops over a human being's life span and whether there are sex differences with regard to the amygdala, for there might be also sex differences with regard to the experience of fear. After all, it seems to be only women who shriek when they see a spider, although this behavior might be also culturally mediated. With regard to the amygdala the following sex differences have been reported (Huesing 2008, p. 108):

"the amygdala ... was found not only to play a key role in emotional responses and emotional memory but also to mediate sex differences in emotional behaviour and to show different levels and temporal-spatial patterns of activity during a given task. Moreover, it develops structurally at different rates in men and women and is significantly larger in male than in female brains (Hamann 2005, 289)."

These results are interesting because they could point to the fact that there might be also individual differences with regard to other parts of the brain and their development which might account for the individual differences with regard to the emotions as was, for instance, found in the case of prefrontal activation.

Besides sex differences with regard to the amygdala further distinctions are helpful in order to understand the functioning of the amygdala with regard to the emotions better. In this regard, LeDoux (2000, pp. 133-134) has pointed out that it makes sense to distinguish between two different pathways with regard to the amygdala, namely the fast thalamo-amygdala pathway and the slow thalamo-cortico-amygdala pathway both of which terminate in the lateral nucleus. These pathways might complement each other, for the fast pathway might prime the slow pathway indicating that even pathways and not only certain regions in the brain might serve different functions and therefore speak in favor of segregation in the brain with regard to the emotions. According to LeDoux (2000, pp. 133-134) the following advantages of the parallel processing capabilities of the amygdala system can be reasonably defended by means of supporting evidence: (1) the fast pathway allows the amygdala to detect threatening stimuli quickly which may confer an evolutionary advantage to the species. (2) The fast pathway may prime the amygdala to evaluate information received along the slow pathway via the lateral nucleus. (3) The fast pathway can function as an interrupt device so that the cortex by means of amygdalo-cortical projections shifts attention to dangerous stimuli in the environment. Considering this list one gets the impression that while different pathways have different functions which speaks in favor of segregation in the brain, nevertheless all of them work together to guarantee the survival of the species which speaks in favor of integration in the brain. Therefore, one might be inclined to speak of a combination of integration and segregation in the brain with regard to the emotions—at least with regard to the amygdala.

With regard to the fast pathway involving the amygdala, speed seems only to be necessary for the detection and evaluation of very dangerous stimuli. That is to say, positive stimuli don't need such a fast processing system because one's survival is not at stake unless humans were a species which could only procreate in the glimpse of an instance which one could easily miss. In the latter case one would also need a fast processing system for one's procreation in order to ensure the survival of the species. As we have ample time for procreation, such a fast processing system is not necessary to secure the survival of our own kind.

Besides evidence for the fact that the amygdala is involved in the emotion of fear, there is evidence for the fact that also the hippocampus is engaged when fearful situations appear which points towards a certain relative limited integration within the brain taken from an overall perspective. In this regard, Strange and Dolan (2006, p. 212) emphasize the following:

"The amygdala is critical for the enhanced memory observed for fearful or aversive stimuli. There is, however, overlap of function; amygdala responds to novel stimuli and anterior hippocampus is engaged by fearful situations. This raises the possibility that an anterior hippocampal role in novelty processing is a component of a more general role in detecting any anxiety-provoking stimulus (Bannerman et al. 2004). Enhanced memory for emotional stimuli depends on amygdala-hippocampal cooperativity, mediated via a noradrenergic system and facilitated by strong, reciprocal connections between anterior hippocampus and amygdala....In addition to a role in modulating hippocampal function during episodic encoding, the amygdala has been shown to influence responses in human visual cortex (Morris et al., 1998; Vuilleumier, Richardson, Armony, Driver,

& Dolan 2004) and modulate perception of emotional stimuli (Anderson & Phelps, 2001)."

Overall, this passage points towards a combination of the segregationist and the integrationist account, for on the one hand it emphasizes the particular role the amygdala plays with regard to memory and visual perception and on the other hand it highlights the fact that amygdala-hippocampal cooperativity is necessary for enhanced memory for emotional stimuli. Bermond, Vorst, and Moormann (2006, p. 343) confirm the results by Strange and Dolan on the connection between visual perception, memory, and the amygdala by citing several studies which show that the amygdala is involved in detecting emotional significant stimuli and in recognizing emotional facial expressions. Likewise Dolan and Morris (2000, pp. 231-232) maintain the following:

"the extrastriate regions with the strongest functional interactions with the amygdala have also been shown to be involved in facial emotion processing in previous functional neuroimaging studies (George et al., 1995; Sergent et al., 1994)....Furthermore, recent neuropsychological data also provide evidence that regions of extrastriate cortex have a role in facial emotion processing (Adolphs et al., 1997)."

The interactions between the extrastriate regions and the amygdala speak in favor of an integrationist account with regard to how the brain works in emotion processing. However, as the results only pertain to facial emotion processing, we actually have a combination of segregation and integration given. It has to be remarked however, while facial emotion processing under most circumstances might reveal the true emotions of another person, it might not always be reliable and therefore doesn't fall under the necessary and sufficient conditions for the emotions.

That the amygdala is engaged by novel stimuli, whereas the hippocampus responds to fearful situations, is partially contradictory to what Strange and Dolan (2006) stated before, namely that the amygdala helps in providing memory of fearful or aversive stimuli. However, one could also advocate the view that any novel stimulus, because one is unable to evaluate it on the spot, might be considered a fearful stimulus. Yet, why do the authors make the distinction between novel and fearful stimuli then? Unfortunately this is inexplicable.

Tranel, Gullickson, Koch, and Adolphs (2006, pp. 219-220) point out where the various results with regard to the amygdala and the perception of fear come from; in particular they highlight the following:

"It has been well established that the amygdala is critical for processing various aspects of emotion, and in particular, for the perception of negative emotions such as fear. Perhaps the strongest evidence for this conclusion in humans comes from an extensive series of investigations in patient SM, an extremely rare neurological patient who has complete, focal bilateral amygdala damage. One question that has remained unanswered, however, is whether SM has a normal phenomenological experience of emotion, especially negative emotion....To explore this issue we designed a study....SM is missing from the experiences in her life some of the deepest negative emotions, in a manner that parallels her defect in perceiving such emotions in external stimuli. These findings have interesting parallels with recent animal work (cf. Bauman, Lavenex, Mason, Capitanio, & Amaral, 2004a)".

In my opinion it is rather problematic to base generalizations mainly on one particular case; SM might differ in many particular ways from the general population, so that it might not be legitimate to absolutely conclude that it is the amygdala which is responsible for the perception of negative emotions; it might be some other kind of defect which might be responsible for the lack of the perception of negative emotions in SM. Yet, we will see later on that also cats with amygdala lesions show different emotional behavior. Moreover, as I said before patients or even animals with damages to the brain might not be a reliable source of how the brain works under normal conditions. Besides SM, also people with alexithymia have reduced emotional capacities, and here we will have to see in the chapter on alexithymia whether these people also have abnormalities with regard to the amygdala or whether some other kind of brain region or neurotransmitter is deficient in their cases.

Dolan and Morris (2000, p. 228) point out that not the whole amygdala gets activated by fearful stimuli which might be of interest for the already discussed thesis that there is a distinction between the hemispheres with regard to the emotions, namely that Ross et al. maintained that primary emotions, such as fear, are related to the right hemisphere and social emotions such as embarrassment are connected to the left hemisphere, while Heilman argued that negative emotions are connected to the right frontal lobe and positive emotions to the left frontal lobe:

> "The a priori hypothesis was that the amygdala activates during processing of fearful expressions. The prediction was confirmed by a robust activation, lateralized to the left amygdala and left periamygdaloid cortex specific to the fear condition (see Plate 11; Morris et al., 1996). There was no activation in the right amygdala, even when the significance threshold was lowered. Other areas of activation specific to the fear condition…involved the left cerebellum, the left cingulate gyrus, and right superior frontal gyrus. A categorical contrast of happy with fearful expressions…was associated with activations in the right medial temporal gyrus, right putamen, left superior parietal lobe, and the left calcarine sulcus.…brain areas that reflected increasing fearful intensity of expression included the left pulvinar, left anterior insula, and the right anterior cingulate cortex. The left amygdala was also identified in this contrast, although at a lower level of significance.…the brain regions that showed an increased neural response to increasing intensity of happy expression were different and included the bilateral striate cortex, bilateral lingual gyrus, bilateral fusiform gyri, and the right superior temporal gyrus."

While these results quite clearly speak in favor of a division of labor with regard to which parts of the brain are involved in fear and happiness also when it pertains to the intensity of emotions, it also seems obvious that with regard to the investigated emotions always several parts of the brain are involved. Thus a combination of a segregationist with an integrationist account seems more and more plausible.

With regard to the hemispheric differences thesis, Heilman's claim that negative emotions are connected to the right frontal lobe goes together with the findings here, for in the fear condition the right superior frontal gyrus was activated, whereas with regard to positive emotions the results here differ from Heilman's thesis. In their study Dolan and Morris (2000, p. 237) also discovered a variable which is of relevance for the hemispheric differences thesis of the emotions; in this regard the authors report that

"When subjects processed innately fearful faces, activation was seen in the left amygdala. When subjects acquired, through conditioning, a fear response to previously nonfearful faces, activation was seen in the right amygdala."

Hence depending on which kind of stimulus you are confronted with, different hemispheres are activated, so that learning might have an effect on which brain parts are affected when emotions are elicited. Similarly, Tranel (2000, p. 202) reports that the amygdala plays a role when it comes to learning information that has significant emotional valence.

In general, Dolan and Morris (2000, p. 230) have come up with the following analysis with regard to amygdala involvement in negative vs. positive emotions: neural responses in bilateral inferior occipital gyri, right middle temporal gyrus, brainstem, left hippocampus, right cerebellum, right fusiform gyrus, and left lingual gyrus are better predicted by amygdala activity during the processing of fearful in contrast to happy expressions.

That the amygdala is not only involved when emotions are elicited in humans, but also in other mammals still needs to be seen. In this regard Bermond, Vorst, and Moormann (2006, pp. 349-350), however, point out the results of a particular study with rats:

"Long Evans rats…can show two styles of maternal care, which are denoted high licking/grooming and low licking/grooming. These maternal styles are not genetically preprogrammed, but transmitted to the next generation on the basis of the received amount of licking during childhood (Francis, Diorio, Liu, & Meaney, 1999). Pups that have received low levels of licking are more fearful and more stress-responsive in adulthood. As adults they also show neurobiological changes, which explain the increased stress responsiveness. This includes higher levels of ACTH and glucocorticoids in response to acute stress, decreased glucocorticoid feedback sensitivity and increased levels of hypothalamic ACTH-RH mRNA expression (Liu & Diorio, 1997), fewer benzodiazepine receptors in various subnuclei of the amygdala and the locus coeruleus, increased ACTH-RH receptor densities in the locus coeruleus, (suggesting enhanced hormonal stress responses), and less GABA inhibition of emotions (especially fear; Caldji et al., 1988)….the combination of high levels of ACTH-RH and adrenal androgens with low levels of cortisol during development, as in humans with congenital adrenal hyperplasia, has been shown to result in significantly smaller amygdalae (Merke et al., 2003)."

While this study is very interesting pointing out the neurobiology of emotions, the study doesn't tell us how different amygdala sizes effect the emotions. That is to say, is a smaller amygdala big enough to cope with its work when an emotion is elicited or is the strain too much? The connection with congenital adrenal hyperplasia, which is an abnormal enlargement of the adrenal glands, might suggest that the strain is too much to bear for a smaller amygdala; yet that is not beyond doubt. But also the fact that rats which received low licking/grooming during childhood tend to be more fearful and stress-responsive in adulthood seems to point into the same direction. While it might be unethical to experiment with humans and see whether children who get lesser attention in the form of hugs, kisses, etc. from their guardians have a smaller amygdala, it might be possible to compare different existing groups with each other and the sizes of their respective amygdalas, such as children who grew up as orphans, who were step brothers and step sisters, or who had to spend much time in hospitals and not with their guardians, in order to see whether these results carry over to humans and what a small amygdala has for consequences.

Besides rats, also cats which are closer to us evolutionary-wise served as experimental subjects in order to find out something about the amygdala (Kolb and Taylor 2000). In this study Kolb and Taylor used two experimental setups: different groups of cats are confronted with a "Halloween profile" of another cat meaning a black silhouette of a cat and a "Picasso profile" where parts of the cat are pieced together arbitrarily. Kolb and Taylor (2000, pp. 63-66) describe the results of the study as follows:

"When cats encounter the 'Halloween profile'…they respond with a similar posture, which is followed by a slow approach to the perineal and/or head area of the stimulus cat. There is piloerection over the back and tail, slowed breathing, perspiration on the foot pads, and pupil dilation. This affective response is specific to the 'Halloween' configuration; cats pay little attention to a 'Picasso' cat…(Kolb & Nonneman, 1975). Cats with visual cortex lesions do not respond to the stimulus, which is reasonable because their pattern perception is severely compromised. Cats with amygdala lesions orient to the stimulus and approach the appropriate regions of the stimulus, but they show no affective response....Cats with frontal lesions also orient to the stimulus, but they do not approach the stimulus; rather, they actively avoid it (Nonneman & Kolb, 1974). They show no piloerection or other obvious autonomic signs that are so salient in the control animals. These results imply that there is a visual pathway to the amygdala that plays an important role in mediating fear responses to species-typical visual stimuli."

While I understand and agree with the interpretation of the results of the amygdala damaged cats, I would like to add that the cats with frontal lesions also show particular affective behavior, namely avoidance which seems reasonable in the case of fear. The latter result goes well together with previous claims and results. For Heilman maintained that negative emotions are connected to the right frontal lobe and Dolan and Morris (2000) showed that in the fear condition the right superior frontal gyrus was activated.

The connection between the amygdala and loss of emotion is also found in a study with rhesus monkeys (cf. Aggleton and Young 2000), so that a generalization across mammals becomes more justified. Moreover, it is also discussed and analyzed in which particular way the amygdala is involved in the loss of emotionality, for Aggleton and Young (2000, pp. 107-108) state:

"The discovery that removal of the amygdala produces a striking loss of emotional behavior can be traced back to Brown and Schafer (1888), who noted that bilateral temporal lobe damage could result in an unusual tameness in the rhesus monkey. This remarkable finding was rediscovered by Klüver and Bucy (1939)....They found that bilateral removal of the temporal lobes produces a highly distinctive pattern of behavioral changes (the 'Klüver-Bucy syndrome'). These changes consisted of visual agnosia...; a loss of emotional reactivity; 'orality', a tendency to examine objects with the mouth; 'hypermetamorphosis,' a tendency to switch rapidly from one behavior to another that is often expressed as an increase in exploratory behavior; hypersexuality; and abnormal dietary change,

108

most notably coprophagia (eating of feces). Subsequent studies showed that bilateral aspiration lesions of the amygdala were sufficient to induce the 'tameness,' the orality, the excessive exploratory behaviour, and the dietary changes (Weiskrantz, 1956). It was also found that disconnecting the amygdala from sensory cortical regions results in components of the Klüver-Bucy syndrome, including the loss of emotionality (Downer, 1961; Horel et al., 1975). It has not, however, been possible to duplicate these Klüver-Bucy symptoms by damaging subcortical projection targets of the amygdala (Butter & Snyder, 1972; Stern & Passingham, 1996). These findings suggest that the dysfunctions responsible for the abnormalities lie in the cortical-amygdala interactions."

Agreeing with the inference stated by Aggleton and Young this conclusion points towards an integrationist account with regard to how the brain works in causing emotions. However, if one considers all the evidence so far a combination of an integrationist account with a segregationist account seems to be mostly plausible with regard to the brain and the emotions. Yet, perhaps more unified results are obtained, if one not only looks at particular emotions, but also at certain aspects of particular emotions, such as their intensity, and at certain aspects of the emotion process, such as the reappraisal of certain emotional situations.

Amygdala, other brain regions, and electrodermal activity. That the skin has something to do with the emotions becomes obvious when one considers cases in which one sweats because of fear and/or anxiety or when one's skin hairs stand on end due to fear or when we get goose bumps in case something is particularly moving. As there is a connection between fear and the amygdala, there might be also a connection between electrodermal activity (EDA), skin conductance response (SCR), and the amygdala. Tranel (2000, p. 197) reports the following observations in this regard:

"We have found that bilateral amygdala damage interferes with autonomic fear conditioning, but not with SCRs to basic orienting stimuli (Bechara et al., 1995), a result that is consistent with animal work along these lines (Kim & Fanselow, 1992; Phillips & LeDoux, 1992)."

Besides in the case of fear, one could also imagine that the skin is involved in the case of disgust, if one considers disgust to be an emotion. For at least in German we have the expression "to wrinkle one's nose" when encountering something disgusting which might lead to a closing of pores and therefore to a change in one's skin.

With regard to the question whether other parts of the brain are connected to electrodermal activity and skin conductance Tranel (2000, p. 218) states the following:

"Our findings suggest that the ventromedial frontal region plays a role in linking EDA to stimulus properties such as social significance and emotional value, but that it is not involved in EDA related to more basic unconditioned stimuli. Our findings, together with those of Zoccolotti et al. (1982) and Vallar et al. (1991), indicate that the inferior parietal region on the right is important for EDA connected to stimulus properties such as emotional significance; however, this region does not appear critical for EDA connected to basic unconditioned stimuli."

While these results are very valuable, because they claim something very particular with regard to emotional value, emotional significance, and basic unconditioned stimuli, it is not so obvious how and whether emotional value and emotional significance differ from each other. It is also unclear whether these findings hold for all the emotions and which kind of phenomena the author considers to be emotions. Hence it becomes difficult to evaluate these findings properly. Yet, it becomes more and more obvious that not only the amygdala is involved with regard to the emotions but also that other parts of the brain are engaged when emotions are elicited.

The brain and moral emotions. When one looks at cases like fear or love one wouldn't necessarily think that these are moral emotions. Love is unconditional as they say, and love does not alter when it alterations finds, such as in the case when one finds out that one's dear friend has intentionally killed an innocent person. However, is it really the case that we don't stop loving our dear murderer friend? Solomon (2007, p. 218) perhaps might reply that we don't have only emotions, but also emotions about our emotions. Perhaps we find it disgusting or embarrassing or we are angry at ourselves that we actually still love our friend. And perhaps this emotion about our emotion, which can be a higher cognitive emotion or a basic emotion, might really have an impact on our love. In this way one might already get an idea how morality and emotions might be connected with each other, that is to say, our emotions might show us which actions and even affections turn out to be morally right.

However, is this really meant when we talk of moral emotions? Perhaps one has to distinguish different cases here: on the one hand are the emotions which direct us to what is morally right, on the other hand there are emotions which involve a cognitive evaluation of the situation, as one finds it in the case of higher cognitive emotions, such as guilt, shame, embarrassment, jealousy, envy, etc. In the case of guilt, for instance, one has to be aware of the fact that one has done something wrong. However, in both cases some kind of reflection is necessary in order to result in the respective emotion. I am embarrassed that I have a murderer as a friend, because I only want to have good people as friends and I don't consider a murderer as a good person. As reflection is necessary in order to result in the respective emotion, one can expect these emotions to evolve during human and perhaps even animal development in some of the higher developed animals. With regard to several higher cognitive emotions, which Damasio calls secondary emotions, this can be confirmed. For Damasio (1999, p. 342, n. 13) points out that they begin to appear later in human development, so that a newborn doesn't feel shame and guilt, but a two-year-old usually does, where the later appearance doesn't indicate that secondary emotions are not at least partly biologically preset.

Jesse Prinz (2007) has a very interesting account of moral emotions. Prinz (2007, pp. 168-169) points out that moral facts are made by our sentiments and once the moral facts are made, they can be perceived. That is to say, you can perceive that it is wrong to hurt a cat. According to Prinz when someone hurts a cat, this leads to an emotional response and that response turns out to be a manifestation of a sentiment that constitutes the belief that animal cruelty is wrong. Prinz maintains that it is the sentiment which makes the action turn out to be wrong and makes the wrongness obvious to us. Hence, if one doesn't have any kinds of emotions, one wouldn't be able to make any kind of moral judgments.

However, why shouldn't it be possible that rationality alone determines what is morally right? After all, if it is only emotions which count why do we still reason about morality? Doesn't Rawls' veil of ignorance make us choose in a rational manner what kind of morality, political system, etc. to adopt? But perhaps even in this case, we feel that we would be better off if we treated everyone equally; that is to say, in the end it is the emotions which have the final say in the matter. Yet, what about psychopaths who are emotionally relatively flat, don't they know what is morally right? Even though they might not agree with what everyone else considers as morally right, why shouldn't they know that they have violated a moral norm when they kill an innocent person just for pleasure? Perhaps Prinz might reply that their knowledge differs from our knowledge. Only knowledge based on the emotions turns out to be proper knowledge. That is to say, psychopaths might not really know that they have violated a moral norm when they kill an innocent person just for pleasure.

Prinz (2007, pp. 72-74) endorses the CAD model by Rozin et al. (1999) where CAD stands for contempt, anger, and disgust. While Rozin et al. found that autonomy violations tend to go together with anger, purity violations with disgust, and community violations with contempt, Prinz believes that moral disgust goes together with transgressions against the perceived natural order, that moral anger is directed at transgressions against autonomy, and that contempt is a blend of anger and disgust. Moreover, Prinz claims that if one maintains that contempt is a blend of anger and disgust this explains why contempt is elicited by violations against community. Yet, not all kinds of violations against community elicit contempt. The successful tax evader might be admired or even envied for his cunningness instead. With regard to contempt being a blend of anger and disgust, might we not also feel contempt for someone just because he or she belongs to a lower class or just because he or she is a looser, although he or she had all the possibilities to rise in the ranks? Moreover, in the last two cases it is also not so obvious how these are violations against community. Perhaps the looser has violated against community because he or she has not done what was expected of him or her by the community, and the person from the lower class has violated against community because he or she has tried to enter my community.

With regard to moral disgust, is it really the case that it goes together with transgressions against the perceived natural order? I am morally disgusted by my colleagues, because they in the face of a very famous philosopher do whatever they can to please him, but behind his back they make fun of him. How is that to be a transgression against the perceived natural order? Does the natural order prescribe that they shouldn't make fun of him? And what is natural order really? According to his rank they shouldn't make fun of him, but one can't call a full professorship at one of the best universities for philosophy a natural order. He has achieved a certain position, but one wouldn't consider this to be something natural. Besides being disgusted by my colleagues I also feel anger, because this famous philosopher is my friend and I believe that it is not right to make fun of another person. However, I don't see how autonomy is violated in this case. Perhaps one might want to reply, if I really believe that it is wrong to make fun of another person, my colleagues have invaded my personal belief space, so that a violation of autonomy is given, but also this sounds rather far-fetched.

Prinz (2007, p. 76) advances that contempt, anger, and disgust arise if one blames someone else for having done something wrong. However, this seems to suggest that one can't be angry at oneself that one has left the apartment door open, that one has left the passport at home, etc., and this seems quite clearly implausible. Also why shouldn't one feel contempt for oneself, if one has betrayed the closest friend one had against one's own better judgment just because for a trifle gain? Similarly, why shouldn't one be disgusted by oneself if one has slept with a person just because one wants to get married, although one doesn't like him or her at all and doesn't even find him or her physically attractive? Hence in my opinion contempt, anger, and disgust arise also if one blames oneself for having done something wrong.

Prinz (2007, pp. 22-23) reports many studies which give empirical evidence that emotions occur when humans make moral judgments and that the insula, anterior cingulate cortex, the temporal pole, the medial frontal gyrus, and oribitofrontal cortex were implicated in these studies which are also found in pure emotion studies that don't involve moral judgments. Prinz comes up with two explanations for the findings that emotions occur when humans make moral judgments: on the one hand one could maintain that moral judgments are constituted by emotional responses, on the other hand there is the causal model which states that moral judgments can have emotional effects. Yet, he also points out that so far the evidence is inconclusive with regard to which explanation is the better one. In my opinion, the constitutional model might have problems with explaining why one has so few emotions if one sees a picture of a murderer on TV without knowledge of the particular crime he has committed, while if one personally knows the person one's emotions might be much more intense. Also a psychopath might have quite clear ideas of what is considered to be morally wrong without feeling anything when he violates these very same moral rules indicating problems with the constitutional model. One might want to reply although he knows what is considered to be morally wrong, this might differ from what he considers to be morally wrong and only if he personally considers something to be morally wrong, will he have emotions.

Prinz (2007, p. 60) points out that the anterior cingulate cortex, the insular cortex, and the temporal poles are activated when guilt is elicited and that the anterior cingulate and the insula are also involved in the regulation and perception of the body, so that guilt is an embodied emotion, as is every other bone fide emotion. Yet, perhaps the embodiment is just a side effect of the emotion and not something which is constitutive of the emotion. However, if one sees a bear ten feet away and one's heart starts racing and one feels fear, then quite clearly the racing heart is preparing the body for a flight or a defense response. So the racing heart is not just a side effect of the emotion, but fulfills a particular function in that situation. However, what kind of function do the physiological reactions going together with guilt assume? That one feels bad and therefore changes one's action? Although this could be the case, this is not as obvious as in the case of the racing heart and fear.

Prinz (2007, pp. 24-25) discusses functional magnetic resonance imaging results with regard to trolley cases, where subjects showed significant activation in emotional areas of the brain when they were asked whether it is appropriate to push someone off a footbridge into the path of a trolley. In the condition where subjects were asked whether it is appropriate to pull a lever to divert a trolley from five subjects toward one person the emotion activation was lower and showed also brain activation in areas associated with working memory, Prinz reports. According to Prinz these results can be explained by two emotion-backed rules, namely that it is bad to kill and a somewhat weaker emotion-backed rule that it is good to save lives. In the footbridge case both rules are activated, but we imagine killing in a very vivid way, so that the bad to kill rule overpowers the other rule, while in the pull the lever case, we don't imagine the harm we are causing very vividly so that the save lives rule overpowers the other rule, Prinz claims. Moreover, in the pull the lever case, working memory is involved because of the calculation of how many people survive, Prinz maintains. Yet, why is there no working memory involved with regard to the footbridge case? After all, also here one would like to know how many people in the end survive. That is to say, trolley cases are usually construed in such a way that there is a moral dilemma that one has to save someone by killing someone else warranting a calculation of how many people are to survive.

Prinz (2007, pp. 27-28) admits that intuitions about trolley cases don't show conclusively that moral judgments involve emotions; however, they suggest that emotions can influence moral judgments. Moreover, Prinz cites a large number of studies on the effects of emotion induction to back up his claim that emotions can influence moral judgments.

The brain and aesthetic emotions. It is rarely the case that pieces of art move us deeply. That is to say, I have not encountered any person yet who fell into a depression, because he has read a piece of fiction, looked at a painting, listened to a piece of music, watched a movie, watched a tragedy in the theatre, etc. Yet, pieces of art might make us break out into laughter, when watching a comedy, might make us cry, because the hero of the movie dies, they might make us smile, because the artist just sings so beautifully, they might make us angry, because the sculpture is provocative, they might induce fear, because the narrative is so dark, etc. Hence, one might want to say that pieces of art rarely have long lasting effects, but more short-term effects.

Besides this distinction to our ordinary emotions and moods, there is another fact of the matter going together with aesthetic emotions, namely that they rarely lead to full blown bodily reactions as in the case of ordinary emotions and moods. That is to say, with the exception of running out of a concert hall, because the performance gives you the creeps, hiding under the blanket, because the horror movie looked so real, throwing raw eggs and tomatoes at the actors, because their acting is so provocative, etc., we are rarely moved to action because of aesthetic emotions. In a similar vein, Prinz (2007, p. 59) acknowledges that our aesthetic experiences are usually not associated with bodily changes; however, he also reports that neuroimaging studies have shown that emotions are elicited when people look at art and that the anterior cingulate which is involved in bodily regulation is activated under these circumstances.

Vagueness and the brain. Changizi (2003, chapter 4) claims that brains might not help us to detect the limits of thought, learning, understanding, and intelligence, because at least until he published his book (1) brains were not well-understood, (2) brain activity was not easily describable, (3) brains were not susceptible for proving theorems about them and their limits, and (4) the brain is just one possibility for how a thinking machine might work and therefore cannot tell us the ultimate limits of thought. Changizi (2003, chapter 4) admits, however, that the first three points might advance with a more mature neuroscience, while the fourth point remains standing. With regard to the fourth point, something similar holds with regard to biology, namely that it is only the scientific study of life on this planet and not the scientific study of life in general (cf. Langton 1996, p. 39; Ray 1995, p. 179; Ledwig 2006, p. 109).

The limits of understanding or knowledge also include the question whether the brain, its features, and/or its various concepts are vague. If there is no significant advancement with regard to the brain, its features, and its various concepts, then it might turn out to be the case that we are factually not able to determine whether the brain, its features, and/or its various concepts turn out to be vague or not which might be problematic. However, even the simple question whether one particular cell belongs to the amygdala or to the neighboring brain part might turn out to be problematic and be indeterminate and therefore leave space open for vagueness. With regard to the emotions in general—with the exception of the amygdala and the emotion of fear—not enough information has been gathered yet to conclude with absolute certainty which brain parts turn out to have which function. Yet, also with regard to the amygdala and the emotion of fear there are many open questions, such as can one come up with functions relating emotional value, emotional intensity, etc. with degrees of amygdala activity, can one relate different amygdala sizes to different possible ranges of emotional value, emotional intensity, etc.

116

Hence it is very difficult to determine whether vagueness is involved with regard to the brain in connection with the emotion of fear and a fortiori also with regard to the other emotions.

Conclusion

With regard to the question how the brain works in the case of the emotions, a combination of a segregationist with an integrationist account seems to be much more plausible to defend. Yet, with the exception of fear, which has been extensively studied, the results so far don't allow for generalizations. As it looks like one has to distinguish in more and more detail in which kind of processes under which kind of conditions certain emotions and their parts and therefore also different brain regions are activated. As there are still many open questions even with regard to fear and the amygdala, it is very difficult to determine whether vagueness is involved with regard to the brain and the emotions. However, as it might be difficult to determine with absolute precision to which region a certain brain cell belongs, vagueness in the sense of indeterminacy might enter the picture even in the case of the emotions.

Chapter 4 The Rational Functions of the Emotions

Functions of emotions in general. In Ledwig (2006, chapter one) I have already dealt with de Sousa's (1987) and Johnson-Laird and Oatley's (1992; Oatley and Johnson-Laird 1987) view on the rational function of the emotions. I have also discussed Elster's (1999) rules of thumb and Damasio's (1994) somatic marker hypothesis to some extent in that regard. Consequently I will not dwell on their contributions any longer unless the subject matter demands it and/or I have some new insights to offer. While in Ledwig (2006) I have dealt more with philosophical accounts of the emotions and rationality, in this book I will consider more psychological accounts of the emotions and rationality including results obtained in the neurosciences, so this book deals with a different kind of literature and will hopefully confirm the results obtained in Ledwig (2006).

When one talks about the rational functions of the emotions one doesn't talk about short term rational functions, but long term rational functions, for what might be short term functional might not be long term functional and therefore might not lead to our overall survival in the end which is desirable. For instance, a psycho- or sociopath might maximize his short term utility by tormenting his victims, yet in the end he will not maximize his long term utility, because he will either end up in a psychiatric institution or in prison. Yet, what about the case where one in the short term has to make a decision on which day to have a doctor's appointment? If one were to always need several hours for picking a choice, this would neither be short term maximizing nor long term maximizing, for in the end such lengthy decision processes would lead to the result that one wouldn't get anything done in one's life which wouldn't be survival enhancing in the long run. So even in this case long term rationality is that which counts.

With regard to the emotions, one could advance the view that although emotions were rational for our ancestors to have, nowadays in our technical, cold, and calculated world emotions stand more in the way of our progress than help us cope with our environment, so that nowadays they are merely a by-product of our evolutionary development, but otherwise useless in our struggle for survival. Yet, I have shown in Ledwig (2006, chapter one) that this is not the case in general. That is, emotions can be considered to be rational even in an evolutionary sense nowadays. However, it should be pointed out that it could be the case that in the future our environment changes so much or we change so much that emotions are more in our way than help us in coping with the problems we encounter in our everyday life. That facts with regard to empirical phenomena might change over time is what we encounter and expect in all empirical sciences, so this in itself doesn't speak against my account. Hence, until such a change takes place my account holds.

Nietzsche, Solomon, Hume, and Prinz. According to Solomon (2007, p. 166) it was already Nietzsche who maintained that every passion involves its quantum of reason and that the passions help us in making decisions. Moreover, Solomon (2007, p. 231) claims that according to Nietzsche reason is just another passion, because reason is never really dispassionate and free from the concerns and perspectives of the self. However, if reason is just another passion, why do we have all this emotional vocabulary? Moreover, isn't there a distinction to be made between a person who coldly deliberates what is best for him or her neglecting how he or she feels about the recommended action and a person who takes his or her emotion into account when making up his or her mind?

Prinz (2007, pp. 64-65) maintains that Hume conceives emotions as arational, for they can be caused by reasonable or unreasonable ideas, but they can't be reasonable or unreasonable themselves. Yet according to Prinz this theory can be easily proven wrong, because fear caused by looking at a caged snake is unreasonable even if there isn't any idea to precede or follow the emotion. Prinz tries to solve this problem by offering an amendment to the James-Lange theory of the emotions; in that amendment emotions represent concerns that can be correct or incorrect. That is to say, given that Jones fears the caged snake, he is representing the snake as dangerous which is incorrect. However, Jones is correct in fearing the venomous snake which is coiled around his leg. Prinz points out though that the issue gets more complicated by the fact that emotions are less under our control than our reasoning capacities. That is to say, the fear we have while on a roller coaster is irrational because it is relatively safe, however agents are not irrational for having the fear. For irrational emotions entail irrational agents only when agents have some kind of control over those emotions as when the emotions are caused by beliefs rather than by low-level perceptions. For instance, if one is afraid of flying this entails irrationality on the part of the agent (because the fear is caused by beliefs) which one doesn't find in the case of fear experienced on a roller coaster (here fear is caused by low-level perceptions). Prinz calls his account the embodied appraisal theory, because emotions are somatic signals, but they are also appraisals insofar as they represent concerns.

However, one can construe cases where it is rational to fear even a caged snake, for how can one be sure that the cage doesn't have a false bottom? Take Lou as the person who is even afraid of caged snakes. He has grown up among magicians in a circus, where lots of magic tricks with cages were performed, so for him cages with false bottoms represent normality and not the exception. So how can he be sure that the snake in the cage cannot escape? Unless he knew of all the possible secret contraptions of a cage and might be able to inspect all of them, he might never be completely sure. Hence, as it seems rational to rather be a little bit too afraid than not being afraid enough, if one's survival is at stake it seems even rational to fear a caged snake. After all one bite of this snake might cause your death.

What about the roller coaster example then? As I have never experienced fear on a roller coaster, I find this claim difficult to evaluate, so I have to find another similar example, such as for instance sky diving. My beliefs tell me that it is irrational to be afraid of jumping, because parachutes are relatively safe, however my low level perceptions tell me that this is just too high up falling from such a height. As a result I experience a moderate amount of fear. However, the most frequently diagnosed phobias, such as phobias of insects, snakes, and heights, are directed at situations that reflect an evolutionary preparation to be sensitive to dangers that ancestral human populations encountered (cf. D'Arms and Jacobson 2003, p. 141) and these are actually survival enhancing. In such cases as the roller coaster and sky diving one might want to argue even if it is highly unlikely that anything might happen in both cases, if something does happen it surely is fatal in the case of sky diving and probably fatal in the case of the roller coaster. Moreover, as sky diving and riding a roller coaster are just done for pleasure and are not a necessity for one's own survival, I consider it not necessarily very rational to pursue any of these endeavors.

With regard to the flying case, I am not so sure whether flying fear is really caused by beliefs. Couldn't it also be possible that the fear is caused by low-level perceptions, such as the perceptions when the plane is taking off and when one feels a little bit odd in the stomach? In this case even imagining taking off might probably lead to these funny feelings in the stomach. Hence, I would like to have some more evidence for the different cases Prinz presents.

Another counterexample to the rationality of the emotions is presented by Solomon (2007, p. 162), for he points out that we sometimes get angry at the stubborn bolt or the recalcitrant jar; he advances the view that such kind of behavior would quite clearly become irrational if one started pleading with the bolt or jar. However, one might want to object that anger directed at the stubborn bolt or jar might actually release energy so that we might finally succeed in opening the jar! While pleading with the bolt or jar might really sound irrational, one could also think that by talking to the bolt or jar one might actually start deliberating and trying to find new ways to open the jar. After all, also Edison tried over 1,000 materials for the filament of his electric light bulb, before he finally succeeded. That is to say, failure comes usually before success and talking about different alternatives actually might help in finding the successful solution.

An even more irrational emotion—at least on first sight—can be found in another example presented by Solomon (2007, p. 185). He points out some prisoners in German concentration camps who were joyful, although they were humiliated and although they were presented with the constant threat of death. Solomon however emphasizes that this inappropriate emotion given the circumstances might have had a contagious effect on the person's fellow prisoners uplifting their spirits, so that it didn't seem irrational at all to have. If one thinks about this situation, what kind of alternatives for emotions are actually given? Despair and sadness might not help you, because your fellow prisoners are in a similar situation, the prison guards are not interested in helping you, and possible help is far away. Hope might help you, because it might give you a positive outlook for the future, a motivation for you to carry on. Joy also might help you, because given that you can't change your circumstances, you can only change your attitude towards the circumstances. Hence, it seems rational to actually try to have positive emotions when put into a concentration camp or similar circumstances.

After having looked at these counterexamples to the rationality of the emotions, let's get back to Prinz's (2006, pp. 65-67) view, for he points towards a problem of his embodied appraisal account having to do with the somatic signals, namely that sometimes different emotions correspond to the same bodily patterns, so that one cannot distinguish the different emotions by means of the bodily patterns. Prinz calls this problem the somatic similarity problem and he solves the problem by liking emotions to the tones emitted by smoke alarms which can do double duty. Similarly a somatic signal of the same bodily pattern can have different meanings in different situations depending on the mental mechanisms that caused that pattern to form. Prinz explains this reuse of bodily patterns in the following way: first, we are innately furnished only with a small emotional repertoire. Second, a basic emotion can be combined with another basic emotion to result in an emotional blend, such as contempt possibly being a blend of anger and disgust. Third, a basic emotion can be assigned a novel set of eliciting conditions, so that this set is a subset of the initial eliciting conditions that have been elaborated through experience to form an independent elicitation mechanism. Prinz calls this process recalibration. An example of recalibration might be pride which is joy recalibrated to one's own successes. According to Prinz in many cases we find blending and calibration going together, such as in the case of jealousy which may be a blend of anger, sadness, fear, and disgust in situations of suspected sexual infidelity.

With regard to jealousy, we will see in the chapter on mixed feelings that besides sexual infidelity there is also emotional infidelity and that jealousy arises under both of these conditions. In that chapter I will also mention that there are also particular sex differences given with regard to sexual and emotional infidelity. Prinz's account of the emotions is a very interesting one, for he might be also able to explain why vagueness might be of relevance with regard to the emotions. If certain emotions turn out to be blends of other basic emotions, such as in the case of contempt, one might understand that under certain circumstances one might have problems distinguishing between contempt, anger, and disgust. Also in the case of recalibrations, where the novel set of eliciting conditions is in fact a subset of the initial eliciting conditions, problems distinguishing between different kinds of emotions might ensue because of the overlap.

While multi-component theories of the emotions in contrast to one-component theories of the emotions already from the very outset might because of the many components leave the possibility open for vagueness to appear in many different ways, a theory which allows for blending and recalibration and even a combination of the two might equally suffer from vagueness in many different ways and perhaps even more so than multi-component theories. However, if one takes basic emotions as the building block for all the other emotions and doesn't distinguish between basic and higher cognitive emotions, vagueness might also be reduced to a certain extent. For if one takes basic emotions to be phenomena which are caused by low-level perceptions, such as in the case of fear, and if conceptual issues and feelings are considered as completely irrelevant for an appropriate account of the emotions, cases of vagueness with regard to basic emotions are only given, if one considers perceptions to be vague. Yet, Keefe (2006, p. 15) pointed out that perceptions might be controversial cases with regard to vagueness (cf. chapter one of this book). However, it is not so obvious to me why visual impressions, such as a bear running towards me in the twilight, might not have vague content (cf. also Williamson 1994, p. 93). However, Prinz also allowed for emotions which are caused by beliefs, so at least in his case vagueness might enter the emotions also at the level of beliefs.

Functions of the emotions and evolution. In general, people are of the opinion that evolution doesn't produce superfluous things, so that there must be a reason why humans and animals have emotions. However, Solomon (2007, pp. 248-249) claims that anger might be just a by-product of a more general sense of aggressiveness which is inherited and which arises in response to violations of territory. Similarly, Solomon maintains that erotic love might just be a culturally refined variation of a natural sense of attachment, which we have developed towards people who are closest to us, combined with a biological desire for mating and

123

reproduction. Hence Solomon concludes just because we have a certain in-born propensity for certain emotions, does not mean that those emotions have been selected for by evolution. As spandrels in architecture are forms that were not designed but naturally occurred with the design of arches in gothic buildings, also emotions might not have been designed but naturally occurred with human beings and animals, Solomon argues. However, even if emotions were just a by-product of evolution, it could nevertheless be the case that by accident they serve a rational function. And it seems to be the case that the racing of the heart when one sees a bear ten feet away quite clearly serves the function to enable the agent for flight or fight.

The evolutionary function of the emotions is in particular stressed by Öhman, Flykt and Lundqvist (2000, p. 297) who claim the following:

"Emotions are means designed to regulate behavior in relation to agendas set by biological evolution. Thus, emotion pervaded the critical ecological problems that our distant ancestors had to solve if their genes were to be represented in the next generation. These problems included finding and consuming food and drink, finding shelters, seeking protection and support from conspecifics, asserting oneself socially, satisfying curiosity, getting access to and engaging with sexual partners, caring for offspring, and avoiding and escaping life-threatening events. These are all activities structured by emotions (see Tooby & Cosmides, 1990). In a biological perspective, therefore, emotions can be understood as clever means shaped by evolution to make us want to do what our ancestors had to do successfully to pass genes on to coming generations (e. g., Öhman, 1993a, 1996)."

While hunger and thirst might lead us to find and to consume food and drink, I am not so sure whether I would call hunger and thirst emotions, because to a certain extent they are more physiological states or simple sensations than emotions. Emotions seem to me more psychological states, although they also have a physiological component. Yet, finding and consuming food and drink might lead to some pleasurable feelings or even happiness in case one has been starving for quite some time. Not finding them on the other hand might lead to sadness or even to despair. To say that all these activities such as finding shelter, seeking protection, etc. are structured by emotions seems to be a bit far-fetched, however. For finding shelter, for instance, might involve lots of deliberation, such as what kinds of objects are good for shelter (such as a cave, a huge overhang, a hut), what kind of an environment does one want to have around one's shelter (such as a river or a lake, some plants that produce fruits or vegetables), etc. And of course one could advance the view that in all these deliberations decisions have to be made and that good decisions lead to pleasurable outcomes, whereas bad decisions lead to not pleasurable outcomes, so that emotions might be involved, but the deliberation itself on first sight doesn't have to involve emotions. If one, however, takes Damasio's (1994) stance seriously that emotions help us in making decisions and one in fact has good reasons for taking him seriously, then the authors seem to be right that all these activities are structured by the emotions.

Functions of the emotions and decision-making. In 2000, p. 14, Damasio makes his position on emotions and their function in decision-making more precise. In particular he advances that on account of current neurological evidence certain compromises of emotion are a problem for the edifice of reason to work properly. Hence according to Damasio emotions are not a substitute for reason nor do they decide for us nor is it impossible that emotional outbursts can lead to irrational decisions.

Damasio (2000, p. 13) elaborates on his previous claims as follows: "emotion is integral to the processes of reasoning and decision making….there is evidence to support the claim. The findings come from the study of several individuals who were patently rational in the way they governed their lives up to the time when, as a result of neurological damage in specific sites of their brains, they lost their ability to make rational decisions, and, along with that momentous defect, also lost their ability to process emotion normally. Those individuals can still use the instruments of their rationality and can still call up knowledge pertinent to the world around them. Their ability to tackle the logic of a problem remains intact. Nonetheless, many of their personal and social decisions are irrational, when considered from the common-sense perspective of a comparable individual. More often than not, those decisions are disadvantageous to them and to persons close to them. I have suggested that the delicate mechanism of reasoning is no longer affected, nonconsciously and on occasion even consciously, by signals hailing from the neural machinery that underlies emotion (Damasio, 1994, 1996). This hypothesis is known as the 'somatic marker hypothesis,' and the patients who led me to propose it had damage to selected areas in the prefrontal region, especially in the ventral and medial sectors, and in the right parietal regions."

What is interesting with regard to Damasio's results is that the amygdala is not mentioned at all with regard to which brains areas were damaged. Damasio's results with regard to damages in the right parietal regions might indicate the involvement of the amygdala, though, for the amygdala and the insula project to the parietal regions (Heilman 2000, p. 330). Also memory might be of relevance with regard to which decision to make, that is, in lots of cases one can simply extrapolate from the past into the future for predicting which decision to make. Furthermore, with regard to memory and the emotions one also finds a connection to the amygdala (cf. the chapter on the brain in this book). Yet, perhaps the scenarios Damasio considered for testing his patients might be ones which don't involve memory at all. For instance, with regard to the question on which day and hour to make a doctor's appointment doesn't necessarily involve memory. That is, one just needs to know on which days in the future one has time at which hour and not necessarily how one made doctors' appointments in the past. Yet, that the patients had damages to areas in the prefrontal region goes together with previously discussed findings in the section on prefrontal activation in the chapter on the brain.

Specific functions of all the emotions. While Damasio just considered which function the emotions serve in cases of reasoning and decision-making, Rolls (2005) tries to capture all the specific functions the emotions serve. In this regard, Rolls (2005, pp. 123-127) comes up with the following list:

"1. *Elicitation of autonomic responses* (e.g., a change in heart rate) *and endocrine responses* (e.g., the release of adrenaline)....

2. *Flexibility of behavioral responses to reinforcing stimuli....*The essence of this idea is that goals for behavior are specified by reward and punishment evaluation and that innate goals are specified by genes....

3. *Motivation.* Emotion is motivating....For example, fear learned by stimulus-reinforcement association provides the motivation for actions

performed to avoid noxious stimuli. Genes that specify goals for action, such as rewards, must as an intrinsic property make the animal motivated to obtain the reward; otherwise, it would not be a reward. Thus, no separate explanation of motivation is required.

4. *Communication.* Monkeys, for example, may communicate their emotional state to others by making an open-mouth threat to indicate the extent to which they are willing to compete for resources, and this may influence the behavior of other animals....

5. *Social bonding.* Examples of this are the emotions associated with the attachment of parents to their young and the attachment of young to their parents. The attachment of parents to each other is also beneficial in species, such as many birds and humans....

6. The current mood state can affect the *cognitive evaluation of events or memories*....This may facilitate continuity in the interpretation of the reinforcing value of events in the environment....

7. Emotion may facilitate the *storage of memories*. One way this occurs is that *episodic memory* (i. e., one's memory of particular episodes) is facilitated by emotional states. This may be advantageous in that storing many details of the prevailing situation when a strong reinforcer is delivered may be useful in generating appropriate behavior in situations with some similarities in the future....A second way in which emotion may affect the storage of memories is that the current emotional state may be stored with episodic memories, providing a mechanism for the current emotional state to affect which memories are recalled. A third way that emotion may affect the storage of memories is by guiding the cerebral cortex in the representations of the world which are established....

8. Another function of emotion is that by enduring for minutes or longer after a reinforcing stimulus has occurred, it may help to produce *persistent and continuing motivation and direction of behavior*, to help achieve a goal or goals.

9. Emotion may trigger the *recall of memories* stored in neocortical representations."

With regard to the **social bonding function**, one encounters something similar already in the common sense philosopher Thomas Reid. That is to say, Reid (1994, p. 561; cf. also Ledwig 2005, p. 55) claims that the upbringing of children takes so much time and requires so much care, that, if one did it merely out of reason and duty and if it were not sweetened by affection in their guardians, then one can reasonably doubt whether many children would be raised in that way.

That there is a connection between emotions and **memories** is in agreement with the findings on amygdala function in the chapter on the brain, so this supports Rolls's account in this regard. Further support for the connection between emotions and memory comes from Ortony, Norman, and Revelle (2005, p. 196), for they maintain the following:

"One of the most fundamental functions of affect is as a valenced index of importance, and indeed, there is some neuroscientific evidence that affect is a prerequisite for establishing long-term memories....A second important function of affect is that it provides occasions for learning, from quite simple forms of reinforcement learning to complex, conscious planning and experimentation. Affect also has important consequences for the allocation of attention. It is a well-established finding in the psychological literature that negative affect tends to result in the focusing of attention on local details at the expense of global structure."

While focusing on local details to a certain extent might help in finding the "culprit" of why something went wrong or why one feels bad, too much focusing on local details, especially if one doesn't get out of that state, might be problematic. For by focusing just on the local details one forgets that there is something else out there, which momentarily is not in the agent's focus and which might also provide a viable solution to the problem or which might relativize the problem to its real status. Thus, too much focusing on local details might not be survival enhancing in the short and/or in the long run.

Yet, perhaps it is not necessarily focusing on local details which is of importance for negative affect, but actually a focusing of attention in contrast to a diversion of attention. Similarly, Breazeal and Brooks (2005, p. 274) state:

"As argued by Isen (1999), negative affect allows us to think in a highly focused way when under negative, high-stress situations. Conversely, positive affect allows us to think more creatively and to make broader associations when in a relaxed, positive state."

Given that this is true, one might want to argue to function perfectly one should be in both affective states at the same time, for in many cases one needs to find out why a particular solution to a problem didn't work out, so that one needs to focus attention on how the particular details of the solution didn't match the details of the to be solved problem. However, at the same time one also needs to find a viable solution to the problem, so that one has to use one's creativity to find it. One might want to object that it seems more reasonable to first find out what is wrong with the not-working solution before one proceeds to find a working solution. Although this procedure is reasonable to follow especially when one is under time pressure, humans are rarely so perfectly rational. However, following that procedure actually might induce a positive state, so that the agent is in the right state for finding the correct solution, for when one encounters a problem, this induces a negative state leading to focusing of attention on the problem; finding out why the solution didn't work creates a positive state, so that the agent can make use of his or her creativity.

In cases where one just encounters a problem without having a not-working solution yet, it also seems reasonable to first focus on the problem in order to analyze is properly and then to use one's creativity to solve it. And one might want to argue that also here the problem puts one in a negative state which leads to a focusing of attention on the problem, and after one is clear about the analysis and has achieved something positive this induces a positive state so that one can make use of one's creativity. Thus also here it seems optimal to follow this procedure and that our emotions help us in finding solutions to problems by generating the appropriate state given certain states of the world.

Function of sadness. That sadness has a function seems on first sight not very plausible, for any normal person wouldn't like to be sad. That is, under ordinary circumstances one wants to get out of that state as soon as possible. Yet, perhaps sadness might actually facilitate that result in an optimal way, if not in the short run then at least in the long run. For Breazeal and Brooks (2005, p. 274) state:

"According to Izard (1993), a unique function of sadness is its ability to slow the cognitive and motor systems....In adults, the slowing of cognitive processes may enable a more careful and deliberate scrutiny of self and circumstances, allowing the individual to gain a new perspective to help improve performance in the future (Tomkins, 1963)."

These claims go together with what was stated earlier about the function of negative affect that it leads to focusing on local details on expense of the global picture. Perhaps this feat is accomplished by sadness' ability to slow the cognitive and motor systems down.

Yet, sadness might not only have the function to slow these systems down, so that attention gets focused on local details of the problem in order to find a solution to the problem, sadness may also serve an interpersonal communicative function as was already advanced by Rolls (2005) and is stated by Breazeal and Brooks (2005, p. 295):

"The expression of sorrow communicates to others that one is in trouble and increases the likelihood that the others will feel sympathy and lend assistance (Moore, Underwood, & Rosenhan, 1984)."

In a similar vein Hendriks, Nelson, Cornelius, and Vingerhoets (2008, p. 87) claim that crying serves

"a variety of interpersonal functions, foremost among these being to communicate distress to others and to facilitate social bonding. It is argued that by way of these interpersonal benefits, crying improves the physiologic and psychological well-being of the crying person."

However, might it not also be the case that the expression of sorrow leads to Schadenfreude in others? After all in lots of cases your loss is my gain. Moreover, that the others will feel sympathy might depend on whether they can understand what you are sad about and this hinges to a certain extent on their capacity for empathy and knowing something about you and the situation you are in and how close they are to you psychologically. Thus it seems rational to express sorrow only in circumstances when one knows of the others that they don't take advantage of your weakness and/or when it is deemed appropriate to show expressions of sorrow following certain display rules, such as crying over a close relative or friend at a funeral.

That crying serves to facilitate social bonding might depend on what one is crying about and how often one is crying. If someone was to cry over the most insignificant detail and was to constantly cry, given that this person was not suicidal, I am sure there are many people who would be appalled by that kind of behavior and who would rather withdraw than bond with that person. Also if the person was to cry in the most impossible circumstances, say in a meeting at work, when one is introducing him or her to one's boss, etc. this would much more likely lead to withdrawal than to social bonding. Hence one has to qualify to some extent under which kinds of conditions do expressions of sorrow and sadness lead to social bonding. Therefore, it doesn't seem very rational to express sorrow and sadness under all kinds of conditions. No doubt this is the reason why we have display rules. They make it easier for us to evaluate when it is rational to show certain kinds of emotions.

Prinz (2007, p. 62), however, claims that sadness might have evolved as a response to all kinds of losses, such as the loss of a loved one by means of a divorce or by means of death, the loss of good weather, failures of achievement, misplaced articles, etc. Moreover, Prinz maintains, someone who has experienced such kinds of losses will seek out coping strategies in order to improve his or her state. Hence according to Prinz sadness serves as a loss detector which is advantageous to our well-being, because we will seek out ways to improve our well-being as a response.

Yet, do we actually need such a loss locator? Isn't it obvious when someone dies that this is a loss or when a marriage fails in some sense this will always be a loss? While in many cases the losses would be obvious there might be exceptions where it is not clear that one has actually lost something or someone, such as when an acquaintance moves to a different city and out of a sudden one feels sadness, because one misses his jokes and his company in evening strolls. Hence in order to help humans for the not so easily detectable cases, sadness might actually jump in and serve such a purpose. Moreover, just because sadness serves as a loss detector, doesn't mean that it cannot also serve other functions. The coping strategies Prinz speaks of might for instance also include seeking help from others leading to social bonding. Furthermore, the loss detection might actually lead to a slowing down of the cognitive and motor systems, for the searching for the loved one, for example, has come to a stop. That emotions might not only serve one function, but actually many, might turn out to be very efficient and therefore also rational to have.

Behavioral functions of emotions. Clore and Ortony (2000, pp. 28-29) claim that there are two routes to emotional appraisal or categorization, namely reinstatement and computation, and that these routes may serve different behavioral functions, namely preparedness and flexibility. The two kinds of categorization are prototype and theory based (Clore and Ortony, 2000, p. 28). With regard to the behavioral function of flexibility we find that also in Rolls (2005). Clore and Ortony (2000, p. 41) claim with regard to their two behavioral functions that

"the goal of being prepared benefits from speed of processing, whereas the goal of flexibility benefits from awareness rather than from speed....it is no accident that the increased capacity for flexibility appears to parallel an expanded capacity for subjective experience. The subjective experience of emotion registers the urgency of a situation, provides information, and allows processing priorities to be revised. Thus, humans can entertain alternative courses of action and sample how they would feel about different outcomes, but...in order to do this, they must be aware of the stimulus that occasions the processing."

Clore and Ortony (2000, p. 54) point out that flexibility of response is better achieved by rule-based processing. Yet, the latter seems counterintuitive, for how can rules allow for flexibility unless there is also a rule which states that under such and such conditions allow for flexibility. Or do Clore and Ortony want to advance that under this circumstance this rule applies, under that circumstance that rule applies, etc.? Here some kind of clarification by Clore and Ortony seems to be necessary. It seems odd to assume that the goal of being prepared and the goal of flexibility are goals which the agent sets himself consciously, for although under certain kinds of conditions, such as in combat, it might be good to be prepared and to be flexible, in lots of other situations it is not a straightforward goal of an agent working towards a specific other goal to be prepared and to be flexible. However, these goals might regardless of which particular goals one wants to achieve in general be goals which are underlying our ordinary processing in a subconscious way and be necessary to achieve any kind of goal.

The signaling or communicative function of emotions. Similarly to Rolls (2005), who advances communication as a function of emotions, Denollet, Nyklíček, and Vingerhoets (2008, p. 3) state that: "There is the interpersonal, communicative function aimed to signal to others information about our internal state and behavioral intentions (Frijda, 1986)." Prinz (2007, p. 75) reports a particular example which is in

132

correspondence with the latter statement, namely smiling and laughter which might not only signal happiness (the internal state), but also dominance (the behavioral intention). However, laughter might be of different kinds, such as the innocent laughter of children over the funny fairy tale or the derisive laughter of the criminal over his unsuccessful persecutors, and also smiles might be of different kinds, such as the grin and bear it smile, when your colleagues make fun of you and you bear it as if nothing happened, or the genuine smile when one is seeing an old friend again after many years of solitude, or the fake smile for a photograph. Hence I doubt that in all these cases smiling and laughter signal happiness and dominance.

While the innocent laughter of the children might signal happiness, it would be difficult to argue that it signals dominance, for even though bad news might not have such an effect on the children when they are happy, it is not so obvious where the intention to dominate their environment might come from. Perhaps already the loudness of the laughter leads them to dominate the situation, though, for laughter is quite clearly louder than any ordinary conversation. With regard to the grin and bear it smile, however, it is not so obvious how that can signal happiness, because already the word "bear" indicates that something is very wrong with the situation. Also the fake smile for the photograph might be hardly interpretable as happiness (let alone dominance) unless the photographer is really good in provoking a genuine smile out of you.

With regard to the signaling or communicative function of emotions Rottenberg and Vaughan (2008, p. 126) report the following:

"It has often been noted that the majority of emotion expressions occur during social interaction (e. g., Ekman, 1992; 1992). Following Darwin's seminal (1872) work on emotional expression, a surge of modern research has elucidated the critical role of emotional behavior in signaling conspecifics. Two primary types of signaling function have been emphasized. One function is *informative*. That is, many facial and vocal displays of emotion communicate information in a fairly reliable fashion to receivers about the senders' emotions and their social intentions (e. g., Ekman, 1993, Fridlund, 1992)....A second function of emotional behavior in social interactions is *evocative*. That is, emotional behaviors elicit responses from others that are relevant to the emotional situation or event.....In this way, emotion expressions can in themselves be a potent emotional stimulus that alters feeling states (Bachorowski & Owren, 2001), behavior (Wexler, Levenson, Warrenburg, & Price, 1993), and/or physiology (Dimberg & Öhman, 1996)."

Yet, not all facial and vocal displays of emotion are reliable. I, for instance, whenever I am very tired because of lack of sleep start crying. That is, my eyes start to fill with tears, and I hardly have any possibility of controlling it. Moreover, I am mostly embarrassed by these tears and don't want any attention by anyone surrounding me, so that quite clearly goes against any kind of social intention tears and sorrow usually have. In this case, my tears also don't have any evocative kind of function, in the sense that I want attention by others. I rather would like to be left alone to make up for the lost sleep.

Also if one cries in a movie because it is just so sad what happens on screen, these are usually not tears which one wants anyone else to see. One is mostly embarrassed by them, because it is just a piece of fiction and not real. Moreover, in plays, movies, etc. not real emotions are displayed but only fake ones, unless the actor completely identified with the role he or she was playing. Furthermore, if one were to live in a society which dislikes any kind of emotional display, such as Victorian England or Prussia, the senders' emotions and their social intentions would not considered to be particularly welcome. Additionally, cultural norms have an effect on which emotional displays are considered appropriate in particular situations by particular members of the culture. For instance, in many cultures there are certain emotional displays which are considered inappropriate for men, such as their explicit expression of sorrow, sadness, or grief by means of crying. For a man in many cultures is supposed to be tough, whereas women, children, or old people might display such kind of behavior, because they are weak by constitution (or at least weaker than most men usually are). Another occasion is at a funeral where one is not supposed to laugh, because it shows disrespect to the people who are mourning and who are dead. Hence, there are many exceptions to the rule that our emotional displays communicate our genuine emotions and their social intentions to their recipients.

134

Öhman, Flykt and Lundqvist (2000, pp. 298-299) also advocate the view that emotions have signal functions, for they claim the following:

"as stated by Izard (1979, p. 163), 'a particular emotion sensitizes the organism to particular features of its environment...[and] ensures a readiness to respond to events of significance to the organism's survival and adaptation.' According to Izard (1991), this sensitization function is most obviously seen in the emotion of interest, but it is also coupled to a powerful disrupt-and-reset function when unexpected stimuli are encountered, the emotional counterpart of which is surprise. The purpose of this function is to redirect the activity of the organism toward significant but unexpected stimuli....The signal function of emotion implies that we attend to different aspects of the environment when in different emotional states. When in a euphoric mood, we may concentrate attentional resources on cues signalling success, which may facilitate performance (Isen, 1993), but sometimes also incur a risk of missing task-relevant signals that call for a change in the course of action if failure is to be avoided."

With regard to this passage the following can be said: Izard's emotion of interest might find its counterpart in the feeling of **boredom**. For when I am interested in something, I am quite clearly not bored. Yet, whether boredom is an emotion is an open question, for there is actually nothing in the environment or in us that causes boredom. It is rather the absence of anything interesting that causes or leads to boredom. As boredom is already questionable as an emotion also interest might be problematical as an emotion.

While both boredom and interest might lead us to do something about that state, in the case of interest to approach whatever is considered to be interesting and in the case of boredom to find something interesting, both boredom and interest very seldom reach such extremes that one would commit a crime because of it. For consider the following case: a scientist— call him Nobel—very much wants to find a cure for the AIDS virus, not because of monetary reasons, not because he wants to help millions of people, not because of the fame, no—just because he is interested in finding it. Now there is someone—call him Daredevil—who has found a cure, but this person wants to destroy it, for he is not interested in the money or in the fame (he already has both) and he actually hates humans.

Then the question is: would Nobel do anything possible to get the cure, such as even killing Daredevil, if he just wants to get it out of interest's sake? While there might be some person out there who is so extremely motivated by this motif, the number of people being so motivated seems to me very small in comparison to the people who kill out of jealousy or for money. And I dare say that the number might really not exceed the fingers of my hands. Hence, although we have the German expression that a certain topic is of "burning interest", we usually don't apply this expression to humans, and the intensity of interest which a person might develop with regard to a certain subject matter is relatively restricted in comparison to other more typical emotions, such as fear, anger, etc. It seems therefore not so much justified to call interest an emotion.

What might speak in favor of interest being an emotion is that it motivates us to do something, that is, interest usually results in approach behavior which interest might have in common with positive emotions, such as love, given that one takes love to be an emotion. Moreover, interest comes in short term form and long term form and the same might be the case with regard to love unless one wants to distinguish between the relatively short term phenomenon of falling in love and truly loving someone or something. Interest might differ from curiosity in that regard, for curiosity one only finds in the short term form in my opinion.

With regard to euphoric moods, I doubt that we concentrate our attentional resources on cues which signal success, for why should one focus on anything at all, if one is euphoric? One already feels great, so why does one need to pay attention to anything at all? Yet, one might have an interest in sustaining the euphoric mood, because it just feels so great, and in order to do so, it might indeed be reasonable to concentrate one's attention on positive cues. Moreover, besides having an interest in sustaining the euphoric mood, there must be actually something which does sustain the euphoric mood, for otherwise we wouldn't call it a mood any longer. That is, moods are usually called that way not only because they have a global effect (cf. Ledwig 2006, chapter six), but also because they are not short term phenomena but are rather long lasting, such as in the case of depression. So, one indeed needs to find cues in one's environment which keep the current state of the mood in its status quo.

Gruber comes up with a further connection between communication and the function of emotions, for he claims (Gruber 2008, p. 322):

"non-verbal communication appears to be a precondition for emotionally intelligent behaviour and for social intelligence. It obviously serves as a basis for the ability to detect other individuals' intentions and to deceive them by means of miming, gestures, and nonverbal utterances, and, as Damasio argues, it is a way of displaying *social dominance* and *dependence* (Damasio 2003, 48)."

While one indeed can use the detection of other people's emotions to one's own advantage by means of miming, gestures, and nonverbal utterances, there might be also persons out there who are very good at detecting such deceptions. Moreover, the closer one knows another person, the more difficult it might become to deceive the other person. Furthermore, society might also have punishments in place for people who deceive and try to manipulate other persons in that way especially if it harms the respective persons.

Sartre and Solomon on the functions of emotions. Considering Sartre's stance on the emotions, Solomon (2007, p. 9) takes from him the idea that emotions serve a purpose. On the basis of Sartre's work Solomon wants to argue that our emotions turn out to be strategies through which we make ourselves happy or not and give our lives meaning. Furthermore, Solomon points out that by cultivating our emotions we determine which kind of virtues and vices make us good or not so good people. When contemplating Solomon's account of the emotions, I found it particularly interesting that Solomon (1979, p. 16) claims that passions are reasons. In my own view, I defended in Ledwig (2006, chapter one) that an emotion can be termed rational, if one has good reasons for the particular emotion in the given situation. This differs from Solomon's account in that Solomon identifies passions with reasons, which I don't do. Nevertheless I find Solomon's suggestion quite interesting and intriguing. For if I have the desire to be happy, this serves as a reason for me to pursue whatever activities are necessary to fulfill that desire. Yet, one might want to object it is not my happiness which serves as a reason, but my desire to be happy which amount to two different things.

If one, however, takes the view that reasons are causes in Solomon's account and that my emotions therefore are the causes of certain actions or decisions which I make, then this can come out as true. For even if my will decides what is going to happen and therefore is the direct cause of my actions and decisions, my emotions might serve as an indirect cause for the subsequent action or decision, for my will might determine that a certain emotion should have an impact on which action or decision to make. One might object, however, that indirect causes might be screened off because of the Markov-condition, yet that this holds is not so obvious and would have to be demonstrated. If not only my emotions but also other factors are of relevance with regard to which action to take or decision to make, at least my emotion can turn out to be a partial cause of what is coming to be. Something similar holds for probabilistic causes.

What would happen, however, if we lived in a deterministic universe? Could emotions still be causes, even if they are only indirect and partial ones? In my opinion this has to be affirmed, for the simple reason that my will would then be determined by for instance my genes and/or my environment, so that these factors exert force on the will which in turn then determines that a certain emotion should have an impact on which action to take or decision to make. But let's get back to Sartre himself. What kind of account does he have with regard to the emotions?

Sartre and the existentialists. In *Existentialism and Human Emotions* Sartre interprets the existentialist's view on the emotions. For Sartre (1957, p. 18) states the following with regard to anguish:

"The existentialists say at once that man is anguish. What that means is this: the man who involves himself and who realizes that he is not only the person he chooses to be, but also a lawmaker who is, at the same time, choosing all mankind as well as himself, can not help escape the feeling of his total and deep responsibility. Of course, there are many people who are not anxious; but we claim that they are hiding their anxiety, that they are fleeing from it."

Yet, perhaps human beings don't need to involve themselves and they don't need to be lawmakers. One might object to that as long as one is not alone in this world, but shares it with other human beings, animals, and plants, etc., one cannot but involve him- or herself and become lawmaker in one way or another. Yet, while being a lawmaker and carrying responsibility for oneself and others might lead to anguish under certain circumstances, one should also consider this as a possibility of changing the status quo and improving things in the future. Moreover, there might be some people out there who don't have and/or who don't show so many signs of anxiety, despite the fact that they are the lawmakers and take responsibility for what is going on. The amount of anxiety a person has might vary from person to person. That is, anxiety might not only be due to current circumstances which cause anxiety to arise, but might also be a character trait which is either inborn or acquired. Furthermore, being the lawmaker gives one also a sense of power to control what is going on and to have that power might feel to some persons pleasurable while others actually dread it.

With regard to the emotion of anguish Sartre (1957, p. 19) makes his position more precise by stating the following:

"Anguish is evident even when it conceals itself. This is the anguish that Kierkegaard called the anguish of Abraham....if it really were an angel who has come and said, 'You are Abraham, you shall sacrifice your son,' everything would be all right. But everyone might first wonder, 'Is it really an angel, and am I really Abraham? What proof do I have?'"

Yet, I don't see why everything would be all right, even if the angel is authentic. For wouldn't one ask oneself what kind of God is it who demands such kind of sacrifices? And even more fundamentally: does one want to worship such a God? Other questions might be: is this just a game and does God only want to test my loyalty? While Sartre characterizes anguish by skepticism, in my opinion anguish can be better characterized by being torn apart by one's doubts. Moreover, normally one would experience anguish only if one's choice in the respective decision situation or the situation itself might lead to some extremely bad consequences seen from the viewpoint of the person who is contemplating the situation and is experiencing anguish.

Sartre (1957, p. 29) maintains the following with regard to the connection between forlornness and anguish: forlornness implies that we ourselves choose what we want to be. Moreover, according to Sartre forlornness goes together with anguish. With regard to despair, Sartre claims that we should confine ourselves to what depends on our will or on the probabilities which make our actions possible. That is to say, whenever we want something, we always have to work with probabilities.

Whether forlornness implies that we ourselves choose our being might depend on since when we have been forlorn. For one could argue since the time we have been forlorn we have to choose our being, but before that time it is unclear whether we ourselves chose our being or whether it was chosen for us. Moreover, couldn't it be possible that I just have been left alone in the desert and am therefore forlorn, but I can't really make any sensible choice, so that not me but the others made a choice for me by leaving me in the desert and I therefore didn't choose my being. Perhaps one might want to reply here that even if I am alone in the desert, I might be able to choose my being, because I have a choice as regards to how I spent my time, whether I just ruminate about the desperate situation I am in or whether I think about the best moments I had in my life, etc. So, Sartre might be right in this regard.

I am not so sure, however, whether forlornness and anguish have to go together. For I might feel anguish whether I should abort the child, although I am not forlorn. I have the possibility of getting advice and help from many people. Yet, perhaps one might want to reply as nobody else is exactly in the same situation I am in, I am indeed forlorn despite all the possible help and advice. With regard to despair, in my opinion one feels despair, if one doesn't see a possibility of hope any longer. Sartre's reference to probabilities makes this obvious, for if there is no chance of hope, then despair results.

Sartre (1957, p. 23) explains the existentialist's view on passion, namely that he believes that passions are not so intense that they can dictate what a person is about to do, so that human beings can be responsible for their passions and can't use them as an excuse. However, this belief of the existentialist has to be based on evidence and Sartre doesn't give us any evidence for that belief. One might want to argue though, it might be better to hold that belief than not holding it regardless of whether it is true or not, because it might lead people to try to lead a more responsible life.

Sartre (1957, p. 32) claims the following with regard to the existentialist's view on love: "for the existentialist there is really no love other than one which manifests itself in a person's being in love. There is no genius other than one which is expressed in works of art". This comparison between love and art, while interesting, seems to have a rather narrow conception of genius or a rather broad view of what art is. For surely one would also consider Isaac Newton and his account of classical mechanics as the works of a genius as one would likewise do with Albert Einstein and his quantum mechanics. Sartre's account of art would be rather broad, though, if he would allow Isaac Newton and Albert Einstein to be considered as artists. Yet, there are people who actually advance the view that mathematical proofs, for instance, are beautiful, and there doesn't seem to be such a difference between proofs in mathematics and proofs in physics. One could alternatively defend the view that everything which is beautiful is art. Yet, people, too, can be beautiful at times. And we wouldn't consider people as pieces of art, unless a person would make quite an effort to beautify or present her- or himself beautifully, in the sense of staging oneself, as one can find it with certain pop-stars, such as Gwen Stefani, Madonna, Pink, etc.

Sartre and vagueness. The only time Sartre refers to vagueness in his *Existentialism and Human Emotions* is when he talks about values. In particular Sartre (1957, p. 26) claims the following: "If values are vague, and if they are always too broad for the concrete and specific case that we are considering, the only thing left for us is to trust our instincts." In this passage Sartre would have to specify more clearly what he means when he evaluates values as vague and as too broad for the to be considered case. Yet, couldn't one equally advance that instead of trusting our instincts we should trust reason or our rationality? Our rationality, however, at least in the form of rational decision theory would have us maximize our expected utility given subjective desires and beliefs the agent has, and the agent's desires and beliefs might include or refer to some values which might make this approach problematical given that values are vague. Thus, Sartre is right that trusting our instincts might be the best option in such a case, unless instincts in general lead to detrimental results. One could also advance the view that instead of following one's instincts one should follow one's emotions, because they fulfill so many rational functions. Yet, perhaps for Sartre following one's instincts might amount to the same thing as following one's emotions.

Sartre and feelings. Sartre (1957, pp. 26-27) has an interesting account of what determines the value of a feeling which might be considered a parallel to Schachter and Singer's (1962) account of the emotions. Before we go to Schachter and Singer's theory in more detail, let's take a closer look at Sartre's (1957, pp. 26-27) account:

"But how is the value of a feeling determined? What gives his feelings for his mother value? Precisely the fact that he remained with her....The only way to determine the value of this affection is, precisely, to perform an act which confirms and defines it. But, since I require this affection to justify may act, I find myself caught in a vicious circle. On the other hand, Gide has well said that a mock feeling and a true feeling are almost indistinguishable; to decide that I love my mother and will remain with her, or to remain with her by putting on an act, amount somewhat to the same thing. In other words, the feeling is formed by the acts one performs; so, I can not refer to it in order to act upon it. Which means that I can neither seek within myself the true condition which will impel me to act, nor apply to a system of ethics for concepts which will permit me to act."

While Schachter and Singer (1962) advance the view that physiological arousal combined with cognitive labeling results in particular emotions, in Sartre one gets the impression that the acts which one performs determine the feeling which one has and therefore result in a certain feeling. Thus if I am nice to my mother on Sartre's account, the feeling of love for my mother arises, regardless of the motives why I am nice to my mother in the first place, whereas according to Schachter and Singer if I am physiologically aroused and have no explanation for it and if someone describes my mother in a loving way, then I will feel love for my mother regardless of how likeable my mother in the first place is. Yet, I might be nice to my mother because I am deadly afraid of her and because I know if I am not nice to my mother, then she will be merciless to me, which speaks against me feeling love for my mother because I am nice to her regardless of whether I have an explanation for my physiological arousal or not and regardless of whether I am physiologically aroused or not.

So on first sight one might want to doubt that feelings of affection can actually be caused in Sartre's way. Yet, if one looks at sufferers of the Stockholm syndrome (cf. Ledwig 2006, chapter three, and this book in the chapter on mixed feelings), then Sartre's theory gets verified. For sufferers of the Stockholm syndrome actually go quite some lengths to defend their kidnappers, which might even lead to marriage in the end. Yet, do affections also develop in less extreme cases, such as when one just wants to be polite? Also here it might be possible that affections arise if not in the short run, then at least very likely in the long run. For, if someone is nice to you, this creates a good atmosphere, which might lead to the other person being nice to you in return and so forth. Hence, in the end affections on both sides develop. However, it seems also to be the case that preexisting emotional dispositions and tendencies might have an effect on whether affections are aroused and to which extent they are aroused as one can see from the person who is nice to his or her mother because he or she is afraid of his or her mother.

With regard to Schachter and Singer's (1962, pp. 302-303) account, they in particular maintain the following:

"1. Given a state of physiological arousal for which an individual has no immediate explanation, he will 'label' this state and describe his feeling in terms of the cognitions available to him. 2. Given a state of physiological arousal for which an individual has a completely appropriate explanation (e.g. 'I feel this way because I have just received an injection of adrenaline') no evaluative needs will arise and the individual is unlikely to label his feelings in terms of the alternative cognitions available. 3. Given the same cognitive circumstances, the individual will react emotionally or describe his feelings as emotions only to the extent that he experiences a state of physiological arousal."

Given these particulars, consider my previous stated case again: I am physiologically aroused, I have no explanation for it, and someone describes my mother in a loving way. According to Schachter and Singer, if these things are given, I will feel love for my mother. Yet, if I know of this person that she always describes everyone as lovable, so that this description is no reliable sign of my mother's character, why should I feel love for my mother? The case might be even worse: I know of this person that she actually always describes someone as lovable who is not lovable at all. In such a case one quite clearly would consider it foolish if I felt love for my mother and I doubt that love for my mother would arise because of that description.

But getting back to Sartre's account of how feelings arise: while indeed certain kinds of feelings result, because of the actions which one performs, such as practicing expressive behavior of various emotions leads to the corresponding emotional feelings in the short term (cf. Ledwig 2006, pp. 26-27), that these results generalize to long term effects and that other kinds of behavior might lead to corresponding emotional feelings is not an established fact yet. Moreover, just because feelings or emotions can be cultivated in this way, doesn't mean that this is the way emotions or feelings naturally and/or usually occur. Additionally, there might be at least one other way to cause emotions or feelings, besides the natural or usual way, namely localized brain stimulation alone can cause emotional behavior patterns to arise (Panksepp 1998, p. 27).

Conclusion

Research has convincingly shown that emotions serve different rational functions which turn out to be evolutionary beneficial in the end. Particularly stressed are decision-making functions, social bonding functions, memory functions, behavioral functions, communicative functions, signaling functions of the emotions, and the function of sadness. Sartre's account of the emotions in *Existentialism and Human Emotions* is discussed and compared to Schachter and Singer's attribution theory.

Chapter 5 Hope and Alexithymia

I. Hope

Hope is usually not considered to be an emotion. Perhaps this is so, because it is usually the case that the feeling component doesn't show high intensity in the case of hope. An exception might be, for instance, that people in America right now have high hopes in Obama that he will solve the economic crisis in America and even of the whole world. Another reason why one might refrain from classifying hope as an emotion might have to do with the fact that the feeling of hope is only necessary if the conditions one lives in are very difficult. So, it might be the case that during both world wars and during the great depression the emotion of hope was more called for. Hence its rare necessity and low frequency might have led to the conclusion that hope is not a prototypical emotion.

Yet, despite the fact that hope is usually not considered to be an emotion, Ortony, Norman, and Revelle (2005, p. 198, note 5) state that in the English language hope usually stands opposite to fear. Evidence for hope being opposed to fear and therefore being an emotion might come from the fact that both in the case of simple forms of hope and fear some minimal form of expectation is necessitated (Ortony, Norman, and Revelle 2005, p. 175). Yet, might it not be possible to hope for something to happen, while not expecting something to happen? That is to say, can't one imagine a scenario where to the best of one's knowledge all resources for help are exhausted, yet, nevertheless one hopes for something good to happen? In such a case one doesn't expect anything to happen, because one doesn't have any grounds for that expectation—one hopes against hope. So, quite irrationally—at least on first sight—one doesn't give up, but hopes for a better outcome.

Yet, perhaps it is not irrational to hope for a better outcome, although one doesn't have any grounds for doing so, for giving up hope amounts to admitting defeat and admitting defeat might lead to despair depending on how one's overall situation looks like. That is to say, if admitting defeat in a particular area is detrimental for one's well-being in a subjective sense, then despair seems likely to result and appears almost immanent; yet, if admitting defeat in a particular area is not detrimental for one's well-being in a subjective sense, despair doesn't seem likely to result. However, despair is such a negative emotion that one usually tries to refrain from having it. The only way out here is then to hope against hope. However, one might want to argue that one doesn't have to hope against hope, because of the fact that we view the future to be open. That is to say, the unexpected can always be hoped for, because of the perceived indeterminacy of the future. Hence despite the fact that one doesn't have any particular grounds—any kind of evidence—for a better outcome one can nevertheless hope for a better outcome. Fatalists or people who believe in determinism, however, might not be able to hope against hope unless they are inconsistent in their beliefs and therefore irrational.

With regard to fear leading to a minimal form of expectation, does this really have to be the case? In my opinion this can be affirmed, for if one fears something or someone, because one definitely knows what is going to happen, then expectations result because of one's knowledge. If one fears something or someone, because it is completely unclear what is going to happen, then, although one might not have any particular expectations, one expects something—whatever that something is—to happen or be the case. From this comparison between hope and fear one might get the impression that hope and fear are opposites of each other after all. For although hope is positive and fear is negative with regard to their valences, hope and fear seems to be accompanied by expectations. Fatalists and people who believe in determinism are not counterexamples to the proposed account, because they don't hope (unless they are irrational) and therefore shouldn't have any kinds of expectations based on hope.

Nevertheless, I don't think that hope and fear are really opposites of each other, but rather hope and despair. For although in both hope and fear we have expectations given and although the first is positive in valence and the second is negative in valence, in the case of hope and despair we have expectations given in the case of hope, but no expectations given in the case of despair (one has given up on everything) and the valences are positive and negative respectively. Thus hope and despair are not only opposites with regard to the valence dimension, but also with regard to the expectation dimension. As the expectation dimension shows the same values in the case of hope and fear, that is, expectations are given in both cases, the expectation dimension doesn't make hope and fear opposites of each other. That hope and despair are related to each other as opposites might already become obvious if one looks at the origins of the verb "to despair", namely coming from Latin "desperare" which already includes parts of the word "hope", namely "spes"—hope—in Latin. Moreover, the prefix "de" in "desperare" refers to the fact that something is being removed. Hence, someone who has lost hope or whose hope has been removed is in despair.

Is hope related to any of the other emotions, or is hope something completely different from the rest of the already considered emotions? In Christianity hope is considered one of the three virtues, namely faith, charity (love), and hope. While in general one might think that hope is directed towards the future, one might also have hopes with regard to something in the past, such as in "I hope that he was right in his evaluation of the situation", or even have hopes with regard to something in the present, such as in "I hope he is at home during the now raging thunderstorm". With regard to fear, something similar might hold, such as in "I fear that he was right in his evaluation of the situation" and "I fear that he is outside during the now raging thunderstorm". Thus we find another parallel between hope and fear besides the expectation dimension. With regard to hope being a virtue, this might depend on who sets it up as a virtue. Also other emotions, such as being happy, being fearless, etc. might be considered as virtues, for one might think it is better to have a positive attitude towards life than a negative one. Thus, just because one considers something to be a virtue, doesn't exclude the possibility that it can also be considered an emotion.

With regard to the question whether it is **rational to hope** Solomon (2007, p. 186) maintains that its rationality depends on the probability and value of what one hopes for; similarly in the case of fear, its rationality depends on the probability and seriousness of the threat or danger. Solomon claims that anger turns out to be rational when one recognizes rightly that an offence has been committed, when one's anger is proportionate to the seriousness of the offence, and when one's anger is appropriate to the offender or to the relationship which one has with the offender. Yet, if one thinks about the AIDS-virus, it seems ridiculous to hope for a vaccine, because the virus mutates so fast. Is it then irrational to hope for such a vaccine or for any other kind of cure? In this case the value of what one hopes for is immense, because there are millions of AIDS-patients in the world, and the probability of finding a vaccine is very small. In my opinion, even if the value of what one hopes for in this case were marginally small, I think it would be rational to entertain such a hope, because with this hope one can simply lead a more positive life than if one already had given up on a vaccine. After all, if one is depressed one sees the world with more objective eyes (cf. Ledwig 2006, chapter one) and here objectives eyes would tell you that there is no vaccine any time soon to be had. Hence, in order to end up not being depressed, it seems rational to look at the world with pink tainted glasses and hope against hope.

Yet, is it also rational to experience hope, if one's hopes are **vague**, such as I hope that the future will look bright, where it is unclear how far into the future I think and when the future actually starts and what bright actually means? Also here I think a positive outlook seems the better starting point to have and therefore rational to hold. What about cases, where one half hopes and half fears that something might happen, such as in Stephenie Meyer's (2005) *Twilight* novel where Isabella, the human, half hopes and half fears that Edward, the vampire and her love, bites her. Are these emotions rational to attain? Granted that this is only a fictional case, yet one can imagine a similar case to take place in reality. As I will argue in the chapter on mixed feelings these emotions can be rational to attain, because each emotion is supported by a different reason, which is considered to be a good reason, so that no inconsistency between the different emotions arises and the minimum condition of rationality, namely consistency, is fulfilled.

II. Alexithymia

What is alexithymia. Bermond, Vorst, and Moormann (2006, p. 333) give a relatively comprehensive account of what alexithymia is by stating the following:

"In the accounts of Marty and M'Uzan, (1963), Nemiah and Sifneos (1970), Nemiah (1977, 1996), and Sifneos (1973a, 1991, 2000), five aspects of alexithymia have emerged. These are reduced capacities for emotionalising…, fantasising, identifying emotions, verbalising emotions, and thinking about or analysing emotions.…Although genetic factors appear to be involved in alexithymia (Heiberg & Heiberg, 1977; Valera & Berebaum, 2001), it has also been suggested that alexithymia could be the result of severe trauma (Krystal, 1988), sexual assault (Albach, Moormann, & Bermond, 1996; Berenbaum, 1996; Cloitre, Scarvalone, & Difede, 1997; Sher & Twaite, 1999; Zeitlin, McNally, & Cassiday, 1993), or childhood in an emotionally dysfunctional family (Lumley, Mader, Gramzow, & Papineau, 1996; Mallinckrodt, King, & Coble, 1998)....The consensus is...that alexithymia and somatic complaints are correlated, albeit possibly weakly (de Gucht & Heiser, 2003; Gündel, Ceballos-Baumann, & von Rad, 2000; Taylor, Bagby & Parker, 1997). The exact interpretation of this correlation also remains unclear, as it may be due to an increased tendency to seek professional help, rather an actual increase in somatic complaints (Lumley & Norman, 1996). This would be consistent with the notion that alexithymics suffer from hypochondria, rather than from psychosomatic disorders (Papciak, Feuerstein, Belar, & Pistone, 1987; Shipko, 1982; Wise, Mann, Hryvriak, Mitchell, & Hill, 1990)."

Hence, there may not be only physical brain damages which might lead to dysfunctions with regard to the emotions, emotional deficiencies might also occur due to genetic factors and/or psychological malfunctioning might be due to environmental stressors.

While in the previous quote alexithymia was characterized as a reduced capacity for emotionalizing, fantasizing, etc., van Dijke (2008, p. 154) maintains almost the exact opposite, namely that alexithymia consists in an overregulation of affect:

"Overregulation of affect can be described as being afraid to feel or experience emotions....Patients suffering from overregulation may be characterized by the following features: (1) being numb or inhibited; (2) suffering from impairments in insight into emotions; (3) having difficulty verbalizing emotions; and (4) having difficulty analyzing emotions. These features form the core of the alexithmia concept (Taylor, Bagby, & Parker, 1997) and have also been described in patients with medically unexplained physical complaints (Kooiman, Bolk, Brand, Trijsburg, & Rooijmans, 2000), with somatization disorder, chronic pain disorder, conversion and undifferentiated somatoform disorder".

150

In my opinion, an overregulation of affect might lead to a reduced capacity for emotionalizing, fantasizing, etc., though. For if every single outbreak of an emotion is regulated, surely every emotion is changed in some way by this measure. Yet, an overregulation might not only lead to a reduction of the emotions, it might also lead to an amplification of the respective emotions, so this doesn't prove how the reduced capacity is reached by an overregulation. Also to describe an overregulation of affect as being afraid to feel or experience an emotion doesn't have to hold generally. For there might be some people who are not afraid to feel or experience an emotion, yet they like to control everything, which might lead to an overregulation of affect, too. Van Dijke (2008), however, quite clearly leaves the latter possibility open by using the word "can" in the above quoted passage.

Van Dijke (2008, p. 153) distinguishes between affect overregulation and affect dysregulation, where affect dysregulation is characterized as follows:

"In the current contribution, affect dysregulation encompasses (1) the inability to regulate and modulate affective experience; this may keep the person unaware of the affective experience as either being numb or overwhelmed; (2) the incapacity to experience all aspects of affect, due to lack of the specific orienting information associated with each emotion; (3) the inadequate communication of emotion (due to being overwhelmed) or the nonexperiencing and/or nonexpression of affect (numbness), which increases the likelihood that one's needs will not be responded to by others. Consequently, this may increase the likelihood of social isolation and/or pattern of quickly changing and emotionally instable social contacts (Gross, 1999)."

Comparing these last two quotes by van Dijke one could get the impression that affect overregulation is just one form of affect dysregulation, for both in the case of alexithymia and affect dysregulation the author refers to the features of feeling or being numb. Moreover, it would make sense to consider affect overregulation as one form of affect dysregulation, but then one would have to explain why van Dijke considers affect dysregulation as the inability to regulate affective experience. For, if one is unable to regulate one's affective experience, one surely is not able to overregulate it. However, van Dijke has never said that alexithymia consists in the ability of overregulation of affect, but just in the overregulation of affect. Hence, van Dijke's account is not inconsistent in this regard.

With regard to the overregulation of affect, this can be done consciously or unconsciously. While Lane (2000, p. 364) has not stated anything with regard to alexithymia being an overregulation of affect, Lane has related alexithymia to the unconscious, though, namely that it goes together with emotional arousal in the absence of conscious awareness. Moreover, Lane (2000, p. 364) points out that:

"As greater conscious awareness of emotion is theoretically associated with progressively greater regulatory control of lower level processes, the relative absence of such awareness may be associated with autonomic and neuroendocrine dysregulation (Lane et al., 1997a; Thayer & Lane, in press). The best recent evidence supporting this view comes from the observations that group psychotherapy designed to promote the awareness and expression of emotions (e. g., confronting fears directly) is associated with enhanced survival in patients with recurrent breast cancer (Spiegel et al., 1989) and malignant melanoma (Fawzy et al., 1993)."

With regard to Lane's thesis, however, one would like to know why one finds lack of conscious awareness of emotional arousal in persons who suffer from alexithymia. Furthermore, one would like to know whether group psychotherapy leads to an improvement of conscious awareness of emotional arousal in patients with alexithymia in comparison to people with alexithymia who don't get such a treatment. Otherwise one would have to conclude that the evidence presented by Lane is not really evidence for the case of alexithymia at all. It seems, however, plausible to assume that confronting fears directly leads to a heightened awareness of the emotions in the respective persons. Yet, just because it seems plausible is no guarantee that it actually takes place.

Measurement devices for alexithymia. As alexithymia differs remarkably from other affective disorders, measurement instruments for its diagnosis had to be devised. In this regard, van Dijke (2008, pp. 156-157) claims:

"Frequently applied instruments for the assessment of affective pathology such as the Symptom Checklist (SCL-90-R; Derogatis, 1994), the Beck Depression Inventory (BDI; Beck, Rush, Shaw, &

Emery, 1979), the Positive And Negative Affect Scale (PANAS, Watson, Clark, & Tellegen, 1988), the State-Trait Anxiety Inventory (STAI; Spielberger, Gorsuch, & Lushene, 1970) all fail to capture the regulatory aspects of emotional experiencing. The concept of alexithymia can be measured with a well-validated self-report instrument: the Toronto Alexithymia Scale (TAS; Bagby, Parker, & Taylor, 1994). However, this instrument measures only the cognitive aspects of emotional dysfunctioning. The concept of alexithymia and emotional functioning can be more fully assessed with the Bermond-Vorst Alexithymia Questionnaire (BVAQ; Vorst & Bermond, 2001) and the EMOtional development Questionnaire (EMOQ; Vorst & Bermond, 2004). These instruments measure the cognitive aspects of emotional dysfunctioning (alexithymia or overregulation) and the emotional factors (impairments in emotionality and impairments in fantasizing) and social aspects (impairments in insight into other's emotions and impairments in analyzing other's emotions) of emotional (dys)functioning."

Subsequently, old measurement instruments were improved, and Lumley, Beyer, and Radcliffe (2008, p. 43) point out that the 20 item revision of the Toronto Alexithymia Scale

"provides not only a global alexithymia score but also scores on three dimensions or facets of alexithymia: (a) difficulty identifying one's feelings, (b) difficulty describing one's feelings, and (c) an externally oriented mode of cognition."

With regard to the effectiveness of measurement devices in psychopathology, van Dijke (2008, p. 151) emphasizes the following, however:

"Especially in complex psychopathology patients, standard psychiatric classification and assessment procedures seem to be inadequate and treatment-as-usual or diagnosis-specific treatment protocols seem to be ineffective."

Hence, in case one person has more than one affective disorder these measurement devices won't be of help in diagnosing the patient's specific illnesses. However, as I have already stated in the introduction to this book, it is not uncommon that a person with one affective disorder has also another affective disorder. Consequently, in order to get clear results with regard to the effectiveness of specific treatments it would be best just to consider persons with one disorder first, before one determines what works best for people with certain combinations of several disorders. This doesn't mean that one shouldn't treat people with several disorders, just that one should be more careful with regard to giving recommendations for combinations of several disorders.

Alexithymia and diseases. In order to link alexithymia to particular diseases or illnesses, it might be helpful to divide people with alexithymia into further subgroups, which Moormann, Bermond, Vorst, Bloemendaal, Tejn, and Rood (2008, p. 29) have already done; the authors state with regard to alexithymia types I and II:

"Type I individuals can be characterized as being concrete and rational, as lacking emotional warmth, as being distant in interpersonal relationships and socially clumsy, and as having a poor fantasy life. It is therefore not surprising that Type I turned out to be positively related to the Schizoid Personality Disorder and negatively to the Theatrical or Histrionic Personality Disorder....Type II individuals are emotionally unstable, which is in line with the established strong association with the Borderline Personality Disorder."

With regard to alexithymia types I and II Moormann, Bermond, Vorst, Bloemendaal, Tejn, and Rood (2008, p. 28) elaborate further that

"*Type I alexithymia* is characterized by low emotionality and a poor fantasy life in combination with poorly developed cognitions accompanying the emotions....*Type II alexithymia* is characterized by high emotionality and a rich fantasy-life in combination with poorly developed cognitions accompanying the emotions."

Moreover, Moormann, Bermond, Vorst, Bloemendaal, Tejn, and Rood (2008, pp. 32-33) state with regard to persons with type II alexithymia that "They lose balance quickly and easily become victims of debilitating anxiety." Yet, it seems surprising that persons with type II alexithymia lose their balance quickly and experience debilitating anxiety, for if people with alexithymia have a reduced capacity for emotionalizing, they shouldn't feel debilitating anxiety. Perhaps a reduced capacity for emotionalizing does refer to the fact that they in fact experience fewer emotions, not that the intensity of the emotions is actually reduced.

While from the above findings it becomes clear that alexithymia is related to certain personality disorders, Bradley and Lang (2000, p. 244) report that one finds alexithymia commonly in connection with psychosomatic disorders. Yet, alexithymia is not only connected to these disorders, Lumley, Beyer, and Radcliffe (2008, pp. 48-49) actually point to a huge list of studies which show that alexithymia is elevated in people with eating disorders, alcohol or drug abuse or dependence, problematic gambling, poorer nutrition and a sedentary lifestyle, a greater body mass index, and less frequent sexual intercourse among women. Yet, the latter kind of disorders might already suggest some of the causes or by-products of alexithymia. Similarly, Lumley, Beyer, and Radcliffe (2008, p. 52) report that "alexithymia is secondary to illness or stressors." That is, according to the authors studies show that alexithymia is higher in people with experienced sexual violence, head injury, severe burns, posttraumatic stress disorder, HIV infection, or kidney failure. Yet, Lumley, Beyer, and Radcliffe (2008, p. 52) make clear that "these studies do not confirm that alexithymia is a consequence of a stressor; rather, they indicate only that alexithymia is a correlate of some stressor." Nevertheless, these correlations might help us in identifying the cause or causes of alexithymia. Moreover, it makes sense to assume that a severe trauma due to sexual violence, head injury, etc. might have the effect of a shock in the respective person, such as feeling numb, etc. Hence, in order to get a good grasp of the situation and to work through the situation, so that one can deal with it properly and manage it, one has to reduce the corresponding emotions, for otherwise the experience and memories wouldn't be bearable at all, which speaks in favor of the **rationality of alexithymia**.

Alexithymia and the brain. While studies on people with brain damage to the amygdala have shown that the amygdala is critical for processing various aspects of emotion, and in particular, for the perception of negative emotions such as fear (see the chapter on the brain in this book), we will see now whether something similar holds for alexithymia. Actually all the studies I have seen so far don't report any kind of connection between alexithymia and the amygdala. Instead there seems to be a connection between the right hemisphere and alexithymia, which goes together with the findings on brain damage and emotional dysfunction in the chapter on the brain. In particular, Bermond, Vorst, and Moormann

(2006, p. 334) report an enormous amount of studies which show that the processing of emotional information takes place mainly in the right hemisphere. They cite studies which show that the right hemisphere is involved "in regulation of the subjective emotional experience, memorising emotions, in the communication of emotions to others, and in emotional physiological responses" (Bermond, Vorst, and Moormann 2006, p. 334). Bermond, Vorst, and Moormann (2006, p. 334) report other studies which interpret these findings: "alexithymia could involve: (1) a malfunctioning of the right hemisphere: or (b) a hyperactive left hemisphere", and they highlight the fact that both positions get supported by the literature. Moreover, Bermond, Vorst, and Moormann (2006, p. 335) cite further studies which support that malfunctioning means underfunctioning of the right hemisphere. In this regard it might be of interest to notice that Bermond, Vorst, and Moormann (2006, p. 336) report a number of studies which support that alexithymia is related to the dysfunction of the corpus callosum, which connects the two hemispheres. In this regard, one may plausibly speculate that the underfunctioning of the right hemisphere is due to the dysfunction of the corpus callosum.

After having discussed the right hemisphere and its connection to alexithymia, Bermond, Vorst, and Moormann (2006, p. 340) turn to the anterior cingulate and point out that "although the literature is unequivocal regarding a role of the anterior cingulate in the regulation of emotions, the literature is far less clear concerning the relationship between the anterior cingulate and alexithymia." In particular, Bermond, Vorst, and Moormann (2006, p. 339) report the following with regard to the anterior cingulate cortex (ACC):

"ACC activity has been related to mood changes, ACC lesions have consistently been associated with change in affect (Luu & Posner, 2003). Emotional lability has been related to reduced cerebral blood flow in the ACC (Lopez et al., 2001). Changes in subjective emotional experiences and deficits in the recognition of emotional expressions have been described in patients with lesions in the anterior cingulate (Hornak et al., 2003). In a PET study, Lane et al. (1998) observed significantly increased ACC activation in response to watching emotion inducing films."

From these observations, one could get the impression that ACC and alexithymia type II persons should go together because these show emotional lability. Yet, also damages to the anterior cingulate could show a connection to the alexithymia type I persons with low emotionality and/or to the alexithymia type II persons with high emotionality, for the changes in emotional experiences could refer to less intense or more intense emotional experiences or even to both.

Alexithymia and moods. While the last quotation already suggests a connection between alexithymia and moods, Rieffe, Terwogt, and Jellesma (2008, p. 187) give further support for this view by reporting the following findings:

> "It is assumed that people with alexithymia can identify their own mood states, but they fail to identify emotions, because they do not link their affective condition to specific situations, memories, or expectations (Bagby & Taylor, 1999). The physical symptoms associated with emotional arousal are also not adequately identified and these physical signals are easily misinterpreted as organic problems. This continuation of negative feelings and the corresponding physical changes explain the predominantly negative mood states and somatizing tendencies that characterize alexithymic individuals (Sifneos, 1996)....chronic negative mood states, such as depression and anxiety, are repeatedly found to be related to somatic complaints in adults and in children."

From this quote one gets the impression that (1) persons diagnosed with depression or an anxiety mood might also suffer from alexithymia or (2) that the concept of alexithymia is actually superfluous, because it is already captured in some mood disorder.

That alexithymia type I goes together with the schizoid personality disorder might support the first notion, for there is a connection between schizoid affective personality disorder and depression as we will see in the chapter on moods in the section on schizophrenia and psychotic depression. With regard to the second notion, the fact that alexithymia type II goes together with borderline personality disorder might suggest that alexithymia is not necessary as a new concept. It would be interesting to see whether the corresponding measurement inventories for people diagnosed with alexithymia and for people diagnosed with schizoid personality disorder on the one hand and for people diagnosed with alexithymia and borderline personality disorder on the other hand are not highly correlated with each other or whether there is no distinction to be found between persons diagnosed with alexithymia type I and schizoid personality disorder and with alexithymia type II and borderline personality disorder. If the latter were the case, alexithymia would become superfluous as a new concept and should be abandoned. Although Moormann, Bermond, Vorst, Bloemendaal, Tejn, and Rood (2008, p. 29) stated that there is a connection between alexithymia type I and schizoid personality disorder and between alexithymia type II and borderline personality disorder, they didn't point out how strong this connection actually is.

Conclusion

Hope turns out to be opposite to despair, although hope also has many features in common with fear. One can argue that it is even rational to experience hope if the probability and the value of what one hopes for turns out to be marginally small. With regard to alexithymia, one can maintain that under certain conditions it seems rational to experience it. There is an overlap of alexithymia to other disorders and it is not clear yet whether alexithymia can be reduced to these other disorders or not. Here one needs to await further studies in order to get clarity into the subject matter.

Chapter 6 Vagueness and Rationality in Mixed Feelings

Introduction. Pugmire (1996) rightly observes that folk psychology presumes that emotions can be ambivalent, because people speak of "having mixed feelings", "being of two minds", or "being at odds" with regard to certain things. Certain experiences are described as bittersweet, such as seeing a loved one, who lives very far away, only for a couple of days, which seems to suggest that human beings can have two different emotions or at least two different feelings at the same time. Similarly, certain relationships are characterized as hate-love relationships, as exemplified by the saying "women: one can't live with them, one can't live without them". Even certain tastes such as in sweet-and-sour sauce and in dark chocolate, which is bitter and sweet, exhibit ambivalence. However, what does ambivalence really mean? According to Merriam-Webster's On-line Dictionary (11/26/2004a), ambivalence has three meanings, namely

1. simultaneous and contradictory attitudes or feelings (as attraction and repulsion) toward an object, person, or action,
2. continual fluctuation (as between one thing and its opposite), and
3. uncertainty as to which approach to follow.

The last meaning does not seem to have any connection with the emotions—at least not on first sight—, for although a person may sometimes be uncertain why he has a certain emotion, having a certain emotion does not necessarily lead to an uncertainty with regard to following a certain approach. In particular, de Sousa (1987, p. 195) even claimed that emotions serve the function of filling gaps left by reason in the determination of action and belief, to solve the philosophers' frame problem (cf. Ledwig 2006, p. 50ff.), so that emotions can draw us to relevant information. Yet, when emotions conflict, which is a case that de Sousa does not consider, a certain uncertainty as to which approach to follow, results.

Do human beings really have two or more different emotions at the same time? Feagin (1997, p. 55), for example, considers the question whether contemptuous amusement is one emotion or two. Feagin then asks: is it then amusement colored by contempt or contempt colored by amusement, given it is only one emotion. Perhaps these distinctions are completely irrelevant, but Feagin's question already makes clear that the difficulty we have answering this question can point towards the direction that these are not two emotions but only one, for they blend into each other so much that we cannot say which is the more dominant. Of course, the intensities of these two emotions could be said to be so similar to each other that it is unclear which is the more dominant. However, as intensities come in degrees there is a continuum involved and one can construe a sorites paradox. Moreover, although the intensities of the respective emotions don't reveal anything about the emotional coloring of the emotions, such as love and hate, the coloring of the emotions becomes more or less extreme depending on the intensity of the respective emotions. Hence, it is no wonder that we might have problems evaluating whether it is amusement colored by contempt or contempt colored by amusement, given that it is only one emotion.

Nevertheless, the expression "mixed feelings" expresses quite clearly that there is more than one emotion involved. The expression says nothing about what the mixture looks like, though, but perhaps this is too much to demand. Similarly, when looking at a mixture of colors, it is difficult to say how many parts of the various different colors are involved unless careful prior note had been made of how much of each color contributed to the mixture. Yet, there is a difference between mixtures of colors and mixtures of emotions, namely that we only use one color word for a mixture of colors, whereas with regard to the case of mixed emotions we use more than one emotion word, which might signify more clearly that emotions even if they are mixed, do not completely blend into each other and therefore quite clearly consist of more than one emotion.

One might want to object that we sometimes do have more than one word for a color, such as in the case of "indigo blue" or "marine blue" or "royal red", just to mention a few. But here these words don't refer to a mixture of colors, but rather to a certain tone the color in fact has in order to distinguish it from other kinds of blue or red or other colors, and/or they might refer to the kinds of contexts in which the color was used. However, even here the persistent inquirer could insist on claiming that "indigo blue" indeed consists in a certain mixture of different colors. Yet, "indigo" and "blue" don't refer to two different colors, but only to one, is my reply, and this is what constitutes the difference to mixed feelings or mixed emotions.

Pugmire (1996) claims that ambivalent emotional states are only possible if emotions can contrast and even oppose each other or differ from each other. Yet, if his examples are considered, it can be seen that he quite clearly only considers contrasting and opposing emotions as possibilities for ambivalent emotional states to arise. This seems in accordance with the first two meanings of ambivalence in Merriam-Webster's On-line Dictionary, for the verb "contrast" actually stems from Middle French and used to mean not only "to oppose", but also "to resist" (cf. Merriam-Webster's On-line Dictionary 11/26/2004b). However, the subject of which emotions can contrast or oppose each other is controversial. For example, Plutchik (1984), with his structural psycho-evolutionary model of the emotions, considers terror and adoration to be more similar to each other, than terror and grief. This seems quite odd, because, at least with regard to the feeling component, terror and grief are both negative, whereas terror and adoration are negative and positive respectively. Hence, theorizers even seem to disagree with respect to what constitutes similarity and therefore, also, opposition, with regard to the emotions. However, one could argue for the similarity of terror and adoration by pointing out that dictators which spread terror and therefore demonstrate power in lots of cases are also adored or even loved. One just has to think of Nazi-Germany. Similar instances can be found in the case of the Stockholm syndrome, which will be discussed in a later section in detail, where kidnapped persons develop affections for their kidnappers. Nevertheless, besides the fact that terror and adoration can arise under the same conditions, this doesn't make it obvious why terror and adoration are supposed to be more similar to each other than terror and grief. For terror and grief could also arise under the same conditions. Perhaps from the examples one could conclude that terror and adoration get both some kind of positive value ascribed, whereas terror and grief differ in that regard. Yet, under ordinary circumstances we would consider it wrong to ascribe a positive value to terror—be it from the first- or the third-person perspective—and would evaluate this as a corruption of our values.

Philosophers might not only disagree, on a factual level, about what constitutes similarity with regard to different emotions, such as terror and

162

adoration, but also on the definitional level. For example, Neu (1977, p. 13) mentions the following definition of similarity: things are similar, if they are partially identical. However, things can also be similar to each other, if they are not identical with regard to any feature at all. They can just be very like each other, with regard to every pertinent feature. Although no one is likely to doubt that happiness and sadness are opposite to each other, and people are not likely to doubt that at least some emotions oppose each other, they might diverge on which emotions they classify as similar or opposite.

Ambivalence of emotional states. With regard to the second meaning of ambivalence, namely continual fluctuation, Pugmire (1996) points out that the state of someone's emotions can be unstable. For example, a powerful person might sometimes be feared and at other times might be viewed as fascinating, or a person's stupidity might sometimes be annoying, but at other times this particular person is merely pitiable. Hence, emotions can be ambivalent in this second meaning; yet these emotional states are not inconsistent, because they are not happening at the same time.

Something similar seems to hold for emotions such as jealousy, if Blackburn's (1998, pp. 61-64) analysis of it is correct, for he claims that there are cases in which one person loves another, but does not want to see him or her, because it is too painful, or wants to hurt him or her, because of jealous revenge. Such cases are, according to Blackburn (1998, p. 61), necessarily parasitic upon the normal cases, in the sense that they demand a background of the normal dispositions, which have become out of order, so that in the case of jealousy, love coexists with hatred. That these emotions really coexist can be exemplified by Othello's jealousy with regard to Desdemona, because, as Blackburn (1998, pp. 63-64) points out, Othello still loves Desdemona when he kills her out of jealousy. Otherwise, the extent of his remorse when he realizes what he has actually done could not be explained (Blackburn 1998, p. 63). However, even here Blackburn (1998, p. 64) says that Othello's love is only temporarily overcome. Thus the inconsistency of hatred and love is not really inconsistent, in the case of jealousy, because they do not happen at the same time. It could even be claimed that hatred and love are not inconsistent with each other, because we are talking about two different emotions. If the two emotions had been love and not-love, then such an inconsistency would have been much easier to substantiate. Is it really necessary to love someone before there can be jealousy? On first sight there is no counterexample, so perhaps Blackburn is right in this regard.

Yet, I recently met a woman who married her husband just for the money, and she was almost pathologically jealous being afraid all the time to lose her husband. She was very poor before she married him, so it is understandable that she wanted to guard whatever she considered as legitimately hers. But she had not hugged or kissed her husband for five years, so one cannot really say that she loved her husband unless one thinks of more platonically loving someone. The only thing which she did for him is washing his laundry, cleaning the house, and buying his favorite foods to keep him happy, which also at the same time fattened him up, so that he was not so attractive any longer. From these facts one would rather conclude that she was jealously guarding her property, instead of really being jealous because she loves her husband. Hence, it doesn't seem to be necessary to love someone before there is jealousy. However, one could also maintain that she didn't love her husband, but actually his money, so that love is actually involved. In favor of the hypothesis that she just loved his money speaks that she used the money for making high stakes gambles, buying expensive things, and going out for lunch and dinner making it rather unlikely that she could get used to live on less money in the future. Hence, contra Blackburn jealousy might not only involve persons as love objects, but also material things, such as money.

Continual fluctuation of the emotions might not only be found among humans, but also be found in the animal kingdom, especially if one considers approach and avoidance behavior as one behavioral manifestation of one's emotions. This can be evidenced by the following example: on Philip Island in Victoria, Australia, each day one can watch the parade of fairy penguins which at twilight come back from the sea to their nests. As one watches them trying to get ashore, one notices that they seem on the one hand to be afraid to get ashore, because they are vulnerable due to their clumsiness on land, and on the other hand that they want to get ashore, because they want and need to rest. Thus there is approach and avoidance behavior in the form of literally making four steps

164

forward and two steps backward until they finally make up their mind, overcome their fear and go all the way ashore to get back to their nests.

Some people might want to object that showing this kind of behavior is no guarantee that fairy penguins have the same emotions as humans do when humans show fluctuating behavior between approach and avoidance. Yet, even if one cannot prove conclusively that fairy penguins have the same kinds of emotions as humans do under similar kinds of conditions, they at least belong like we to the amniota according to the Tree of Life Webproject which is a collaborative effort of biologists from all over the world to provide information about the diversity of organisms on Earth, their evolutionary history, and characteristics. In order to determine whether fairy penguins like humans belong to the amniota, one first goes to the website for the fairy penguin (Tree of Life Web Project 2007), after that one continues clicking on the containing group leading in the end to the amniota to which also human beings belong. Belonging to the same group suggests that there is not a parallel evolution of human emotions to fairy penguin emotions. Belonging to the same group rather suggests that the respective emotions of fairy penguins and humans at least have the same origin; it might also suggest, because human beings seem intellectually superior to fairy penguins, that human emotions have developed further than fairy penguin emotions.

With regard to fluctuation, this cannot only be possible with regard to the emotions, but can also be possible with regard to beliefs, although we don't have the expression mixed beliefs or ambivalent beliefs as we have it with regard to feelings. An example for such a fluctuating belief is the following: an agent might at one instance believe that she betrayed him, but a little bit later the agent might believe that she didn't betray him, where the evidence for the betrayal hasn't changed in the meantime. Sometimes the agent just thinks that she is not such a kind of person who does something like that, but at other times the agent thinks appearances might be deceiving.

If one takes emotions not only to include feelings but also beliefs, then it is not so obvious where the emotions get their fluctuation from, from the feelings or from the beliefs. Yet, the fluctuation of beliefs is possible without any emotions going together with them, such as when a detective deliberates about whether the wife betrays the husband and sometimes thinks that she does, because appearances can be deceiving, and at other times, the detective thinks that she doesn't, because she is not the kind of person who does something like that. However, there is also the possibility of emotions going together with the fluctuation of beliefs, such as when the husband deliberates about whether his wife betrays him and sometimes thinks that she does, because appearances can be deceiving, resulting in jealousy of the husband, and at other times, the husband thinks that she doesn't, because she is not the kind of person who does something like that, resulting in a reduction of jealousy in the husband.

Now with regard to the question where do the emotions get their fluctuation from, from the feelings or from the beliefs, if one conceives emotions to not only include feelings but also beliefs, the following can be said: couldn't one come to the conclusion that the above mentioned case of the more or less jealous husband is evidence for the fact that the emotions get their fluctuation from the beliefs, because due to the beliefs, which can take the form of reasons, certain emotions result? Certainly this seems to be possible. Yet, if even animals can show mixed approach and avoidance behavior, the question upraises do also animals have mixed emotions due to certain alternating beliefs which they have?

One could argue that a penguin does not have the same kinds of reasons or beliefs at its disposal that a human has. For, even if penguins don't have the same kinds of reasons at their disposal, this doesn't mean that they don't have any kinds of reasons at their disposal. In this regard I pointed out in Ledwig (2006, pp. 29-30) that according to Jones (2003)

"it is probably necessary to distinguish between reason responders and reason trackers when comparing animals with human beings. A reason responder guides its action by means of a concept of its reasons as reasons, but a reason tracker is able to register reasons and to behave in accordance with them (by means of innate and learned behavior in the case of animals) and does not need a concept of a reason nor have a self-conception. This can explain why animals that lack critical reflective capacities are not as flexible in their actions and are not as sensitive, to the implications of changes in their environment, as reason responders are (Jones 2003, p. 190)."

Perhaps penguins are even reason responders, for they might have higher cognitive emotions at their disposal, such as jealousy which perhaps can take the form of territorial behavior. For in German we have at least the expression that he or she watches jealously over his or her territory or possessions and territorial behavior quite clearly is shown by many higher developed animals. Yet, perhaps their territorial behavior in the end doesn't amount to more than innate or learned behavior, so that only reason trackers and not reason responders are given. Here only empirical facts can decide the matter conclusively.

Yet, fluctuating between an intense amount of jealousy and a minimal amount of jealousy might not be considered mixed feelings or mixed emotions as such, so that my previous claims about mixed beliefs and the parallel to mixed feelings might not hold after all. In order to accommodate that objection one might consider switching from jealousy to emotions such as love and hate as opposites as one finds it in Othello's love for Desdemona to demonstrate the parallel.

As there are not only mixed feelings, but also ambivalent beliefs possible, perhaps there might be also ambivalent perceptions? Because there are ambivalent pictures, such as Wittgenstein's duck rabbit, and cases of anamorphosis, such as the skull in Holbein's painting *The Ambassadors*, which is only visible from certain points of views, ambivalent perceptions might be possible, too. One might even think that ambivalent pictures might go together with ambivalent perceptions. For what is it actually, when we say that a picture changes from one impression (the duck) to another impression (the rabbit) and vice versa? Is it just that from one viewpoint the duck comes into the foreground of our perception, while under another viewpoint the rabbit comes into the foreground of our perception? It seems to be that here a switch in emphasis or perspective which even can be obtained gradually in the case of *The Ambassadors* leads to a switch in our perception, too, so that indeed there exists something like ambivalent perceptions.

In all three cases, in cases of mixed feelings, ambivalent beliefs, and ambivalent perceptions, it would be really interesting to see whether the brain states, when they fluctuate from one feeling to another, from one belief to another, and from one perception to another, really differ from each other or whether our instruments are not good enough to capture any kind of difference within each category yet. In this regard, it is obvious that the preciseness of the measuring instruments is of utmost importance to obtain reliable results.

With regard to the first meaning of ambivalence, namely simultaneous and contradictory attitudes or feelings, this seems—at least on first sight—quite clearly to be possible with regard to the emotions. Greenspan (1980, p. 228), in particular, considers the case of mixed feelings and asks whether the following two statements, ascribing contrary emotions with the same propositional object, can both be true at the same time:

1. She is happy that he won.
2. She is unhappy that he won.

According to Greenspan (1980, p. 228) they could be true of the same agent, if the agent is the rival of a close friend whose feelings the agent tends to share. Thus the agent can have mixed feelings. Against the objection, that contrary feelings cannot be felt toward a rival at the same time, Greenspan (1980, p. 229) replies that although feelings might waver over time between happy and unhappy feelings, it could be concluded that mixed feelings are possible throughout the time span involved and not that there is a continually changing attitude. However, is this really the case? Is it not also possible to conclude that the person is torn apart by his feelings, which might resemble the continually changing attitude, rather than mixed feelings? However, in principle, someone can be torn apart by his feelings at the same time and also over a time-span, so this is no solution to our problem.

Of course, it could even be claimed that (1) and (2) do not constitute a real inconsistency, because it can be said that she is happy that he won, due to reason A, whereas she is unhappy that he won, due to reason B. Yet, without these qualifications, a real inconsistency appears. The question of whether P and not-P really constitute an inconsistency, with regard to the emotions, might depend on which kind of situations P arises in and might depend on which kind of aspects (for instance, she loves him when he talks like that) are to be considered. For example, in situation s1, the agent loves a certain person, because of characteristics a, b, c. However, in situation s2, the agent simply does not love this same person, because of characteristics a, b, c. Here, it is worth distinguishing between synchronic and diachronic inconsistencies:

Synchronic inconsistency is assumed if emotions P and not-P are present at the same time, and are directed at the same object o and in the same situation s, with regard to the same aspects a, b, c, etc.

Diachronic inconsistency is assumed if emotions P and not-P are present at different times, and are directed at the same object o and in the same situation s, with regard to the same aspects a, b, c, etc.

Diachronic inconsistency is considered to be a very weak form of inconsistency or even no inconsistency in the strict sense. It has been already captured in the continual fluctuation of an emotion. Yet, emotions might be also fluctuating between emotions that are not directly opposite to each other, in the way that P and not-P oppose each other, and these types of emotions do not fall under the definition used here for diachronic inconsistent emotions.

With regard to this definition of synchronic inconsistency one might wonder whether such an inconsistency is ever given. Are there any real life examples for that? Actually none come to my mind. However, with regard to diachronic inconsistencies one could imagine such a case. For instance, she loves him at t1 when he talks like that, because it sounds so intelligent and caring. But at t2 she stops loving him when he talks like that, because although it sounds so intelligent and caring she has discovered in the meantime that he just does that because he is opportunistic. However, one might want to object to this case that the aspects have changed why she loves respectively stops loving him, so that this is no proof that diachronic inconsistencies are possible in reality. Hence human beings seem to be more consistent with regard to their emotions than they appear to be on first sight.

Greenspan (1980, p. 229, p. 238) qualifies her statement that mixed feelings can be held, throughout the time span involved, if the person is basically a rational person and not under the consideration of some ideal of perfect rationality, for a perfectly rational agent would take a detached view and would consider it more rational to reconcile the emotions as time passes. Yet, a reconciliation of the emotions is not necessary, because emotions are rather short-lived anyway, so that it would be a waste of time to make the effort of detaching from them. Later on, Greenspan (1980, p. 238) argues against the detached view, for, on a standard of rationality that evaluates emotions with regard to their behavioral consequences, such as social identification with others, ambivalence might sometimes be more rational than an emotion that resolves the conflict. Greenspan (1980, p. 239) argues that mixed feelings are perfectly rational, relative to the non-cognitive functions of emotion, where emotions are considered as motivating attitudes, for she says that human beings have some control over how they act on their emotions, except in extreme cases. Thus, in the case of mixed feelings, by controlling their behavior, she claims that human beings can express their commitment both to someone else's interests and their own interests. This sounds almost as if it would be best for people to strive for mixed feelings, although Greenspan does not advance that, for, as humans are social beings and cannot evade being that, and as they need to survive, it would be best for them to always commit themselves to someone else's interests and their own interests, at the same time. However, people do not always want to commit themselves to someone else's interests, for the simple reason that not everyone is so close enough to deserve that commitment. Moreover, people also do not always need to commit themselves to someone else's interests, because in lots of cases there are enough people around to choose from.

Greenspan (1980, pp. 233-234) even advances that emotions may remain stable, although the reasons for them have changed, so that a change in judgment need not give rise to any change in the corresponding emotion. Greenspan (1980, pp. 235-236) points out, though, that the idea of contrariety must be understood differently for emotions than for judgments, so that emotions cannot be identified with judgments, because contrary judgments are defined as judgments that cannot both be true at the same time, whereas she contends that the friendly rivalry case makes clear that contrary emotions might be instantaneously true for an individual. Yet, given my analysis of what a real consistency would amount to in the case of mixed feelings, synchronic inconsistencies with regard to emotions don't seem to be possible at the same time either. Hence, there is no difference between contrary judgments and mixed feelings in this regard, so that at least from this point of view nothing speaks against identifying emotions with judgments. Consequently, any account of emotions which includes judgments doesn't have to be inconsistent on the basis of how synchronic inconsistencies are defined here. Of course, there may be other possibilities for inconsistencies to arise in an account of the emotions which, however, will not be discussed here.

While the form of inconsistency Greenspan talks about still seems reasonable, or even rational, it seems a bit unreasonable that people go to the movies in order to enjoy a horror film. That is, how can one explain the fact that people actively seek mixed feelings, if they could have something wholly positive instead? Perhaps this can be explained as a playful preparation for real life, so that in principle they know how that feels in real life and how they might react to horrific encounters in the future. After all, during childhood, humans and the higher developed animals play a lot, which, besides being a nice distraction, also prepares them for encounters in real life, such as role playing and hide and seek in the case of humans and playful fights between lion cubs. Alternatively, Matravers (1998, pp. 1-2) suggests that the content of fiction occupies a different space to that occupied by real objects, that is, the relevance to us of events in fiction differs from that of similar events in real life. However, it is difficult to see why he should say this. If a person is seen in a movie struggling with a problem, similar to one recently experienced by the watcher, under the same circumstances, and the movie shows a solution to this problem, which the watcher had not considered before, then why should this not be relevant, especially if this solution is then discussed with friends and they agree that this is a good solution to the real life problem. Just because it is part of fiction, this does not affect whether it is a feasible or even a successful solution.

An alternative explanation for the fact that audiences enjoy a horror movie is that they actually don't experience any fear themselves, but rather can enjoy the movie because of a contrast effect. That is to say, they are sitting in a comfortable place, they don't have to fear anything, and now they can watch someone else fearing something. This sounds very much like someone experiencing Schadenfreude or people being sadists. Yet, what about people who have nightmares because of horror movies? It seems to be the case that people differ with regard to whether they can enjoy horror movies or not.

But even given the contrast effect, how can audiences enjoy something *really* horrible? That seems not only immoral, but also really paradoxical, especially if considering normal people and not sadists, psychopaths, people who feast on Schadenfreude, etc. This paradox can be solved by claiming that the fear which is experienced in watching a horror movie is not real fear, for real fear can only be experienced when one is personally involved in the situation. The fear experienced during a horror movie can only be a diminished form of fear, resulting from identification with the fear portrayed by the actor. The fear might be even diminished by the fact that people sometimes can recognize whether emotions are true emotions or not. Ekman (2003) has discovered, with respect to smiling, that there are many different features which distinguish voluntary from involuntary facial expressions, and that some people are even able to recognize micro facial expressions, which Ekman says are a sign of concealed feelings.

Yet, is it really the case that the fear experienced during a horror movie is a diminished form of fear, such as in the case of the paralyzed person, who doesn't have as intense emotions as a normal person (Panksepp 1998, p. 57)? At least this might not hold generally, for I for one tend to have nightmares from horror movies for several days, whereas this has not happened to me with regard to real life threatening events in my life which factually and objectively were quite horrific events. Perhaps with regard to real life events these are not enhanced by means of music and different lighting conditions, whereas this is usually given with regard to movies; even silence might be used in order to enhance the mood of the movie. Hence, there might be reasons why real life events don't appear as threatening as events watched in a movie.

In this regard, it might also be of interest to consider when watching surgery or the birth of one's own children, it is usually the onlooker, who either feels sick to the stomach or faints, and not the person undergoing the surgery or giving birth. That the patient him- or herself doesn't feel sick to the stomach or faints might actually be advantageous from an evolutionary standpoint, because losing consciousness or feeling sicker than one already is might not be such a good thing to have, whereas such an adaptation function doesn't seem to be necessary for the onlooker, because nothing vital is actually happening to the onlooker per se. This phenomenon might explain why we are so much more moved by watching something than if we are ourselves directly involved in the situation.

When considering the emotions aroused by a movie, one might wonder whether imagining a situation might lead to all aspects of an emotion. If one takes an emotion to have as basic components cognition, evaluation, motivation, feelings, and physiological and neurological responses, then one might want to think whether any of these components are given when imagining an emotion might depend on one's imagining capacity. That is to say, some people might be better in imagining an emotion than others. Moreover, as there are some people who are even able to change their heartbeat by means of autosuggestion, it might be possible to imagine an emotion in such a way that it perfectly resembles the natural emotion elicitation. Something similar might hold for a certain acting technique where the actor puts himself into a strong imaginative situation which then induces an emotional reaction. So, one doesn't necessarily have to command oneself to release endorphine or to have the amygdala activated in order to put oneself in such a position that one's imagining of an emotion might lead to the agent having the respective emotion.

It could be objected to the position that one can only experience real fear when one is personally involved in the situation that one can experience real fear even when one is not personally involved in the situation. For example, many people experienced genuine fear in the U.S.A. on September 11, when the Twin Towers and the Pentagon were attacked, even if they did not have any friends or relatives in the respective planes or buildings. Perhaps they did not see the attack as a personal attack against the actual persons in the buildings and planes, but as an attack against their country, the U.S.A., so that they were after all personally involved in the situation and therefore experienced real fear. Even in cases where a neighbor's child is missing, some kind of personal involvement is assumed, because the child is reasonably familiar and there may be a level of affection—negative or positive—towards the neighbor's child, and therefore genuine emotions might evolve as a result of the disappearance. In the movie case, however, there is no personal involvement given unless there might be some personal experience similar to the scenes instigating fear in the movie. For example, a woman who has been raped before might be reminded or even relive her past experience when she sees a rape scene in a movie, and therefore there might be some personal involvement given and real emotions might evolve. Yet, in ordinary cases no such similarities are assumed.

That identification with someone might be part of having mixed feelings has been already observed by Greenspan (1980, p. 227), for she points out that it seems appropriate to have mixed feelings toward a person who is both identified and competed with, as in the case of sibling rivalry. To make it even more explicit, both in the sibling rivalry case and in the movie case, the person identifies, but also does not identify, with their sibling and with the fear-playing actor. That is, the person does not completely identify with their sibling, because the siblings are each in competition. A moviegoer does not completely identify with the actor who portrays fear, because the audiences know that it is only a movie. Something similar might hold with regard to the case where a mother has to decide between the lives of her two children, for she identifies herself with both of her children, but she does not completely identify herself with them, because they have only half of her genetic material. Yet, in this case, it is not quite clear whether the mother would have mixed feelings: that she is happy that she saved one of her children and at the same time sad that she did not save the other child. Can a decision where someone whom one loves is definitely lost ever leave someone happy? Identification might be said to be a psychological activity that is not necessarily connected to the possession of the agent's own genetic material, so that the mother might completely identify herself with both of her children and, hence, no reason to develop mixed feelings exist. Yet, if the mother identifies herself with her children, on the basis of her genetic material, then the possibility of developing mixed feelings seems much more likely. Furthermore, it seems reasonable to suppose that it seems much more likely to identify with someone who is very similar.

Yet, perhaps it is not identification which might be part of having mixed feelings, but only empathy or sympathy. When someone empathizes they can imagine themselves to be in the other person's place and therefore understand the other person's emotions, desires, beliefs, and actions.[10] Why should there be mixed feelings in this case? It is possible to empathize with another person without feeling anything with regard to that

---

[10] For an interesting account of empathy see Goldie (2000, p. 195).

other person. After all, sadists use empathy to inflict even greater pain on their empathee (cf. Sorensen 1998, p. 79). So it must be more than empathy. Yet feeling sympathy for another person might be enough and, of course, if there is sympathy for another person, it is also possible to identify with that other person. Is it not more likely that sympathy will be felt for another person, because of identification with that other person to a certain extent? That is, is it at all possible to feel sympathy for another person, if there is no identification with that other person? Agreeing with this, Pizarro (2000, p. 362) reports that cueing similarity between self and others can be sufficient to produce a sympathetic response in subjects. Pizarro (2000, p. 363) maintains that this sympathetic response can be explained by the mechanism of kin selection, because in that way a person would protect the interests of those that share their genes.

Sorensen (1998, p. 79) claims that intensive empathy can lead to fanatical over-sympathy, and he offers sufferers of the Stockholm syndrome as examples. In this example kidnapped people are usually only exposed to the kidnapper's perspective and therefore can very much empathize with the kidnappers, which in the end might lead, via identification, to sympathy for the kidnappers. The so-called "Stockholm syndrome" is named after the behavior of four hostages in a bank robbery in Stockholm (cf. also Wesselius and DeSarno 1983). How the Stockholm syndrome arises is still an open question and is much debated in the literature (cf., for example, Auerbach, Kiesler, Strentz, and Schmidt 1994; Graham, Rawlings, Ihms, Latimer, Foliano, Thompson, Suttman, Farrington, and Hacker 2001; Graham, Rawlings, and Rimini 1988; Huddleston-Mattai and Mattei 1993; Kuleshnyk 1984; Rawlings, Allen, Graham, and Peters 1994) and will be discussed in another section of this chapter.

Another question of relevance in the case of mixed feelings, is whether there is really a conflict between the emotions going on, because the expression "mixed feelings" actually does not suggest a conflict, it only suggests that there are several feelings present which do not completely blend into each other. So, what is an emotional conflict and when does it arise? Human beings become mostly aware of emotional conflicts when they have to make decisions, as in the case of the mother who has to decide between the lives of her two children. The arising emotions would have to oppose each other more in cases of emotional conflict than in cases of mixed feelings, because mixed feelings could be claimed when the feelings are relatively similar to each other, so that the overall situation would not be evaluated as a conflicting situation. Of course, it is also possible to have mixed feelings where the two emotions oppose each other, such as is the case with hate and love, but this doesn't have to hold for all mixed feelings. Furthermore, it is constitutive of emotional conflicts that the emotions lead us to make decisions that exclude each other. Hence the mother's affection for one of her children leads her to decide in favor of that child, and the mother's affection for her other child leads her to decide in favor of that particular child.

Yet, aren't there also compromises possible when there are emotional conflicts? Imagine the following scenario: you are a friend of the two persons competing for the departmental chair position. You like them both and are torn apart by the feelings which you have for them. So the optimal solution for you would be that either both act as departmental chairs at the same time or one of your friends acts as departmental chair the first half of the year and the other one acts as departmental chair the second half of the year. Hence, in cases of emotional conflict there are also compromises possible, so that our emotions don't necessarily lead us to make decisions that exclude each other.

In cases of emotional conflict, where there are both positive and negative feelings, such as when two friends are rivals for the same departmental chair, Greenspan (1980, pp. 240-241) has a suggestion for a solution. She suggests that focusing on the happy feelings and congratulating the winner enables the loser to take part enthusiastically in victory celebrations and to avoid dwelling on his disappointment. Whereas this seems to be quite reasonable on first sight, one might want to argue that enthusiastically celebrating the winner might be rather too much to demand from the loser. There is a German saying which states that the heart should not be made into a murderer's pit, which actually means that the emotional capacity should not be overstrained, for this might backfire in the end, even allowing for it not being very human to suppress feelings so much. Perhaps such suggestions for action, such as taking part enthusiastically in the winner's victory celebrations, might depend on how big the loser's own disappointment is. If it is very big, celebrating seems out of the question, though. Yet, the loser's negative emotions might even serve the function of motivating the loser to be a better candidate the next time. So there might be several different ways of dealing with these negative feelings and some of these ways seem to be more feasible than others.

Another form of emotional ambivalence might be found in some claims of psychoanalytic theory, such as that a child unconsciously hates a parent it consciously loves, where the parent is its rival in the Oedipal triangle (cf. Greenspan 1980, p. 223; Pugmire 1996).[11] To prove such claims is rather problematic, although Neu (2000, pp. 212-213) seems to be right in maintaining that evidence of the unconscious has to be indirect and cannot be direct. However, even if evidence of the unconscious can only be indirect, what would this evidence look like in the case of the Oedipus complex and how can we ever be sure that this evidence really is evidence for the Oedipus complex? Having contrary emotions on different levels, such as the unconscious and the conscious, is not a direct inconsistency, but only an indirect one and therefore does not seem so problematical, from a philosophical perspective. From a psychological perspective, this type of inconsistency does not seem to be so healthy, though, since this would be like being of two minds at the same time. Hence, this should be avoided. If the unconscious and the conscious influence each other or if unconscious phenomena can become conscious and vice versa, even from a philosophical perspective this kind of inconsistency might be problematic, for how should these inconsistencies be resolved, if there is no way of directly manipulating the unconscious?

De Sousa (2004) proposes that, besides consistent emotions there are also inconsistent emotions, for example: resentment of loved one, surprise for the expected, fears for the desired, etc. Perhaps the inconsistency of these emotions depends on the time factor, for resentment for a loved one usually refers to a previous time when that certain person was loved, but perhaps because of a rejection by this person or because of a stupid remark by this person, the agent then starts hating him or her. A more interesting case is where the two attitudes are present at the same time. Such a case

---

[11] Neu (1977, p. 148) points out that Spinoza already anticipates Freud's doctrine of ambivalence, that is, the possibility and importance of contrary emotions felt towards a single object.

can be explained by showing that the agent holds two different perspectives at the same time. Thus from one perspective, he loves her, because, for example, she is beautiful; but from another perspective he resents her, because, for example, she is manipulative and makes him behave in an immoral manner. Hence, the important factor to consider is which aspect the agent is currently considering when he is evaluating the object of his emotion. The phenomenon of surprise for the expected might be due to the time factor, for although something was expected to happen either in general or at a certain time, there is surprise because it was not expected at the particular time it actually happened. That the time factor is of relevance for the emotional inconsistency might also hold with regard to the last example. As long as the desired item has not been obtained, the uncertainty with regard to certain factors might lead to fear for one of the desired items. For example, someone very much desires to be loved by a certain person, but might fear it at the same time, because of not knowing what this might lead to or even definitely knowing that this situation might lead to disastrous results. Hence, in all three cases, the emotions seem to follow the pattern of ambivalence by fluctuation, although it is not continual fluctuation back and forth, but rather fluctuation from the first emotion to the second emotion.

Goldie (2000, p. 229) claims that jealousy lacks reason in its inconsistencies, meaning that it is all right for the agent to betray his partner, but not allowing the same freedom of action to his partner. Goldie (2000, p. 229) particularly observes that some men get more and more jealous with regard to their partner, the more they themselves betray their partner. As evidence, he provides a line from Mozart's *Marriage of Figaro*. This is not very convincing, for, as long as this is only a fictional example not supported by any empirical evidence, it seems that this is of no interest for us, because emotions in our real world are more valid to our decision-making than any fictional world. In this regard, Schuetzwohl (2008, p. 98) points out the following interesting results:

"Faithful participants showed no sex-specific preferences of the intention objects of their jealousy neither for suspected sexual nor suspected emotional infidelity. In complete contrast, unfaithful participants' decisions confirmed both hypotheses revealing a strong sex difference in the preferred target of jealousy which was especially pronounced for the adaptively primary infidelity type: confronted with suspected sexual infidelity 74% of the men facing sexual infidelity selected the partner as the intentional object of their jealousy, whereas 94% of the women confronted with suspected emotional infidelity chose the potential rival women."

While these results don't confirm Goldie's hypothesis that some men get more and more jealous with regard to their partner, the more they themselves betray their partner, this study nevertheless points towards differences between faithful and unfaithful persons. However, the study also makes clear that the situation is actually much more complicated than implicated by Goldie. For there are also interesting sex differences found and two different forms of infidelity distinguished, namely emotional infidelity and sexual infidelity. The adaptively primary infidelity type is female sexual and male emotional infidelity, for female sexual infidelity deprives the partner of reproductive opportunities and might lead to years of investment for someone genetically unrelated and male emotional infidelity deprives the mate of necessary resources for her offspring (Schuetzwohl 2008, pp. 93-94).

Goldie (2000, pp. 234-235) cites another reason why jealousy might be inconsistent, for a jealous person wants the loved person to be a person, but also to be owned in a similar way to an object. Yet, does this really have to be the case? Could it not be said that a jealous person just wants all the love and attention directed freely towards him, and if this is not happening, then the jealousy becomes so big that the jealous person does not care anymore whether the other person gives him love and attention freely?

Another inconsistency, with regard to jealousy, could be that jealousy usually does not achieve what it is supposed to achieve, namely to get love and attention. Instead, jealousy usually leads to resentment. Since we usually know that is the likely outcome, the question upraises: why are people jealous in the first place, if it does not lead them anywhere successfully? There might be two answers to this question. First, the view that we do not know for sure that jealousy in all cases and at all times leads to resentment; to show jealousy might also be a way of intimidating the other person, by signaling that the latter's actions are being watched and that these are not approved of and that this may lead to the obedience of the partner. Second, the view that jealousy can be interpreted by the other person as a reassurance of the agent's love. Hence the partner might deliberately give the agent reasons for being jealous, in order to obtain reassurance and find out if the agent still loves him or her. Hence it does not seem to be cogent that jealousy is inconsistent.

The function of jealousy might not be to get love and attention from a partner at all. It might just be to ensure that only the agent's own offspring gets the agent's support, and not the offspring of someone else. This offspring might serve as an explanation for the hypothesis that men seem to be more jealous than women, as evidenced by the greater number of homicides committed by men than by women out of jealousy (Daly, Wilson, and Weghorst, 1982). However, one could also explain the greater number of homicides committed by men than by women out of jealousy that men perhaps tend to be more aggressive than women, that their threshold for aggression is lower than that of women, or that they have different conflict resolution techniques than women. However, Schuetzwohl's (2008) study quite clearly points towards an evolutionary function of jealousy.

Ben-Ze'ev (1993) advances the view that there is something in the nature of romantic love, which connects with tending to hurt the loved one, which seems quite paradoxical. If Griffiths (2003) is right, that emotions are Machiavellian, to the extent that they find their dominant evolutionary function in social competition, then this does not seem so paradoxical anymore, for, if emotions have their dominant evolutionary function in social competition, then people should even compete against their loved ones, which might lead to the hurt of the latter. Yet, how is it possible to be happy about winning, if the loved partner loses? Do we really do this? Do we ever compete against loved ones or is it rather that loved ones form a unit of their own? Although there are unequal love relationships in which one partner dominates the other, it is not quite clear whether this is due to social competition between the partners. Such an unequal partnership could also be the result of one partner telling the other what the former's strengths are and then acting on that knowledge.

Ben-Ze'ev (1993) makes his position more precise by claiming that, even if the lover does not intend to hurt the beloved, there is something in the nature of romantic love, for example sincerity and trust, that leads to

180

hurting the loved one. For example, because the partners trust each other, they share confidences about everything, even things that might hurt the other partner, such as one finds another person very attractive or that one considers one's partner as overweight. Another feature of romantic love is mutual dependency and this may become too great, so that one partner hurts the other. Hence, there is something paradoxical in the nature of romantic love, which leads to hurting the loved one.

The Stockholm syndrome. There are some even more extreme cases, such as where kidnapped people develop affections for their kidnappers, whom they should actually fear and hate. This is part of the so-called "Stockholm syndrome". According to Auerbach, Kiesler, Strentz, and Schmidt (1994) the Stockholm syndrome refers to the development of reciprocal, positive feelings, between hostages and their terrorist captors, which are reputed to enhance the hostages' ability to cope with captivity. Kuleshnyk (1984) claims that psychoanalytic explanations for the development of the Stockholm syndrome involve an analogy between identification, in the Oedipus complex and in the hostage situation, while behavioral explanations focus on the human survival instinct and on principles of normal interaction. While psychoanalytic explanations are difficult to test for their truthfulness, the behavioral explanation fits well with the reputation of reciprocal positive feelings' potential to enhance the hostages' ability to cope with captivity. However, there is even one way to defend this view, for the condition of 'traumatic psychological infantilism' could cause the victim to cling to the person who is endangering her or his life (cf. Graham, Rawlings, and Rimini 1988, p. 220). After they are freed, kidnapped victims may stay in contact with their kidnappers, may not want to testify against them, may join their political movement, or even marry them. A reason for these types of action might be because they might be afraid of retribution from their kidnappers. So, even if they are physically free from their kidnappers, they might not be psychologically free from them (cf. Graham, Rawlings, and Rimini 1988, p. 220). The apparently inconsistent behavior by the hostages can be explained and made consistent in that way.

It might be objected that it is not actually love and hate that are involved in the Stockholm syndrome, but fear and admiration, and, therefore, the emotions are not inconsistent (assuming for the sake of the argument that love and hate are opposite of each other). Why should the hostages actually admire their kidnappers?—The victims might admire their kidnappers for having the courage to do what they would not themselves have the courage to do. However, what if kidnapping goes against the victim's fundamental beliefs? Why would the victim feel able to admire someone who holds beliefs completely contrary to his or her own? The victim might say that these beliefs are already so crazy that someone who holds such beliefs just has to be admired. Nevertheless, ordinarily a person would not admire someone who holds beliefs completely contrary to his or her own. Furthermore, people usually marry (as has happened to victims of the Stockholm syndrome), because they love the other partner and not just because they admire him or her. It seems possible to love a kidnapper and also more reasonable than admiration, because it is generally claimed that love is not very reasonable, but rather that people "fall into" it, whereas admiration goes together with having good reasons for this admiration, so it could be claimed that admiration has less involvement in the Stockholm syndrome. However, dictators and tyrants have been admired, so why not also kidnappers? Here only empirical results can bring more clarification with regard to which emotions are involved in the Stockholm syndrome.

Graham, Rawlings, and Rimini present the conditions for the development of the Stockholm syndrome:

"(1) A person threatens to kill another and is perceived as having the capability to do so;

(2) the other cannot escape, so her or his life depends on the threatening person;

(3) the threatened person is isolated from outsiders so that the only other perspective available to her or him is that of the threatening person; and

(4) the threatening person is perceived as showing some degree of kindness to the one being threatened." (Graham, Rawlings, and Rimini 1988, pp. 218-219)

For female hostages there is an additional element to the terror, namely rape (Graham, Rawlings, and Rimini 1988, p. 219). Condition (3) seems to be in accordance with what Sorensen (1998, p. 79) has claimed, namely that intensive empathy can lead to fanatical over-sympathy. Do the victims

182

really feel over-sympathy? Or are they just afraid of any kind of retribution and therefore follow the saying "Keep your friends close but your enemies even closer"? For in that way they have a better control of what their potential enemies are doing and up to. Whether over-sympathy is given in the Stockholm syndrome or whether the saying is implemented has to be determined by empirical means. If one for instance knew which brain areas are activated when sympathy is felt, one could find out whether over-sympathy is given in the Stockholm syndrome. If one, however, were just to follow the verbal reports of the victims, it could be possible that these might not be completely truthful or reliable, because the victims might repress their emotions, might suffer from memory loss because of trauma, might be too intimidated to answer truthfully, and/or might even be threatened by their former captors.

While there have been some studies which suggest that the Stockholm syndrome doesn't only appear in kidnapping cases, but also in certain kinds of marriages (Graham, Rawlings, and Rimini 1988; Graham, Rawlings, Ihms, Latimer, Foliano, Thompson, Suttman, Farrington, and Hacker 2001; Rawlings, Allen, Graham, and Peters 1994), there might be two other areas where the Stockholm syndrome could have shown itself, namely in concentration camps and in societies with dictatorships. Yet, I have not heard of any study which shows that concentration camp victims actually have developed affections for their captors. This might be due to the fact that complete isolation from outsiders might not have been given in the case of concentration camps, if one were still able to exchange mail or have some form of contact to the outside world by means of telephone, radio, or television. The exchange of letters was to my knowledge still possible in Nazi concentration camps. Whether this was also given with regard to camps for Japanese-Americans and Japanese people during the second world war in the U.S.A., in concentration camps in the Soviet Union, etc., I don't know. Hence, at least with regard to Nazi Germany the Stockholm syndrome might not have arisen in concentration camps, because the third condition of the Stockholm syndrome was not given. One might also think that there is never any complete isolation from the outside world in concentration camps given, because usually new people arrive all the time.

Also with regard to dictatorships, the third condition of the Stockholm syndrome might not have been given in many cases, because there still was some kind of connection to the outside world. Yet, perhaps the Stockholm syndrome might account for the longevity of dictatorships in many cases. Hitler was a person who quite clearly could frighten people (already his public voice is kind of frightening, if one thinks about it; moreover, his natural private voice was never heard on TV or the radio), and actually it was kind of obvious that people who were not conforming to Nazi Germany style and behavior had problems living in Germany. So the first condition of the Stockholm syndrome is fulfilled. On the other hand, Hitler also did a lot for his people, such as building many of the German highways, and therewith employing many people. (The economic situation of Germany after the first world war and before Hitler took power looked very bleak because of the enormous reparation costs.) Also finding more space for Germans to live in didn't look like a bad idea to Germans. Hitler also did raise the self-confidence of many Germans after the humiliation of the first world war. Hence, the fourth condition of the Stockholm syndrome is fulfilled. It is not so easy to escape one's own country, so also the second condition of the Stockholm syndrome is fulfilled. While there was a connection to the outside world, lots of rural places in Germany were relatively isolated from outsiders with the exception of radio- and television-connections, newspapers, etc. Moreover, the latter and even the churches became victims of the Gleichschaltung (enforced political conformity), so that the isolation from the outside world increased. Hence, also the third condition is to some extent fulfilled.

What is also of interest with regard to dictatorships and the Stockholm syndrome is that at least in the case of Hitler one could quite clearly characterize the Germans of the Nazi era as showing fanatical over-sympathy for Hitler which would support Sorensen's analysis of the Stockholm syndrome, namely that intense empathy can lead to fanatical over-sympathy. Of course there were also other psychological mechanisms at work during Nazi Germany, especially mechanisms which pertain to groups and mechanisms which pertain to obedience, yet no one to my knowledge has tried to explain the immense support for the Nazi regime and the extreme willingness for sacrifice which the Germans showed during the second world war by means of the Stockholm syndrome, so that would be quite innovative and new.

The rationality of emotional inconsistencies. Are emotional inconsistencies irrational? Of course, an answer to this question hinges on what we mean by rationality. In Ledwig (2006, chapter 1) I argued that emotions can be rational, in the sense that they can be reasonable, justified, warranted, and/or appropriate for a given situation. An emotion is reasonable, justified, etc. for a given situation, if the agent has good reasons for this particular emotion in the given situation. If this is applied to the different examples given, the following results: for continually changing emotions, such emotional inconsistencies can be claimed as rational, if good reasons can be given for the different emotions, such as if there are good reasons for fearing a powerful person at some times, but at other times is more fascinated by him or her. For example, at the times when a powerful person is feared, this might be due to the fact that the individual is currently in a more vulnerable position or that they are currently more aware of the fear-arousing properties of this powerful person. So these facts might very well serve as good reasons for the emotion of fear. Something similar can be found to ground the agent's fascination.

With regard to the departmental chair example, the view can be defended, that the agent has good reasons for being happy that his friend has won, but also has good reasons for being unhappy that his friend has won. However, on first sight, it would seem to be difficult to ascribe solidity to such reasons, which might be one quality exhibited by a "good" reason, for reason a is solid relative to belief set K, in the case that a is robust against the removal of inconsistencies in this respective belief set K. However, as we are capable of simultaneously believing that someone is happy that their friend has won and also that they are unhappy that the friend has won (= inconsistency), solidity does not seem to be a quality of a good reason. Yet this inconsistency is only an indirect one, for the reasons for the respective emotions differ, so that solidity can be ascribed to a good reason.

Perhaps we should be more tolerant towards inconsistent emotions, for, as Priest and Tanaka (Winter 2004) have advanced that a very good reason for paraconsistent logic is the fact that there are inconsistent, but not trivial theories, the view might also be advanced that emotions can be inconsistent, but not trivially so. Priest and Tanaka have pointed out that people always have inconsistent beliefs and that they may even be rational in having them, for there may be evidence for both X and its negation. Furthermore, according to Priest and Tanaka, there may even be cases, as in the following "paradox of the preface", where it is impossible to eliminate the inconsistency. After thorough research, a rational agent writes a book in which he claims $A_1,..., A_n$. However, he is also aware of the fact that no book of any complexity contains only truths. So he rationally believes $\neg(A_1 \&...\& A_n)$, too. Something like that may be true of the emotions of the mother who has to decide between the lives of her two children, too, because at the same time she has good reasons for being happy about saving child A and also for being unhappy about losing child B.

Vagueness of emotional inconsistencies. In the case of continually changing emotions, such as when a powerful person is feared and then admired, vagueness is given, because it will be very hard to determine at which particular instant or over which time interval the change actually did take place. Needless to say, also all of the other different possibilities for vagueness with regard to emotions and feelings exist in the case of continually changing emotions, such as feelings might vary with regard to their intensity, valence, familiarity, duration, etc. and lie on continua and are therefore open to sorites paradoxes, emotions might have judgments as a component, where these judgments include vague terms or are about vague objects, etc. In the case of simultaneous inconsistencies, such as in the departmental chair case, vagueness is given, because the agent might have difficulties identifying his or her emotions, differentiating the emotions from each other, and even more so explaining the emotions and/or feelings he or she has. Also here all of the other different possibilities for vagueness to arise with regard to emotions and feelings are given.

If, however, vagueness is given with regard to emotional inconsistencies, can the emotions or feelings still be rational? Yes, for even though the reasons why the agent has a certain emotion at a certain time might not be known to the agent, but only known to a third person, due to these reasons a change in the emotion takes place, such as when the powerful person is not feared any longer because the agent has gained in self-confidence, and these emotions can be identified by a third person or by means of physiological measures. Also even if the agent him- or herself is not able to differentiate between the emotions and feelings he or she has, a third person might be able to do so due to his or her knowledge of the agent. Yet, what about determining the point in time or the time interval, when the agent switches from one emotion to the other? Even though it might not be possible to determine this with precision, one could always argue that an emotion turns out to be rational at a given time t given that such and such reasons are given at the respective time.

Conclusion

When we speak of emotional inconsistencies, it is necessary to distinguish between two different kinds: first, the possibility of having two different emotions at the same time and second, the possibility of having continually fluctuating emotions. In the case of mixed feelings, there do not have to be opposite emotions present, whereas in the case of emotional conflicts this has to be the case. Agreeing with Ben-Ze'ev, determines that the apparent paradox, that one hurts the person which one loves, finds its resolution in the nature of romantic love. Yet, paradoxical phenomena, such as the Stockholm syndrome, are not so easily solvable, for, even if it might be rational in the hostage situation to identify with the kidnapper (for the victim is in the same situation), this is no good reason for later on marrying the kidnapper, as has happened in reality. Finally, emotional inconsistencies can be rational, even if they turn out to be vague.

Chapter 7 Vagueness and Rationality in Anxiety Disorders

I. Introduction

One finds a huge variety of anxiety disorders, such as acute stress disorder, agoraphobia (being afraid of open spaces) without history of panic disorder, anxiety disorder due to general medical condition, generalized anxiety disorder, obsessive-compulsive disorder, panic disorder with agoraphobia, panic disorder without agoraphobia, posttraumatic stress disorder, specific phobias (spider phobia, snake phobia, etc.), social phobia, and substance-induced anxiety disorder. Here we will just concentrate on generalized anxiety disorder and social phobias, because they in particular appear quite irrational. For in the case of generalized anxiety disorder the anxiety pertains to everything and therefore in its entirety might be difficult to justify and in the case of social phobias they pertain to human beings who might actually also be beneficial for us, so that we might even harm ourselves by having this disorder which wouldn't be very rational. Yet, before we go into more detail of why generalized anxiety disorder and social phobia appear prima facie so irrational, we first have to get a good grasp of what anxiety disorders are and where they come from.

Characterization of anxiety disorders. LeDoux (2000, p. 130), who spent quite some time on how the fear system works, relates fear to anxiety disorders as follows:

"Fear is a normal reaction to threatening situations and is a common occurrence in daily life. When fear becomes greater than that warranted by the situation or begins to occur in inappropriate situations, a fear or anxiety disorder exists (e.g., Marks, 1987; Öhman, 1992). Excluding substance abuse problems, anxiety disorders account for about half of all the conditions that people see mental health professionals for each year (Manderscheid & Sonnenschein, 1994). It seems likely that the fear system of the brain is involved in at least some anxiety disorders, and it is thus important that we understand in as much detail as possible how the fear system works."

I agree with LeDoux that it seems reasonable to suppose that the fear system should be involved in at least some of the anxiety disorders. For why should one be anxious, if there was no reason to fear something—whatever that something may be? However, there may be people who in general are very restless and therefore anxious with no particular reason for their restlessness. It is just part of their personality. Yet, the anxious personality could also be acquired through constant exposure to fearful circumstances and/or because someone has convincingly installed fear in this particular person. Nevertheless the possibility exists that the anxious personality is inborn or inherited. Hence, it is not so obvious whether the fear system is involved in all of the anxiety disorders, yet one can reasonably assume that it is instilled in at least some.

That anxiety disorders are so widespread and ubiquitous makes clear that on the one hand the fear system seems to be a very powerful one and on the other hand that it easily can get out of balance—at least what we ordinarily would consider out of balance. Also fear seems to be one of the more intense, if not the most intense emotion that we are capable of. One could kill out of fear, die because of fear, overcome obstacles because of fear, etc. I am not so sure, though, whether one could kill oneself because of fear, whereas one could kill oneself because of love for another person or even for one's own country. So here there might be a limit for the emotion of fear. Yet, perhaps one could even kill oneself out of fear of what one would become or do, if one didn't kill oneself. Hence, perhaps love and fear are the most intense emotions, in the sense that they are capable of the highest intensity and therefore could lead to the most far-reaching actions. As hate could be considered as opposite to love, the same should apply for hate.

Also jealousy can be quite intense. Yet the range of actions which one is capable of doing because of jealousy might be rather more limited than in the case of love and fear, for to kill oneself out of jealousy would be quite difficult to justify. In reality, however, it happens quite often that in cases of jealousy also the jealous person kills him- or herself. Yet, that could be the result of realizing what he or she has done to his or her loved one and could be justified by having no reason to live any longer after one's loved one is gone. Also shame seems to be a powerful emotion at least in some cultures, for how should one otherwise explain the desire of

Japanese people to kill oneself after one has lost one's face? However, in this case also cultural expectations play a role with regard to which actions turn out to be appropriate and therefore should be performed.

But we should be getting back to the general phenomenon of anxiety. If the fear system is such a powerful system to have and if fear serves a function, then individuals with high anxiety should differ in some relevant way from individuals with low anxiety. In particular, one would think that fear should protect us from harm. But how can fear do that? It can do that by first making us perceive the dangerous object reliably and fast, second by making us perform the appropriate kind of action, meaning in its most primitive forms either fleeing from the dangerous object or freezing, so that the dangerous object cannot detect us or mistakes us for dead, and third by preventing encounters with the dangerous object in the future by means of either avoiding areas where the dangerous object is located or by means of killing the dangerous object. More sophisticated reactions could be that one makes the dangerous object one's ally or friend, if that is at all possible, so that it no longer poses a threat or danger. On the one hand one would expect that individuals with high anxiety are better in detecting dangerous stimuli, because they might be more alert than individuals with low anxiety, on the other hand one could expect that individuals with high anxiety might be slower in reacting to dangerous stimuli unless the reaction didn't involve much thinking, because they might have problems thinking clearly because of their high anxiety.

With regard to the first point, namely detection of dangerous stimuli, Öhman, Flykt, and Lundqvist (2000, p. 305) report the following data which are in accordance with my hypothesis that individuals with high anxiety are faster in detecting dangerous stimuli than individuals with low anxiety:

"Byrne and Eysenck (1995) examined detection latencies for real angry and happy faces against a background of neutral faces and happy faces against backgrounds of neutral or angry faces. Highly anxious subjects were faster than subjects low in anxiety to find angry faces against a background of neutral faces, whereas the two groups did not differ in latency to find happy faces against a neutral background. When the background consisted of angry faces, anxious subjects were slower to find happy faces than were nonanxious

190

subjects, suggesting a powerful distracting effect from angry background faces. These findings suggest that high anxiety enhances the normal bias to be faster in discriminating threatening than nonthreatening stimuli. Bradley and Mogg (1996) used normal controls and persons diagnosed with generalized anxiety disorder or depression as subjects....The results showed a bias of the generalized anxiety disorder patients to look at angry faces, with reliably shorter latencies than for other expressions."

As detection latencies lie on a continuum and as persons with high respectively low anxiety differ in their detection latencies with regard to angry faces and this even holds for persons with generalized anxiety disorder, vagueness might be of relevance for anxiety disorders. With regard to the other two areas I didn't find any particular studies done yet. Yet, we will see later on that in the case of social phobias one finds evidence with regard to the third area, namely that the social phobic individual tries to prevent encounters with the dangerous object in the future by avoiding it.

Gender differences. As women in lots of cases don't have such a powerful physique as men do, they have from the very outset more reason to be afraid of physical dangers than men do. As a result one can expect that women have more reason to develop anxiety disorders than men at least with regard to physical dangers. However, this doesn't have to hold for many specific phobias, such as spider phobia, height phobia, phobia of open spaces, and even snake phobia, because in all these cases human size and strength doesn't matter—unless one encounters one of the few large snakes, such as a Boa Constrictor. So with regard to these particular phobias there shouldn't be a particular gender difference. However, one could also argue in such a way that even here a gender difference is established: as men have more power than women from the very outset, they are the ones who protect women from physical danger regardless of which kind of physical danger is encountered. (One could argue to distinguish between different kinds of physical dangers or dangers differing in size could amount to too much work and lead to too many problems in borderline cases, so that this approach is abandoned.) As a result even with regard to dangerous objects which are very small, such as spiders, it is women which develop anxiety disorders more likely and/or often than men. In agreement with the latter kind of reasoning, Lane (2000, p. 350) claims the following:

"These data suggest that on average women are more sensitive to emotional cues in themselves and others than are men. This greater sensitivity has clear advantages in the realm of interpersonal relations and problem solving, but may also contribute to the finding that women are approximately twice as likely to suffer from affective and anxiety disorders than are men (Breslau et al., 1997; Gater et al., 1998)."

One could argue that as women need men or use men for their defense in case of physical dangers, women also have to communicate their needs to men. Consequently one could expect women to give more emotional cues to men than to women in case of physical dangers and also cues of higher intensity, given that men are less sensitive to emotional cues in themselves and others. With regard to this hypothesis I have not found any confirming data yet. While one could maintain that the greater sensitivity to emotional cues in themselves and others appears rational to have for women, for dangerous objects are then more easily detected and another person's sympathy to one's needs can be ascertained and made use of, there might be other reasons why anxiety disorders are rational to have.

The rationality of anxiety disorders. In this regard Rodebaugh and Heimberg (2008, p. 144) point out the following:

"all anxiety disorders, on either an individual or evolutionary basis, involve stimuli that, in different contexts, could have posed a real possibility of death (e. g., the stimuli that provoke anxiety in post-traumatic stress disorder are directly associated with an event that either caused or threatened to cause physical harm to oneself or others; APA, 2000)."

Hence, at least the stimulus which caused the disorder seems to be the right kind of stimulus and not something which is completely unrelated to the disorder. Moreover, given that anxiety disorders also lead to the faster detection of dangerous stimuli in the future (for proof of this see one of the previous sections) and the appropriate behavior going together with it, one could quite clearly ascertain the rationality of anxiety disorders and that would be even so if the detection latency of dangerous stimuli lies on a continuum.

Anxiety and depression. Rodebaugh and Heimberg (2008, pp. 142-143) pose a very plausible connection between anxiety and depression:

"This observation that anxiety often leads to depression may initially appear counterintuitive....However, this sequence is explainable if failure to prevent a negative outcome is perceived as blocking one's ability to achieve positive outcomes at a satisfactory rate. For example, consider a person who struggles with social anxiety and consistently perceives social failures that lead to humiliation and embarrassment. An obvious strategy for preventing perceived social failures in the future is to no longer try to interact with people but instead actively avoid being around people. In turn, this strategy interferes with the person's ability to develop intimate relationships with others. Given that intimate relationships are a source of important rewards for many people, difficulty developing or maintaining these relationships would lead the person perceive a lack of rewards. Indeed, when much of a person's activity is devoted to preventing harm, it is difficult to exert sustained efforts toward obtaining rewards. Thus, upon the adoption of a self-regulatory framework, it appears inevitable that high comorbidity between anxiety and depression should occur."

That anxiety leads to depression might make it appear not very rational to develop an anxiety disorder. However, as we saw in the chapter on the rational functions of emotions, depression or at least sadness may serve a rational function, so that it might not be so bad actually that anxiety leads to depression. For if the function of a depression is to slow one's cognitive and motor functioning, so that one can focus on the problem at hand more clearly, the cause of the anxiety can be more thoroughly analyzed, so that a solution to the problem at hand seems more likely to come into view. Moreover, the individual's depression, particularly his or her sadness, might also elicit helping responses by others—even if it meant sending you to a psychologist or psychiatrist for help—which might make it even more likely to find a solution to the problem.

Yet, the results of van Honk and Schutter (2006, p. 290) seem to go against the latter hypothesis, for they claim the following:

"It seems that a continuum of prototypical psychopathology can be constructed on the basis of the relative imbalanced involvement of approach- and withdrawal-related emotion. Anxious depressed subjects can be characterised by extreme forms of social withdrawal, whereas the psychopath shows uninhibited approach tending towards a violent, antisocial level."

Yet, even social withdrawal might signify to some close friends and/or relatives that something is wrong and that one therefore needs to help the respective individual.

That there is a continuum between anxious depressed subjects on the one hand and sociopaths on the other hand on the emotional behavior level, however, might open up the possibility of vagueness to appear on a yet unforeseen dimension. Moreover, also the comparison between anxious depressed persons and sociopaths seems rather astounding and unique. However, although there might be a continuum on the emotional behavior level, there might not necessarily a continuum with regard to the valence level given, for while anxious depressed individuals quite clearly feel miserable, it is not so obvious how sociopaths feel.

Cortisol, testosterone, the brain, and anxiety disorders. We saw in the chapter on the brain that the amygdala seems to be crucial with regard to the fear system. Yet, besides a certain brain structure, one also needs particular neurotransmitters for the processing of the respective emotions and stimuli within the brain and transferring the respective outputs to the rest of the body. With regard to fear, van Honk and Schutter (2006, p. 294) point out the following in this regard:

"cortisol is a crucial neuroendocrine mediator of the emotion fear....High levels of cortisol have been observed in anxious depressed patients (Schulkin, 2003) and also in nonclinical anxious (Brown et al., 1996) and depressed subjects (Van Honk et al., 2003a)."

The latter facts are very interesting because they suggest that on the basis of cortisol alone one wouldn't be able to distinguish depressed from anxious subjects, so that the line to be drawn between depression and anxiety would be a blurry one. However, given that not all individuals with anxiety disorder will become depressed there must be something more than cortisol that is responsible for the distinction between anxiety and depression.

Perhaps the following facts provided by van Honk and Schutter (2006, p. 299) give us the necessary supplementary information:

194

"Several reports link fearfulness and high levels of cortisol to right-sided dominance in frontal asymmetry (Buss et al., 2003; Kalin, Larson, Shelton, & Davidson, 1998; Tops et al., 2004) but there is no evidence for such interrelationships between testosterone, aggression, and left-sided dominant frontal asymmetry."

Yet, unfortunately the respective information with regard to depression is missing, so that we can't draw a reliable conclusion with regard to the distinction between anxiety and depression on the basis of these facts.

Van Honk and Schutter (2006, p. 295) point out a certain connection between testosterone and fear: "Opposed to the amplifying effects of cortisol on fear, testosterone has not only rewarding properties, but also leads to reductions in fear (Boissy & Bouissiou, 1994)." Moreover, van Honk and Schutter (2006, p. 295) emphasize the fear-reducing and antidepressant properties of testosterone. Thus there is not only a substance which is co-present in anxiety and depression, namely cortisol, but also there is a substance which leads to the reduction of anxiety and depression, namely testosterone. Hence, one might be tempted to draw the conclusion that anxiety and depression are one and the same phenomenon which seems rather counterintuitive and implausible. For sadness, which is one of the ways depression might express itself, doesn't seem to be a proper part of anxiety. Perhaps we are confronted here with Prinz's somatic similarity problem (see the chapter on the rational functions of the emotions in this book), where different emotions show the same bodily pattern to account for this coincidence, although I am not so sure whether Prinz considers levels of testosterone and cortisol as bodily patterns.

II. Generalized anxiety disorder

In order to evaluate the rationality and vagueness of generalized anxiety disorder properly one first has to get an idea of what it actually is, how it is caused, and how it can be changed. As a starting point we will take a look at the *Diagnostic and Statistical Manual of Mental Disorders* by the American Psychiatric Association (APA). For a critical evaluation of the manual and the APA see the chapter on moods in this book.

Diagnostic criteria for generalized anxiety disorder according to the* Diagnostic and Statistical Manual of Mental Disorders, *fourth edition, text revision by the American Psychiatric Association (2000).

A. Excessive anxiety and worry occur most days for at least six months including a number of different events or activities ranging over work or school performance.

B. The individual has difficulties controlling the worry.

C. The excessive anxiety and worry are associated with at least three of the following six symptoms (with at least some symptoms present for most days for the past six months). It should be noted that in children only one item is required:

(1) restlessness, feeling keyed up, or feeling on edge,

(2) easy fatigue,

(3) difficulties concentrating or mind going blank,

(4) irritability,

(5) muscle tension, and

(6) sleeping problems of any kind.

D. The focus of the anxiety and worry is not confined to the following features: the anxiety or worry is not about having a panic attack as one finds it in panic disorder, being embarrassed in public as it happens in social phobia, being contaminated as it is given in obsessive-compulsive disorder, being away from home or close relatives as it is present in separation anxiety disorder, gaining weight which is given in anorexia nervosa, having multiple physical complaints as one finds it in somatization disorder, or having a serious illness as it happens in hypochondriasis, and the anxiety and worry don't refer to posttraumatic stress disorder in any way.

E. The anxiety, worry, or physical symptoms cause significant distress or impairment in social, occupational, or other areas of important functioning.

F. The disturbance is not caused by the direct physiological effects of a substance, that is, it is not caused by drug abuse or by medication, or a general medical condition, such as hyperthyroidism, and does not refer to a mood disorder, a psychotic disorder, or a pervasive developmental disorder.

With regard to these characteristics, vagueness enters with regard to the question how much is most of the days of the past six months as we find it in criteria A and C. Because it seems relatively arbitrary where to set the boundary between when most of the days of the past six months are given or not and that a small difference of one day shouldn't make a difference as to when most of the days of the past six months are given, a sorites paradox can be construed, so that vagueness is present in this characterization of generalized anxiety disorder. It is unclear what excessive anxiety and worry in criteria A and C amount to. Also where significant distress begins or ends in criterion E might be relatively arbitrary. With regard to criterion E, it is also unclear where to set the boundary between important and not important areas of functioning. Moreover, how can one really distinguish between social, occupational, and other important areas of functioning? Lots of occupations are also important areas of functioning and are even social, so that there might be an overlap between these categories. With regard to criteria C, D, and also F it becomes clear that some of the symptoms of generalized anxiety disorder overlap with other diseases which might make it problematic to come up with a proper diagnosis. For instance, with regard to C, there might be some people who have a certain sleep disorder, are hyperactive, so that they have problems concentrating, and who because of skeletal deformations have high muscle tension, which already would make them prone to being classified as having generalized anxiety disorder. Hence the possibility of misdiagnosis is quite clearly given.

Characterization of generalized anxiety disorder. Rodebaugh and Heimberg (2008, pp. 140-141) state with regard to generalized anxiety disorder (GAD):

"The primary characteristic of GAD is excessive, uncontrollable worry (American Psychiatric Association [APA], 2000). A recent conceptualization of GAD…suggests that worry serves the function of helping people with GAD temporarily avoid aversive emotional experience generated by poor emotion regulation strategies (Mennin, Turk, Heimberg, & Carmin, 2004). Research…has demonstrated that individuals with GAD report greater intensity of emotional experience and greater fear of depression than nonanxious participants or participants with social anxiety disorder; compared with nonanxious participants, individuals with GAD also report less clarity regarding emotions, more difficulty identifying emotions, and more difficulty describing emotions, as well as more fear of anxiety, anger, and positive emotions (Turk, Heimberg, Luterek, Mennin, & Fresco, 2005). Individuals with GAD have also reported more difficulty repairing negative moods in their daily lives and in response to a negative mood induced in the laboratory (Mennin, Heimberg, Turk, & Fresco, 2005). Such findings are supportive of the general conclusion that people with GAD are motivated to avoid aversive experiences, and, more particularly, aversive emotions. They may turn to worry in an attempt to avoid these experiences. Indeed, participants who, by self-report, meet criteria for GAD are best discriminated from other groups by their endorsement of worry as a strategy for avoiding thinking about more emotional topics (Borkovec & Roemer, 1995)."

What is interesting with regard to all these results is that there is an overlap of alexithymia with generalized anxiety disorder, because individuals with GAD have difficulties identifying and describing emotions which is also characteristic of persons suffering from alexithymia. Hence also here the possibility of misdiagnosis exists.

Generalized anxiety disorder and quality of life. One would expect that someone who suffers from generalized anxiety disorder is not able to enjoy life very much. Moreover, this dissatisfaction with life of individuals with GAD might have an impact on their social relationships. Especially a person who worries about almost everything might also worry about his or her partner, his or her friends, etc. In this regard, Rodebaugh and Heimberg (2008, p. 144) report studies which demonstrate that individuals with GAD show lower marital satisfaction and are more likely to report having no close friends. In my opinion, the reason why people with GAD more likely report that they have no close friends might be due to the fact that they even worry about their friends, in the sense that they worry whether their friends can be trusted at all, and therefore break up with their friends. Yet, if it were the case that a person with GAD indeed had good friends, one might wonder how such friends were able to cope with all the worry of the GAD inflicted person. Hence, also the possibility exists that perhaps his or her friends desert the person who suffers from GAD.

Generalized anxiety disorder and the brain. All this anxiety and worry of the GAD has to leave some trace somewhere in the brain. While I already discussed the connection between anxiety disorders, cortisol, testosterone, and depression, Rodebaugh and Heimberg (2008, p. 144) add the following to the previous results:

"in GAD, anxious apprehension about a number of topics…and symptoms of excessive central nervous system activation are required for diagnosis (APA, 2000)."

While excessive central nervous system activation is not very specific with regard to which brain areas are involved with regard to GAD, it corresponds to the excessive worry. Further studies have to be awaited to get more specific results with regard to which brain parts are activated in a person with GAD in order to be able to draw proper comparisons to other affective disorders, though.

With regard to the question whether it is **rational** to suffer from generalized anxiety disorder, this is very difficult to answer, for one would have to know more about the individuals diagnosed with GAD. Perhaps there is a corresponding basis for the excessive worry, in the form that these individuals indeed have very good reason to believe that they cannot trust their friends any longer. Also their life circumstances could be so difficult and problematic that it seems rational to worry about them very much. They might have had also very difficult living conditions in their past which might even resurface, so that excessive worry is understandable. Furthermore, avoiding aversive emotions by focusing on worrying might be rational if one cannot do anything about these aversive emotions and/or if one cannot change the conditions under which these aversive emotions arise.

The reason why certain people might stay depressed has to do with the fact that they can't focus on anything else (see the introduction to this book and the chapter on the rational functions of the emotions). In cases of GAD people have found a coping strategy to divert them from unwelcome emotions. So in a certain sense one might want to conclude that people with GAD turn out to be more rational than people with depression. Yet perhaps an optimal diversion would consist in not only employing one coping strategy, but actually several different ones to avoid another psychopathology. One might want to object also depressives have a coping strategy to counter their loss, because their sadness might alert others to help them. However, also dwelling on the loss might be of value, because one can analyze what went wrong and how one can handle similar situations in the future. Hence, it seems unclear whether people with GAD are more rational than people with depression.

III. Phobias

To claim that phobias are rational seems preposterous on first sight. After all, phobias might determine one's life to such an extent that one might not be able to live and/or work properly any longer. Thus to advance the rationality of phobias needs some elaborate justification and evidence. This is especially so, if some of the most common phobias might not be learned but are already present in our genes. Yet, Clore and Ortony (2000, p. 56, n. 4) report that the universal fear of snakes among primates is not learned, but the readiness to learn such a fear. That phobias, such as fear of heights, crowds, darkness, snakes, and spiders are learned is also highlighted by Ortony, Norman, and Revelle (2005, p. 192), who additionally claim that these phobias are relatively easy to acquire, but are very difficult to extinguish. In this regard, LeDoux (2000, p. 143) points out two different explanations for the difficulty one has in extinguishing these fears:

"it has been proposed that some clinical fears (especially phobias) involve a special kind of learning, so-called prepared learning, that involves stimuli that were dangerous to our ancestors (Öhman, 1992; Seligman, 1971). Although there appears to be support for this view, it is also possible that the kind of learning that takes place is the same for laboratory and clinical fears, and what differs is the kind of brain that does the learning. We found that following lesions of the ventromedial prefrontal cortex, the extinction of conditioned fear is greatly prolonged (Morgan & LeDoux, 1995; Morgan et al., 1993; but see Gewirtz et al., 1997a). Extinguishable fear is thus converted into extinction-resistant fear by altering the integrity of the medial prefrontal cortex."

Yet, even if one grants that what holds for the brain-damaged cases also holds for the undamaged brains and that therefore how we learn is determined by what part of the brain does the learning, the question comes up are the so acquired phobias then rational? While our brain might be determined by our genes to a large extent, one cannot exclude the possibility that the environment has an influence on our brain and that there might be interactions between nature and nurture with regard to our brain which might contribute to extinction-resistant fears. After all alcohol consume (nurture) can lead to quite some brain damage (nature), just to mention this as an example. Yet, even if our brain were completely determined by our genes, one could advance the rationality of phobias given that they lead to our overall survival. Moreover, the most frequently diagnosed phobias, such as phobias of insects, snakes, and heights, are directed at situations that reflect an evolutionary preparation to be sensitive to dangers that ancestral human populations encountered (cf. D'Arms and Jacobson 2003, p. 141), so that they helped in our overall survival. Furthermore, as I already advanced in Ledwig (2006, chapter one) it is rational to be rather too afraid than not being afraid enough, given that the thing one is afraid of has the power to harm one fatally.

One might want to advance that nowadays it seems irrational to be afraid of snakes, spiders, etc., because one rarely encounters these things in one's real life. Yet, actually where I am currently living, namely in Las Vegas, there are tarantula migrations, black widows can be found in the desert, scorpions can be found in one's apartment, and rattle snakes and other dangerous snakes are present in our surrounding deserts.

Scabies and other mites and ticks belong like the spiders and the scorpions to the group of the Arachnida according to the Tree of Life Web Project (1995) and these (scabies, mites, ticks, and many different spiders) are present in lots of different climates. While the mites and ticks form a group of their own apart from the spiders and scorpions and while mites and ticks are not as instantly deadly as some of the spiders and scorpions are, their relationship to the spiders and scorpions besides the diseases which they can carry might be very good reasons why we don't like them. So even if deadly spiders and scorpions are not as ubiquitous as mites and ticks, it would be rational for us not only to be afraid of all of them including the mites and ticks, but as some of the spiders and scorpions are deadly, it would be rational to develop phobias with regard to at least the spiders and the scorpions. With regard to the mites and ticks it isn't necessary to develop a phobia, as they don't lead to instant death. With regard to fleas and lice which belong to the insects one also doesn't need to develop a phobia as they are like the mites and ticks not deadly. With regard to snakes, it seems rational to develop a phobia, for although some snakes are neither poisonous nor do they strangle you, as most humans are not snake experts and are therefore not able to identify the dangerous snakes with any kind of certainty, it seems rational to withdraw in any case and not to take an unnecessary risk.

Besides the results on medial prefrontal cortex and phobias, there have been other studies on the brain and phobias. Reiman, Lane, Ahern, Schwartz, and Davidson (2000, p. 398) report the following findings with regard to cerebral blood flow (CBF) and snake phobia:

"snake-phobic anxiety was associated with significant CBF increases in the vicinity of occipital visual association areas, a region that includes anterior cingulate and medial prefrontal cortex, anterior insular cortex, motor cortex, supplementary motor area, thalamus, caudate, midbrain, cerebellar vermis, and lateral cerebellum (Reiman, 1996)."

That motor areas of the brain are involved with regard to snake phobia are of relevance with regard to the effectiveness of a phobia. For in order for a phobia to be effective one might want to think that people who have a phobia should also be more ready to respond to a phobia specific stimulus in order to enhance their survival. This not only includes a faster detection of the stimulus, but also an adequate response towards the stimulus. With regard to the detection of the stimulus, Öhman, Flykt, and Lundqvist (2000, p. 307) have discovered that individuals specifically fearful of snakes or spiders are very fast to discover the respective fearful stimulus. Moreover, one would think that the earlier in the processing of a phobic stimulus a phobic response occurred the better it is for the survival of the person who has such a phobia. In agreement with this reasoning, Öhman, Flykt, and Lundqvist (2000, p. 313) maintain on the basis of a study that preattentive processing of a phobic stimulus is sufficient to elicit at least part of the phobic response. This only agrees with my reasoning, though, if one takes preattentive processing to be faster than conscious processing which I, however, do. Therefore, persons with a phobia show the necessary behavior for insuring their survival. Hence, to have a phobia seems to be rational.

So far we have only looked at the brain and whether parts of it are of relevance for acquiring a phobia, yet, the rest of the body is also involved with regard to an adequate response to a phobic stimulus. Bradley and Lang (2000, p. 268) point out that also the heart shows a different behavior in phobic individuals:

"Only at the highest activation level, just before action, does the vagus release the heart, giving way subsequently to a sympathetically driven acceleration that is the classical defense response. Thus, for phobic subjects, cardiac acceleration, rather than deceleration, occurs when processing pictures of their feared material because these subjects are further along in the 'defense cascade' than normal subjects processing standard unpleasant pictures."

The defense cascade encompasses three phases (1) the pre-encounter, (2) the post-encounter, and (3) the circa-strike (Bradley and Lang, 2000, p. 269). During the pre-encounter phase cardiac deceleration begins, the heart starts accelerating again when the circa-strike phase begins (Bradley and Lang 2000, p. 269).

The results of Bradley and Lang (2000) show that not only the perception of a phobic stimulus might be faster in individuals with a phobia, but also that their physiological arousal is faster than the arousal in non-phobic individuals. Yet, whether this is evolutionary advantageous is an open question. On the one hand one might think, the earlier the defense response happens the better it is for the individual. On the other hand one might want to reason that the classical defense response should appear just before action and not when the individual is still processing the pictures of the phobic stimulus assuming this to be the case here for the sake of the argument, although also an earlier processing of the pictures might be possible in the case of an individual with a phobia. Here it would be of interest to see whether the responses shown by phobic individuals are more adequate not only in the speed of the perception and the speed of the response, but also in the right reaction—an action which is considered to be appropriate with regard to the phobic stimulus.

In general, one might wonder whether persons with a phobia actually show other kinds of disorders or diseases as well, in the sense that phobias might go together with psychosomatic disorders, which might not be considered as so evolutionary advantageous for the particular person to have. In this regard, Rieffe, Terwogt, and Jellesma (2008, p. 184) report the following results:

"Many studies performed in adults have shown a relationship between somatic complaints and impaired emotional functioning. Emotional problems such as increased levels of stress, excessive experience of negative emotions, and symptoms of depression or feelings of fear often co-occur with an increase in somatic complaints. There is strong evidence that these factors are also important in children (Campo et al., 2004; De Waal, Arnold, Eekhof, & Van Hemert, 2004)....It is currently widely recognized that severe and chronic stress has a negative effect on people's biological functioning and in the long-term may cause (irreversible) organic damage (Bhatia & Tandon, 2005; Segerstrom & Miller, 2004)."

Because these studies don't give any specific results with regard to phobias and somatic complaints and because the authors just state that feelings of fear often go together with an increase in somatic complaints (leaving the possibility open for exceptions), on first sight this doesn't sound very promising. However, one would have to await further studies which unambiguously show evidence for or against the hypothesis that phobias go together with somatic complaints. As somatic complaints might either impact just the individual person and not necessarily his or her offspring or the individual person and his or her offspring (for one cannot care as much for one's offspring if one is sick), it could be possible that even in the long run phobias would turn out to be harmful for the species. Yet, perhaps one could argue that this harmfulness would still be outmatched by the fact that in particular instances the phobia has saved the particular individual's life and therefore has also protected his or her offspring in some way. In the case the person has not had a chance to have offspring yet, it might protect the potential offspring a person might have in the future, and in the case the person already has had offspring it protects the offspring in such a way that the parent is still there and can provide for the offspring. Hence in the overall balance phobias turn out to be rational.

With regard to vagueness and phobias, if one thinks of someone who has a phobia of heights, it seems rather vague where a dangerous height actually starts for such a person. Similarly for a person with a spider phobia or a snake phobia, does a very tiny spider or a very small snake already elicit that phobia or has it to be a relatively big one and where actually is the starting point for the phobia to manifest itself? Here one might want to think even if there is vagueness involved and even if it is relatively unclear when a phobia is set off as long as the human and his or her offspring survive the phobia seems to be justified and rational.

IV. Social phobias

So far we have only considered phobias which mainly relate to animals which might turn out to be deadly for us. Yet, sometimes we are ourselves our worst and deadliest enemy as the history of wars can quite clearly illustrate. Hence, one can also expect that there are phobias which are related to humans. The latter are called social phobias (SP for short). In order to evaluate social phobias for vagueness and rationality one first has to be clear about which kind of features are characteristic of them. While the *Diagnostic and Statistical Manual of Mental Disorders* published by the American Psychiatric Association may not be flawless, because after all it is humans who produced that manual—humans who might even have a political agenda on their mind by defending their take on psychology—, it is nevertheless a good starting point to get an idea of what social phobias actually consist in.

Diagnostic criteria for social phobias according to the Diagnostic and Statistical Manual of Mental Disorders, *fourth edition, published by the American Psychiatric Association (1994).*

A. A significant and persistent fear of one or more social or performance situations in which the individual is exposed either to unfamiliar people or to possible scrutiny by others. The person is afraid that he or she will act in such a way (or show anxiety symptoms) that he or she will be humiliated or embarrassed. It should be noted that children have to show evidence of the capacity for age-appropriate social relationships with familiar people and the anxiety has to occur in peer settings.

B. Exposure to the feared social situation almost always causes anxiety, which may take the form of a panic attack. It should be noted that in children the experienced anxiety may be expressed by means of freezing, tantrums, crying, or avoiding social situations with unfamiliar people.

C. The individual is aware of the fact that the fear is excessive or unreasonable. It should be noted that this feature may be absent in children.

D. The social or performance situations which are feared are either avoided or they are endured under intense anxiety or distress.

E. The avoidance, anxious anticipation, or distress in the feared social or performance situation or situations has a significant effect on the person's normal routine, occupational or academic functioning, or social activities or relationships, or the individual experiences significant distress about having the phobia.

F. In case the individual is under eighteen, the duration has to last at least six months.

G. The fear or avoidance is not caused by the direct physiological effects of a substance, such as medication or a drug which is abused, or a general medical condition, and is not better explained by another mental disorder, such as separation anxiety disorder, body dysmorphic disorder, schizoid personality disorder, panic disorder with or without agoraphobia, or a pervasive developmental disorder.

H. In case the individual has a general medical condition or another mental disorder, the fear in the first criterion isn't related to it. That is to say, the fear isn't fear of stuttering, trembling in the case of Parkinson's disease, or exhibiting abnormal eating behavior as is the case in anorexia nervosa or bulimia nervosa.

Finally, in the case that the fear includes most social situations one should also consider the possibility of the additional diagnosis of avoidant personality disorder.

With regard to this characterization it is obvious that vagueness enters with regard to the question what a significant and persistent fear is, where it seems unclear where exactly significance and persistency start and where they end. While persistency according to the DSM-IV amounts to six months in case one is younger than eighteen years, the justification for this duration is not obvious. One might want to argue that there is no difference between six months minus one day and six months. Similarly, one might want to argue there is no difference between eighteen years and eighteen years minus one day. Also where a significance level starts might be set quite arbitrarily. In all three cases boundarylessness is given, and as one is able to construe a sorites paradox with regard to significance and persistency and the age criterion, vagueness enters this characterization of social phobias.

With regard to criterion A, one might want to argue that vagueness might also be given with regard to the question what unfamiliar people are, what age-appropriate social relationships are, and what kinds of characteristics social and performance situations and peer settings have to show. For one might be able to construe a continuum between familiarity and unfamiliarity, between age-appropriate social relationships and not-age-appropriate social relationships, social situations and not-social situations, performance situations and not-performance situations, and peer settings and not-peer settings. With regard to criterion B, the expression "almost always" turns out to be vague, too, because as it stands it is very difficult to quantify it properly. With regard to criterion C, awareness comes in degrees, so that vagueness enters the scene. With regard to criterion D, intensity might vary in degrees, too, so also here vagueness is given. With regard to criterion E, here it is vague what a significant effect and what significant distress amount to. Finally, with regard to the addition at the end, it is not obvious what "most social situations" amount to, so that is vague, too.

What is of particular interest with regard to the rationality of social phobias, the person who has such a phobia recognizes that the phobia is excessive or unreasonable, while in children this feature may be absent according to the DSM-IV which might indicate the influence the person's environment has on the person classifying his or her phobia as irrational. However, it might also indicate that the person has matured so much that due to personal insight he or she is able to acknowledge that his or her phobia is irrational, whereas in the case of the child such a maturity is not given yet or at least is not expected yet.

Social phobia and the function of avoidance of eye contact. While one might want to think that avoidance behavior, which is referred to in characteristics B, D, E, and G, is actually not adaptive, because the person instead of dealing with the issue directly and immediately leaves it untouched, one could also advance the view that it might serve some evolutionary beneficial purpose. Similarly, van Honk and Schutter (2006, pp. 287-288) argue that "In social phobia and melancholic depression, sensitivity for the punishing consequences of (threatening) social encounters should result in socially avoidant behaviour." Yet, here it is already assumed that a certain sensitivity for the punishing consequences of social encounters is already given in the individuals who have a social phobia. In this regard, one might want to know where does this particular sensitivity have its origin?—In a harmful encounter in the past or in a certain genetic predisposition or even in both? Previously we observed that all anxiety disorders involve stimuli which have the possibility to cause death. Such an encounter might make an individual sensitive to dangerous stimuli; moreover, if the individual in general seems to be a very sensitive person, whether this is due to an acquisition of this sensitivity or due to a genetic predisposition, this might make the acquisition of an anxiety disorder appear much more likely. If one, however, is sensitive to dangerous stimuli, because of a very negative encounter with this stimulus or because of a genetic predisposition, one might want to argue that the best way to handle such kind of stimuli is to avoid them, because, if encountered, these stimuli might upset the individual too much to be of any further value.

With regard to one particular avoidance behavior, namely the avoidance of eye contact, Hermans and van Honk (2006, pp. 312-313) maintain the following:

"Whereas persistent thoughts of social rejection and negative self-evaluation may play an important role in SP, everyday life of SP patients is characterised by avoidance of social scrutiny rather than excess attention towards it (cf. Clark, 1999), which is manifested in evading eye contact....submission gesturing, such as gaze aversion, and provocation using angry or contemptuous facial expressions, may subserve peaceful organisation of primate social systems (Öhman, 1986; Sapolsky, 1990). Within this evolutionary framework, facial expressions are viewed as vehicles of communication, each of which has evolved to communicate a specific message (Fridlund, 1994)."

Moreover, Hermans and van Honk (2006, p. 313) point out that self-reported social anxiety does predict attentional avoidance of angry faces and that this avoidance effect also covers SP patients. If avoidance behavior is mostly shown in order not to upset the social hierarchy, one might want to assume that in the absence of any hierarchy or in the absence of an evaluation of the quality of a performance, avoidance behavior is absent unless social phobias are so much ingrained in our system that it is difficult to abstain from showing avoidance behavior. Here new empirical studies have to tell us how much social phobias are part of us already.

If one takes the stance that avoidance behavior actually serves the function to maintain social hierarchies, one might want to conclude that it is actually rational to do so. However, maintaining a social hierarchy might not always be the best thing to do, because the hierarchy might not reflect the qualities of the respective individuals in the hierarchy any longer, so that avoidance behavior might not always be the best thing to do. If, however, the individual who shows avoidance behavior is not a high performer anyway or the individual is very vulnerable, avoidance behavior might be rational even if the social hierarchy needs some kind of reform quality-wise.

Social phobia and the brain. As we have already seen in the chapter on the brain, the amygdala is particularly responsive when fear is experienced. Hermans and van Honk (2006, pp. 314-315) agree with that and point out that there is an emerging consensus among researchers that the amygdala serves as a protection device that is at least involved in emotional aspects of social behavior. Moreover, Hermans and van Honk report that neuroimaging studies of social phobias can for the most part support the notion of hyperexcitability of the amygdala in social phobic patients. That is to say, social phobic patients show above average amygdalar responses to neutral faces, higher responses to angry and contemptuous faces, and higher responses to symptom provocation.

With regard to these findings, one might want to maintain that exaggerated amygdalar responses to neutral faces might not be very rational to have. However, one can likewise ask who is to set the standard with regard to what normal and therefore right is? Yet, one might wonder why should a neutral face elicit an exaggerated response? If one looks at the DSM-characteristics one might answer this question by hypothesizing that a neutral face will most likely be an unfamiliar person, so that our social phobic patient doesn't know what to expect of this unknown individual. This uncertainty which quite clearly seems justified and therefore rational might then leave an exaggerated mark with regard to the amygdalar response. With regard to the higher amygdala responses in the case of angry and contemptuous faces and symptom provocation, it might be of interest to know where the social phobic patients stood in the social hierarchy in order to evaluate their amygdalar responses for their rationality properly. However, one might want to object that the social phobic patients were unrelated to the persons with angry and contemptuous faces. Nevertheless it might be possible that the social phobic patients implicitly assume or expect that only people who have a higher position in the social hierarchy show such kind of faces.

In the chapter on the brain, it became also obvious that not only the amygdala, but also the prefrontal cortex (PFC) is involved when emotions are elicited. In this regard, Hermans and van Honk (2006, p. 317) explain the connection between social phobias, prefrontal cortex, and the amygdala as follows: one doesn't only find hyperactivity in the amygdala in patients with social phobia, but also hyperactivity in several frontal sites. On the basis of these findings, Hermans and van Honk paint the following course of events when social phobic patients encounter a social cue: first the amygdala will most likely hyperreact to the event which will bring about peripheral autonomic nervous systems reactions, so that the peripheral feedback will converge with a slower, more cognitively guided assessment of the same event in the orbitofrontal and dorsolateral parts of the PFC and produce a distorted reassessment in this area. This results in less negative feedback to the amygdala, leading to a sustained activation in this area, according to Hermans and van Honk.

Social phobia and genes. Hermans and van Honk (2006, p. 318) state with regard to the connection between cortisol, corticotropin-releasing hormone (CRH) gene expression, and the amygdala that

"there is evidence that cortisol increases CRH gene expression in the central nucleus of the amygdala (Rosen & Schulkin, 1998), which results in hyperactivation of this area, presumably to maintain a state of heightened vigilance while at the same time restricting demanding overactivation of the axis....in (melancholic) depressive disorders, which have a high comorbidity rate with SP and other anxiety disorders, basal levels of cortisol are by-and-large above average."

Hermans and van Honk (2006, p. 324) add to the previous findings that one has found a significant genetic contribution to SP, with heritability estimates being as high as 0.5.

Given the partial heritability of social phobias one might wonder whether social phobias can still be considered rational. Yet, also here one might want to think that the principle applies that it is rational to be too afraid than not being afraid enough given that our immediate survival or even the survival of one's family and therefore of one's genes are at stake. Thus it would be evolutionary beneficial to have a high significant genetic contribution to SP. Moreover, given the violence of our species—one just has to think of the wars humans have fought and our ability to construct weapons of mass destruction or the fact that in the U.S.A. currently every 100th person is in jail—, it seems rational to assume that our immediate survival could be at stake. Therefore it at least doesn't sound irrational to have a social phobia. Yet, there is an argument which might make the rationality of a social phobia and even any other kind of common specific phobia, such as spider phobia, snake phobia, etc. almost sound like an impossibility, and I will get to that immediately in the next section.

The Rationality of social phobias. Hermans and van Honk (2006, p. 308) present the following compelling argument against the rationality of phobias:

"Intuitively, it would seem likely that the prevalence of car phobia, for instance, should be much higher than spider phobia, as it is reasonable to suppose that fewer people have suffered traumatic experiences with spiders than in traffic. Similar puzzling but striking observations have been reported in relation to SP: The mean age of onset of this disorder differs substantially from other anxiety disorders, and roughly corresponds to pubertal age, a developmental period when social hierarchies start to emerge (Öhman, 1986). Furthermore, SP also contrasts with other anxiety disorders, such as specific phobias, panic disorder, and generalised anxiety disorder, in the absence of a strong preference for the female sex (although epidemiological data indicate that SP occurs slightly more often in women Merikangas et al., 2002), which can be taken to suggest a connection to the stronger hierarchical organisation of male social order."

Given the traumatic experiences many of us have had with cars, we should rather have a car phobia than a social phobia or a spider phobia, so why is there not something like a car phobia? If one compares a spider phobia with a car phobia, one can observe the following: spiders and also many snakes are so small that it seems on first sight irrational to develop a phobia with regard to them, whereas cars are already bigger than we are and therefore sheer size should remind us of the fact that it is dangerous to sit in a car. Hence a car phobia doesn't have to develop. Moreover, cars as such are not dangerous at all. They need humans to operate them, so why should we develop a phobia for cars? It should be rather the case that we develop a phobia for the people who drive the cars, but that would be already given in the case of a social phobia.

Yet, there are also phobias with regard to heights, which is like the car an object and therefore not alive. Moreover, heights and cars share one further property in common, namely size, and we have previously argued, because of the sheer size one doesn't have to develop a phobia with regard to cars. Hence the same should hold for heights, unless size also doesn't really matter for the development of a phobia.

Now, if there is a phobia of heights, why is there not a phobia for cars? Here again, cars in themselves are not dangerous, whereas heights in themselves might quite clearly be (just imagine yourself standing on the Nanga Parbat, the most dangerous of the 8000 meter mountains of the Himalaya, looking down). Hence, it is understandable that we have not developed a car phobia yet. Moreover, the same holds also for spiders and snakes that they themselves can turn out to be lethal, whereas this doesn't hold for cars themselves.

Cars bring us also many advantages—of course there are also disadvantages, such as the air-pollution, the waste, and the costs—, but we can travel from one place to the next faster with a car, we can transport more than on foot, bicycle, or train, and can therefore accomplish so much more. One cannot say the same with regard to spiders and snakes that they bring us so many advantages unless one keeps them as a pet or uses them as part of a show to make money out of them or uses them naturally for killing insects respectively mice. Heights might have some advantages going together with them, such as a better overview of the area and a better position for defense. Yet, in general also heights don't bring to each single person such an advantage as cars do. Hence why should one develop a phobia for a car? That doesn't seem to make sense at all.

Social phobia and vagueness. So far vagueness and social phobias have only be connected by means of the DSM-characteristics of social phobias as we have seen in a previous section of this chapter. Yet there might be another area where social phobias and vagueness go together. For Hermans and van Honk (2006, p. 308) state with regard to social phobias that they "can plausibly be conceived of as the far end of a spectrum of normal fears (Rapee & Spence, 2004), which have adaptive value when within normal range (cf. Rosen & Schulkin, 1998)." Hermans and van Honk (2006, p. 323) come up with the following evidence in order to support the view that social phobias are not as unnatural or irrational as is commonly assumed to be:

"most people have experienced some mild form of the symptoms of SP, and diagnosed SP and severe shyness have proven to be hardly separable in several aspects (Turner, Beidel, & Townsley, 1990). An explanation in terms of a functional defect would therefore be contradictory to a spectrum approach that emphasises the utility of social anxiety and treats SP as the far end of a broader dimension (Rapee & Spence, 2004)."

That severe shyness, a character trait, and social phobia overlap might be obvious if one considers avoidance behavior. If someone can only be diagnosed with a social phobia after a duration of six months has passed showing the respective symptoms, one might also think that a social phobia will turn out to be a character trait and not an emotion any longer. Yet, if there is an overlap with another phenomenon, the boundaries between these two phenomena could turn out to be unclear, that is vague, given that these two phenomena consist of one dimension or several dimensions of which at least one is held in common and given that boundaries exist at all.

One might want to know how it is possible that one can ascribe utility to social anxiety. Besides the fact that social anxiety solidifies and/or maintains given social hierarchies, there doesn't seem to be anything which social anxiety is good for. Moreover, one might even wonder what social hierarchies are good for. Yet, while social hierarchies might not always be the best ones depending on the values social hierarchies embody, human beings cannot live in isolation. We are fundamentally social beings depending on others for our upbringing, education, nourishment, care in case of sickness and old age, and work. Yet our dependability on others might not necessarily lead to social hierarchies, for we might just want to pay the one or ones who give the very best service for the lowest price in a free market competition and this might change over time quite drastically.

In order to promote the individual good, however, it seems rational to always turn towards the very best for help. Moreover, if the best is not available, one would have to go to the second best in order to obtain the next best outcome, and if the best and the second best are not available one would have to go to the third best, etc. Hence, in order to promote the individual good social hierarchies seem inevitable. Yet, social hierarchies might not always reflect the performance level of the persons in the hierarchy, for power and connections play a role with regard to social hierarchies as well. While we cannot do away with factors such as power and connections, social hierarchies cannot completely leave performance factors out of count, for otherwise our survival or the survival of our offspring might be at stake.

Conclusion

In the case of generalized anxiety disorder, humans have found a coping strategy for dealing with aversive emotions, namely to worry. It is not so obvious whether this coping strategy turns out to be more rational than the coping strategy of depressives. The DSM-IV characterization of generalized anxiety disorder leaves the possibility open for vagueness to appear with regard to several criteria. However, as long as the individual and his or her offspring survives, it doesn't harm to be a little bit too afraid than not being afraid enough, so this wouldn't speak against the rationality of generalized anxiety disorder. With regard to social phobias, there is a significant overlap to severe shyness which might make the concept of social phobias superfluous. Social phobias seem much more rational to have than car phobias. The DSM-IV characterization of social phobias leaves the possibility open for vagueness to appear with regard to several criteria. Nevertheless, one might want to argue that social phobias are justified because they maintain social hierarchies and that social phobias turn out to be rational given the danger human beings can present to their fellow human beings.

Chapter 8 Vagueness and Rationality in Moods

I. Introduction

Moods. I already dealt with the different theories of moods, such as the feeling theories of moods, the dispositional theories of moods, and the computational theory of moods, in Ledwig (2006, chapter six). Moreover, I also started to consider the rationality of moods in that publication. I will therefore not repeat what I already said but deal with material which I have not worked on before. In order to do that one might want to turn to the existentialists for a change. Yet, Solomon (1979, p. 4) states that "Heidegger, despite his famed mention of *mood* in *Being and Time*—hardly any analysis, given how little is dissected there—leaves the emotions in general and the structure of moods unresolved." Also in Sartre one doesn't find more on moods and the emotions as I already presented in the chapter on the rational functions of the emotions.

In order to understand what moods really are, it makes sense to distinguish moods from other phenomena. In this regard, Damasio (1999, p. 286) distinguishes moods from background feelings:

"Prominent background feelings include: fatigue; energy; excitement; instability; balance; imbalance; harmony; discord. The relation between background feelings and drives and motivations is intimate: drives express themselves directly in background emotions and we eventually become aware of their existence by means of background feelings. The relation between background feelings and moods is also close. Moods are made up of modulated and sustained background feelings as well as modulated and sustained feelings of primary emotions—sadness, in the case of depression."

If one considers Damasio's distinctions one might wonder, though, whether so many different categories, such as background feelings, background emotions, moods, primary emotions, etc. are actually necessary. Moreover, it doesn't seem so obvious why moods are constituted both by background feelings and feelings of primary emotions. However, one might want to argue that the particular atmosphere you are in actually creates background feelings, so that a mood is a blend of the situation you are in (background feelings) and the person you are (feelings of primary emotions).

Mixed feelings, mixed moods, and vagueness. If emotions have as a necessary component subjective feeling states, one can reason as follows: as there are mixed feelings but not mixed moods and as feeling states are constitutive of the emotions, there is a categorical boundary between moods and the emotions and therefore there is no vagueness with regard to the distinction between moods and the emotions given. Yet, one could even advocate the view that there is such a thing as a mixed mood, for what else is a bipolar disorder, if not a change from mania to depression and vice versa? Moreover, there are even some people who claim that mania and depression can happen at the same time, where mania and depression summate and cancel each other out (Swartz and Shorter 2007, p. 83). Hence there wouldn't be only mixed moods in the sense of a fluctuation of one mood to the other, but also a simultaneous existence of two moods at the same time possible. Consequently, one couldn't conclude on the basis of mixed moods that there is a categorical boundary between moods and the emotions. Hence, so far still the possibility of vagueness exists with regard to the distinction between moods and the emotions.

Moods, feelings, cognition, and processing. I already argued in Ledwig (2006, chapter six) that moods in opposition to emotions don't have an object. In a similar vein Clore and Ortony (2000, p. 54) maintain that in order to account for cases in which affective feelings precede cognitive appraisals, one should characterize moods as feeling states without salient objects and emotions as feeling states with objects; given that moods lack salient objects one may experience moods as information about other suitable objects, though. This information can then contribute to appraisals that cause genuine emotions, Clore and Ortony claim.

The hypothesis that moods can contribute to appraisals that cause genuine emotions, although an interesting one, could be problematic for the following reasons: first of all, one would like to know when moods in fact contribute to appraisals and not only when they can. The can clause leaves room for too many exceptions as it stands. That is to say, one would like to know under which kind of conditions moods in fact contribute to appraisals and under which not. Second, it seems rarely to be the case that moods cause emotions, for if this were really given all the time, one would like to know how it comes that moods are actually so long lasting. If moods were to cause emotions all the time, then moods shouldn't be long lasting, but short. However, Clore and Ortony never stated that moods cause emotions all the time, so they are off the hook in this regard.

Clore and Ortony (2000, pp. 45-46) convincingly explain the effects moods have on judgments:

"Judgments of just about anything are more positive in good moods than in bad moods. According to the affect-as-information hypothesis (Schwarz & Clore, 1983), the information on which judgments and decisions are made routinely includes information provided by affective feelings. Bechara et al. (1994) have published dramatic data that suggest that choices...may be mediated by feedback-produced feelings before the formation of relevant beliefs can play a role. And other results show that feelings from an irrelevant source can influence judgments even when varied independently of beliefs about the object of judgment (Clore et al., 1994). However, this phenomenon is dependent on not experiencing...the affective feelings as relating to the other (irrelevant) source. When the default linkage or attribution to the target stimulus is eliminated, the effect of mood on judgment also disappears. This kind of pervasive influence of affective feelings on judgement is most easily observed when the source of affect is a mood because a distinguishing feature of moods is that any situational causes are not generally salient. Unlike emotions, which are generally focused on a causal object..., moods are relatively undifferentiated feeling states with less salient cognitive content (Clore, 1994b, Ortony & Clore, 1989). As a result, mood-based feelings are easily misattributed to whatever stimulus is being processed at the time. Hence, general moods...are much more likely than are specific emotions to result in contamination of judgments and decisions. Our explanation for this phenomenon is the same as our explanation for the influence of unconsciously primed affective meaning. The feelings associated with moods can have runaway affective meaning because they are unconstrained by any episodic harness."

218

If good and bad moods lead to certain distortions of judgments, one might want to argue that to have such moods, doesn't seem very rational. For a distortion of judgments is something undesirable and doesn't help us in our overall survival. Yet, if Carroll (2003, p. 530, cf. also Ledwig 2006, chapter six) is right that moods very likely give the organism information about the individual's level of energy and tension, then a positive distortion of one's judgment if one is in a good mood and a negative distortion of one's judgment if one is in a bad mood might correspond to the individual's level of energy and tension and therefore wouldn't pose extra obstacles for our overall survival. Hence, to have moods that distort our judgments in this sense seems rational after all.

Similarly to Clore and Ortony, Rolls (2005, p. 126) claims that "The current mood state can affect the *cognitive evaluation of events or memories....*This may facilitate continuity in the interpretation of the reinforcing value of events in the environment." In my opinion Rolls is right in his evaluation, for as mood states are rather long lasting their influence on judgments should be continuous. Moreover, as stability might make life easier, because there are fewer adjustments to be made, our overall survival would be improved which contributes to the overall rationality of moods. However, if our environment were of such a kind that it changed continuously, to have stable moods might be a problem, because they wouldn't adjust well to our different living conditions. As this is not in fact the case, we don't have to worry about the rationality of moods yet.

Besides the fact that moods as a general category can be termed rational, is there also some evidence for the fact that positive moods as a category and negative moods as a category serve a rational function? In this regard, Clore and Ortony (2000, p. 51) maintain that one finds a steadfast association between positive moods and inclusive, integrative, category-level processing on the one hand and between negative moods and piecemeal, analytic, and item-level processing on the other hand. The latter corresponds to what we discovered with regard to the function of sadness in the chapter on the rational functions of emotions and therefore can be considered as additional evidence for it.

APA, DSM, and depression. The book *Psychotic Depression* by Swartz and Shorter (2007) gives an interesting insight into the politics of the American Psychiatric Association (APA) and how their *Diagnostic and*

Statistical Manual of Mental Disorders (*DSM*) with its different versions up to the *DSM*-IV got developed. Especially the shortcomings of the different versions of the manual are highlighted and even inconsistencies with the *International Classification of Diseases*, Tenth Edition (*ICD*-10), are pointed out. Here we will just concentrate on what Swartz and Shorter (2007) have to say with regard to depression and the *DSM*. Swartz and Shorter (2007, p. 10) claim that the basic problem with the *DSM* is that it doesn't recognize endogenous depression as a disorder and therefore also not the distinction between endogenous and reactive depression. Another problem with the manual is that it doesn't make any assumptions about causation, so that it is more agnostic than diagnostic, Swartz and Shorter maintain.

In a similar vein Swartz and Shorter (2007, p. 61) point out that the *DSM* not only dismisses causation, but also background factors. Moreover, if there is a probable but unknown medical cause, the diagnosis doesn't change, but remains for instance psychotic depression, so Swartz and Shorter. Furthermore, causation by drugs or anything else are not considered as a tool for a proper diagnosis, if the drug exposure occurred more than three months before the symptoms, even if the symptoms started at the same time as the drug exposure and continued without interruption during the drug exposure, according to Swartz and Shorter.

While the question whether there is endogenous depression or not is a question for scientific dispute and not necessarily a question for a manual which just tries to help in finding the best diagnosis in a given case (although manuals should reflect the current state of the art of science), that causation should figure in an adequate diagnosis makes perfect sense. For if the cause is not there, the effect, that is the disease, will also be not there at least in cases of deterministic causation. So knowledge of the cause or knowledge of which causes lead to which effects is central for a correct diagnosis. Moreover, knowing the cause or causes might in many cases be a precondition for a successful treatment of the disease. Also in cases of probabilistic causation knowing the cause or causes might still be beneficial to the psychologist or psychiatrist treating the patient. For even if they can't influence all the causes, some of them may be removed which might have an effect on the effect, especially if there is an interaction between different causes.

Endogenous depression, reactive depression, and psychotic depression. Swartz and Shorter (2007, p. 4), who are in favor of the distinction between endogenous depression and reactive depression, because endogenous depression roughly corresponds to their favorite category psychotic depression, report the following with regard to the history of endogenous and reactive depression and support the distinction by their own observations: in 1920 the German psychiatrist Kurt Schneider proposed the term endogenous depression for depressed patients who were terribly slowed. The term "endogenous" stems from the German nosologist Emil Kraepelin, which meant biological, indwelling in the brain, and dominating the body, according to Swartz and Shorter. Schneider contrasted endogenous depression with reactive depression which is usually seen outside of hospital settings, Swartz and Shorter maintain. Reactive depression has maybe sadness in common with psychotic depression, but otherwise not much; moreover, reactive patients are not psychotic and don't experience their thought and action being slowed, Swartz and Shorter claim.

Swartz and Shorter (2007, p. 7) support the distinction between endogenous and reactive depression further by the following evidence: psychotic depression consists of a variety of endogenous depressions which may end up in hospital. Reactive depressions differ from endogenous depressions by starting slowly under conditions of stress and are filled with anxiety, anger, or dissatisfaction, Swartz and Shorter maintain. Furthermore, the symptoms of reactive depressions tend to be vague, take on no specific form, and are primarily subjective, according to Swartz and Shorter. Here it would have been helpful to know what Swartz and Shorter meant by vague for a proper evaluation of the vagueness and rationality of reactive depressions. Because this was not further specified, we have to leave it like this as an open question for future clarification.

Swartz and Shorter (2007, p. 11) elaborate further on the distinction between endogenous and reactive depression and convincingly compare endogenous and reactive depression to tuberculosis and pneumonia to advocate that endogenous depression and reactive depression are two different diseases: while endogenous and reactive depression may have sadness in common or a diminished self-confidence and distress and both may be triggered by stress, endogenous depression must also have a biological trigger, such as jet lag, high cortisol, insomnia, starvation, and stimulant drug abuse. Moreover, patients with endogenous depression in contrast to patients with reactive depression think that they have sinned a lot and therefore don't deserve any better, Swartz and Shorter point out. We have therefore two diseases which is similar to the case of tuberculosis and pneumonia which are two diseases, although they have fever and coughing up phlegm in common, Swartz and Shorter conclude.

Swartz and Shorter (2007, p. 39) provide the following evidence for the connection between endogenous depression and psychosis and therefore justify the classification psychotic depression:

"when Leslie Kiloh at the University of new South Wales and a co-worker did a cluster analysis in 1977 of the data on the sixty-one patients whom Lewis had treated at the Maudsley in the early 1930s, they discovered at least two clearly defined subtypes of depression: endogenous and neurotic. In the endogenous groups, 'ideas of influence' received the second heaviest weighting, meaning that the endogenous patients were largely psychotic (Kiloh and Garside, 1977)."

Catecholamine hypothesis of affective disorders. Swartz and Shorter (2007, p. 5) report the following with regard to the influential catecholamine hypothesis of affective disorders, namely that in 1965 Schildkraut claimed that depression and mania are a result of disturbances in the metabolism of the neurotransmitter norepinephrine which belongs to the "catecholamine" class of neurotransmitters. Moreover, Swartz and Shorter (2007, p. 215) cite studies which show that major depression seems to involve a deficiency of dopamine and other catecholamines.

Vagueness. Vagueness might not only pose a problem for the rationality of the emotions, but also be an obstacle to good research. In this regard, Swartz and Shorter (2007, p. 119) point out that there have been many publications which considered the question of whether psychotic depression differs from nonpsychotic major depression in a significant way. It is Swartz and Shorter's opinion that the *DSM* classification "major depression" poses problems for answering the question, because its components are indistinct and the boundaries between them turn out to be vague. To evaluate Swartz and Shorter's claim properly we have to have a look at the diagnostic criteria for major depressive disorder according to the *Diagnostic and Statistical Manual of Mental Disorders*, fourth edition, published by the American Psychiatric Association (1994). The manual states with regard to major depressive disorder that for a person to be diagnosed with this disorder he or she must have had at least one major depressive episode, but no hypomanic, manic, or mixed episodes. So far this seems pretty clear, yet we should go into further detail by evaluating the criteria for major depressive episode point by point.

The criteria for a major depressive episode according to the *Diagnostic and Statistical Manual of Mental Disorders*, fourth edition, published by the American Psychiatric Association (1994) are as follows:

A. At least five of the following symptoms have been present during the same two-week period and these symptoms differ from previous functioning; at least one of the symptoms is either (a) a depressed mood or (b) a loss of interest or pleasure. It should be noted that symptoms which quite clearly result from a general medical condition or are due to mood-incongruent delusions or hallucinations should be excluded.

(1) Depressed mood most of the day, almost every day, based on either subjective report (e. g., the individual feels sad or empty) or on observations made by others (e. g., the person appears tearful). It should be noted that in children and adolescents it can be an irritable mood instead.

(2) Significant reduced interest or pleasure in all, or almost all, activities most of the day, almost every day (based on either a subjective account or on observations made by others).

(3) Significant weight loss, given the person is not dieting, or significant weight gain (e. g., a change of more than five percent of body weight in a month), or decrease or increase in appetite almost every day. It should be noted that in children one should consider failure to make expected weight gains as a characteristic.

(4) Insomnia or hypersomnia almost every day.

(5) Psychomotor agitation or retardation almost every day, which are observable by others, not merely subjective feelings of restlessness or of being slowed down.

(6) Loss of energy or fatigue almost every day.

(7) Feelings of worthlessness or excessive or inappropriate guilt are present (which may be delusional) almost every day that excludes cases of self-reproach or feeling guilty about being sick.

(8) Reduced ability to think or concentrate, or indecisiveness, almost every day based on either a subjective account or as observed by others.

(9) Recurrent thoughts of death, which excludes cases of fear of dying, recurrent suicidal thoughts without a specific plan, a suicide attempt, or a specific plan to commit suicide.

B. The symptoms differ from the criteria for a mixed episode.

C. The symptoms lead to clinically marked distress or impairment in social, occupational, or other areas of important functioning.

D. The symptoms are not caused by the direct physiological effects of a substance in the form of drug abuse or medication and are not due to a general medical condition such as hypothyroidism.

E. The symptoms are not better accounted for by the loss of a loved one, the symptoms persist for longer than two months or are characterized by significant functional impairment, suicidal thoughts, morbid preoccupation with worthlessness, psychotic symptoms, or psychomotor retardation.

Going back just for a brief time to Swartz and Shorter's complaint that the *DSM* doesn't take alternative causes into account, criterion A quite clearly mentions medical conditions, as does criterion D. Moreover, criterion E also mentions the loss of a loved one as an alternative cause. Furthermore, criterion B states that the symptoms of the patient should differ from the criteria for a mixed episode. So there are alternative causes mentioned. Perhaps these are not all possible causes; however, Swartz and Shorter's complaint doesn't hold in its generality.

If one considers the criteria for a major depressive episode with respect to vagueness, starting with A(1) one would have to specify further what a depressed mood is. Moreover, expressions, such as "most of the day" and "almost every day", which can be found in A(1)—A(8) leave the possibility for vagueness open. In A(2) expressions, such as "significant reduced interest", are open to vagueness, too, for one can construe a continuum from insignificant reduced interest to significant reduced interest. While in A(3) a boundary for a significant weight loss or gain is set, there is no justification given why it should be set in that way; hence, also here vagueness might be given. With regard to A(4), one might wonder where does insomnia and hypersomnia start and end? One hour less respectively more sleep? With regard to A(5), psychomotor activation or retardation is not very specific. Moreover, one could construe a continuum from significant psychomotor activation or retardation to insignificant psychomotor activation or retardation. With regard to A(6), one would like to know when a significant loss of energy is given opening up the possibility for vagueness to occur. With regard to A(7), it is unclear what an excessive or an inappropriate amount of guilt amount to, for this appears not specific enough, and as one might want to question whether a certain amount of guilt is excessive/appropriate or not, vagueness enters the picture even here. With regard to A(8), a reduced ability to think or concentrate is also problematic, for when is a reduced ability given? Here the justification of a particular boundary might be only possible in pragmatic terms, so that vagueness enters the picture. With regard to A(9), one might want to know how many times thinking about death amount to recurrent thoughts of death. Hence, there is an abundance of vagueness given in criteria A(1)—A(9).

With regard to criteria C and E, it might not be clear what is meant by clinically marked or significant distress and by significant functional impairment. Also here there is a continuum between marked and not marked distress and between significant and not-significant impairment possible. Furthermore, clinicians might differ about what important areas of functioning in contrast to not-important areas of functioning amount to in criterion C. Moreover, how can one really distinguish between social, occupational, and other important areas of functioning? Lots of occupations are also important areas of functioning and are even social, so that there might be an overlap between these categories. Additionally, what distress or impairment amount to, might be difficult to distinguish, because impairment usually is accompanied by distress. With regard to durations in A and in E, that it has to be exactly two weeks and at least two months appears arbitrary. One might want to argue that what holds with regard to two weeks should also hold with regard to two weeks minus one hour. For an hour is just such a small difference that it shouldn't make a difference with regard to the diagnosis. Also with regard to two months, what holds with regard to two months should also hold with regard two months minus one day, for a day is just such a small difference that it shouldn't change anything drastically. Hence, Swartz and Shorter were right with regard to the criteria for major depressive disorder being indistinct and vague. Yet, one has to admit that it might be not so easy to come up with better criteria especially if the phenomena themselves are vague.

With respect to vagueness, Swartz and Shorter (2007, p. 3, n. 1) furthermore report that according to Goldberg and Huxley (1980) there might be a continuum with regard to depressive illness. Similarly, Swartz and Shorter (2007, p. 46) state:

"According to Myrna Weissman...the disease designers were influenced by Gerry's and Gene Paykel's notion, published in 1970, that in depression there was a smooth continuum from mild outpatient depression to the severe inpatient variety, with no demarcation points along the way."

Yet, if there are two different kinds of depression with markedly different symptoms and/or causes, one would have to establish independently whether these also differ only in degree between mild outpatient depression and severe inpatient depression. With regard to what we know so far of endogenous and reactive depression, this continuum doesn't exist going from endogenous severe inpatient depression to endogenous mild outpatient depression and going from reactive severe inpatient depression to reactive mild outpatient depression. It rather seems to be that severity goes together with endogenous depression and mildness goes together with reactive depression.

With regard to the debate whether there is such a thing as psychotic depression, Spitzer (1974, p. 5) comes up with the following reason why it might be problematic to have such a classification: "It was...agreed that 'psychosis' and 'neurosis' are useful possibly as adjectives, but not as classificatory principles. The term psychosis has become vague in usage". Yet, if the term "psychosis" has indeed become vague, then in which sense could the term "psychosis" be used as an adjective? One might want to argue that if the term is vague, the term remains vague, whether it is used as an adjective or as a noun. And if one wants at least to be consistent, which many consider a minimal condition of rationality, then one shouldn't use the term at all given that one wants to avoid vagueness. In the section on psychotic depression we will consider in a more detailed fashion whether the term "psychosis" is vague or not.

Besides the evidence for psychotic depression which we have seen before, there is further evidence for the disease. Moreover, this evidence is

226

also connected to vagueness. Swartz and Shorter (2007, p. 156) report the following results with imipramine as a treatment for depression:

"Imipramine reached the United States in January 1957, as two psychiatrists in Saginaw, Michigan, received a supply....They administered the drug to in- and outpatients with a wide variety of diagnoses. Of those with 'psychotic depression,' 42 percent were 'markedly well,' slightly smaller percentages of patients with involutional and neurotic depression. So the news from Saginaw was promising: 'Patients frequently reported that delusional thoughts and hallucinations become more vague...' (Ruskin and Goldner, 1959)."

While the evidence here doesn't speak in favor of a distinction between psychotic and involutional and neurotic depression, for the positive treatment results didn't differ markedly across the different categories, it was interesting to see that psychotic depression, which is characterized by delusional thoughts and hallucinations as we will see in the section on psychotic depression, quite clearly seems to be characterized by vagueness. For the effect of imipramine was to make these features more vague.

II. Psychotic Depression

Classification. Swartz and Shorter (2007, p. 80ff.) give their own classification of seven different forms of psychotic depression, which cannot be found in the *DSM*-IV manual. According to the authors (Swartz and Shorter 2007, p. xi) psychotic depression is an amalgam of psychosis and depression which cannot be separated into psychosis and depression. Swartz and Shorter claim that in psychosis thought and behavior have become unrelated to reality, that is to say, psychosis is a sign of madness which is just as biological as delirium; depression on the other hand is an illness one of whose characteristics is the disability to think things through. Hence Swartz and Shorter conclude psychotic depression is an illness which shows disordered thought, behavior, and mood; consequently, patients with psychotic depression are delusional and suffer from a mood disorder. The seven different forms of psychotic depression by Swartz and Shorter (2007) are: (1) melancholic psychotic depression, (2) psychosis-dominant depression, (3) catatonic psychotic depression, (4) psychotic-equivalent depression, (5) tardive psychotic depression, (6) drug-induced psychotic depression, and (7) coarse brain disease psychotic depression. I will characterize what these different forms amount to in the following.

Swartz and Shorter (2007, p. 80) come up with the following characterization of melancholic psychotic depression: patients with melancholic psychotic depression show behavior which appears sickly and slowed as in melancholics; they suffer from delusions, such as poverty, nihilism, dying, worthlessness, guilt, or body illness that portray misery and are presented in an emotionally flat way without any signs of drama. Sickness delusions are about organ dysfunction, being rotten or full of waste, poisoning, cancer, or infestation, according to Swartz and Shorter. Patients with melancholic psychotic depression show signs of passivity and apathy, Swartz and Shorter point out. The marked psychomotor slowing may be responsible for the patients not mentioning their psychosis, Swartz and Shorter claim. Finally, Swartz and Shorter maintain that some patients with bipolar disorder experience depression that looks like melancholic psychotic depression. That some patients with bipolar disorder have similar episodes of depression might suggest that the boundary between bipolar disorder and this form of psychotic depression is vague. It might, however, also suggest that some forms of bipolar disorder are a combination of mania with melancholic psychotic depression.

Swartz and Shorter (2007, p. 53) present the following characterization of psychosis-dominant depression: patients with psychosis-dominant depression show clear signs of psychosis without the obvious signs of sickliness, slowing, sadness, or apathy, although the patients don't enjoy living. The delusions are about paranoia, contamination, religion, or self-importance, Swartz and Shorter report. According to the authors one can distinguish between two subtypes of psychosis-dominant depression, namely bipolar mixed state and deteriorative, which should be treated differently. Swartz and Shorter admit that some patients could be classified as having a mixed manic-depressive episode with psychotic features, so that there is an overlap to other existing categories.

If one considers Swartz and Shorter's first characterization of psychotic depression as an alloy, which cannot be separated into psychosis and depression, one might wonder how the distinction between melancholic psychotic depression and psychosis-dominant depression can ever be justified, for both illnesses don't appear to be alloys at least on first sight. Yet, even in the case of psychosis-dominant depression one still finds the feature of not being able to enjoy life and in the case of melancholic psychotic depression one still has delusions. One might also wonder whether Swartz and Shorter's further subclassification of psychosis-dominant depression doesn't lead to an unnecessary explosion of different illnesses. However, if one considers different cancer forms, one also finds a multitude of different forms. Moreover, it seems reasonable to assume that if different treatment methods lead to success in the case of bipolar mixed state and deteriorative psychosis-dominant depression, that a subclassification of psychosis-dominant depression seems necessary.

Swartz and Shorter (2007, pp. 91-92) characterize catatonic psychotic depression in the following way: while catatonic depression is a manifestation of episodic catatonia, there is also catatonic schizophrenia which is unremitting. Swartz and Shorter explain that catatonia is a motor disorder that accompanies a major psychiatric illness, where the movements may either be abnormally slowed or they may be pathologically quickened. Catatonia is further characterized by disturbances of emotion and thought expression, by appearing puzzled or bewildered, not saying much, not moving much, and staring a lot, Swartz and Shorter point out. Moreover, according to Swartz and Shorter catatonic patients show signs of echolalia, echopraxia, and involuntary limb movement in response to light pressure if one checks for them.

If one looks at this characterization closer, one wonders where the psychotic depression is in catatonic psychotic depression. For appearing puzzled or bewildered or having disturbances of emotion and thought expression one wouldn't necessarily consider as psychotic. Moreover, wouldn't it appear plausible to be puzzled or bewildered, if one were to experience something like catatonia? I even would say that it is no wonder to be emotionally disturbed or to be disturbed in one's thinking if one had catatonia. That is to say, thoughts like what is going on with me, why I am so strange, etc. one would consider as reasonable to have while one is in a catatonic state. Moreover, it seems reasonable to assume that such kinds of thoughts disrupt one's ordinary expression of one's thoughts under that condition. So even if one would consider these features as characteristics of psychosis, it seems rational to have them.

Swartz and Shorter (2007, pp. 100-101) claim that psychotic-equivalent depression is depression with reversible dementia and was formerly called pseudodementia. Moreover, patients with psychotic-equivalent depression show incoherent speech or other deficits in reasoning, in emotional expression, or in motivation, so that problem solving and appreciation of complexities in human relationships are problematic for such patients, Swartz and Shorter maintain.

With regard to psychotic-equivalent depression, one might want to know how deficits in emotional expression amount to depression. That is, this characterization of psychotic-equivalent depression doesn't make clear where the depression fits into the classification. However that may be, one would nevertheless think that it seems plausible to assume that significant deficits in reasoning and problem solving might lead to a depression. For given that one's memory functions normally, one knows of oneself that one was able to accomplish similar tasks before one got sick which might not only lead to a depression but also to changes in motivation. Yet, while some people get de-motivated by deficits, others consider such a deficit as a challenge that needs to be overcome. So it seems reasonable to assume that not all patients show a deficit in motivation.

If one realizes, however, that it is not a question of effort, but an ability that has changed, one might realize that however much more energy one puts into it, it won't change the end result, so that in the end one asks oneself why should I make such an effort, if it doesn't change anything, leading to a deficit in motivation. Yet, other patients might reason to themselves, this is just a temporary thing, so my ability in general won't be affected, so my motivation doesn't have to be affected either. This might then explain why a deficit in motivation can be given but doesn't have to be given in the case of psychotic-equivalent depression.

Swartz and Shorter (2007, pp. 101-102) maintain that tardive psychosis is an amalgam of psychosis and depression that eventually occurs after having taken a dopamine-blocking drug, such as an antipsychotic tranquilizer:

"New-onset hallucinations and delusions were observed in men of ages 65 and 74 years after taking metoclopramide for just 3 and 6 months, respectively. This was to treat gastrointestinal distress, and neither patient had a psychiatric history (Lu et al., 2002). Similarly, in young adults who were taking antipsychotic drugs for nonpsychotic mania, mood-incongruent psychotic phenomena began occurring after 3 years (Downs et al., 1993)....As with tardive dyskinesia, tardive psychosis appears to be a long-term rebound phenomenon. In rebound, a drug that produces a particular therapeutic effect in the short term produces the opposite effect when taken long term."

What is problematic about this characterization of tardive psychosis is that Swartz and Shorter (2007, p. 61) themselves have criticized the *DSM* that in cases of medical causes of depression the diagnosis remains the same (see the section on APA, DSM, and depression), and here they basically do the same, although I think it is an improvement to have two extra categories (see this and the next category) for the medically induced forms of depression. The reason for the distinction between this category and the next seems to be that in the case of tardive psychotic depression one finds a rebound phenomenon, while in drug-induced and hormone-induced psychotic depression (the next category) no such rebound is given, although to be strict also the rebound phenomenon is actually an effect that is caused by a drug initially, so that one shouldn't need another category for a proper classification. Also with regard to the next category, Swartz and Shorter's own criticism of the *DSM* applies to their own case that in cases of medical causes of depression the diagnosis remains the same, that is they stay within the psychotic depression category. However, what other alternative do they actually have? They can't just say that the person is actually not sick at all, because the illness is just drug-induced, so that different categories for medically induced psychotic depressions seem reasonable to pose after all.

Swartz and Shorter (2007, pp. 104-105) state with regard to drug-induced and hormone-induced psychotic depression that corticosteroid administration, fast withdrawal of androgenic or estrogenic steroids, thyroid hormone deficiency, and amphetamines can lead to psychotic depression that continues to last for quite some time, although the drug or hormone has been discontinued in the meantime. Swartz and Shorter put postpartum psychosis into the very same category, for the simple reason that there is a large fall in female steroid hormones at the time of parturition, although these decreases include estrogen, pregnanolone, and allopregnanolone, none of which is known to be involved in psychotic depression. Swartz and Shorter point out that the same holds for postabortion psychosis. Swartz and Shorter report that in five percent of steroid-treated patients one finds severe psychiatric reactions, such as depression, mania, psychosis, and mixtures of these; in five percent of anabolic steroid abusers one finds mania-like symptoms, and in five percent one finds depression when they stop using these hormones. Swartz and Shorter highlight the fact that postpartum psychotic depression, which starts usually within one month after delivery, occurs once in a thousand births particularly in women with a personal or family history of serious depression or bipolar-I disorder.

When the authors state that postpartum psychosis involves a decrease in estrogen, pregnanolone, and allopregnanolone, although none of them is involved in psychotic depression, this sounds contradictory, especially if they consider postpartum psychosis as a hormone-induced psychotic depression. However, it could be the case that although estrogen and these other hormones are not directly involved in psychotic depression, they could be involved indirectly whose connection to psychotic depression we have not observed yet.

With regard to coarse brain disease psychotic depression, Swartz and Shorter (2007, pp. 106-108) explain that the term "coarse brain disease" refers to illnesses that include brain lesions which are observable by means of EEG, brain imagining, angiogram, or abnormal neurological signs on physical examination, such as spastic paralysis. As examples of coarse brain disease Swartz and Shorter mention epilepsy, cerebral lupus erythematosis, Alzheimer's disease, cerebrovascular disease, multiple sclerosis, neurosyphilis, Huntington's chorea, and Parkinson's disease. Swartz and Shorter report that patients with coarse brain disease are at risk of psychoses and depressions, because risks of psychosis and depression increase with greater severity of the neurological illness, especially if the patients have dementia and are at an advanced age. Swartz and Shorter cite studies which show that patients with Parkinson's disease that has progressed into dementia, thirty-six percent had delusions and/or hallucinations. Swartz and Shorter report with regard to all Parkinson's patients one finds five to twenty percent with psychosis, while in Parkinson's disease with dementia forty percent have psychosis with visual hallucinations being the predominant psychotic symptom. Swartz and

Shorter cite a study in which forty percent of Parkinson's patients with psychosis were depressed. Swartz and Shorter point out Alzheimer's disease is very similar to Parkinson's disease with respect to occurrences of psychosis and depression with the exception that delusions are more predominant than hallucinations in Alzheimer's disease. Finally, Swartz and Shorter report that a quarter of Alzheimer's patients has major depression, another quarter has minor depression, delusions were predominant in those with major depression, and Parkinson's disease was predominant in those with major depression.

With regard to Parkinson's disease and Alzheimer's disease, one might want to question whether it is such a good idea to classify people into one category as patients with coarse brain disease psychotic depression. For not all patients with Parkinson's and Alzheimer's show this kind of a disease. Because Parkinson patients and Alzheimer patients can be without psychosis and depression and because Parkinson patients differ from Alzheimer patients with coarse brain disease psychotic depression in the amount of hallucinations versus delusions they have, it seems to make more sense to just state which other kind of diseases are co-present in the Parkinson and Alzheimer patient. This is especially so, if one considers that someone with Parkinson's or with Alzheimer's has good reasons to be depressed, so that the depression might just be a side-effect of Parkinson's or Alzheimer's. Also the psychosis in its different forms in Parkinson's or Alzheimer's might just be another side-effect of the respective diseases, for damages to the brain should have some kind of adverse effect on the normal functioning of the brain. After all, in one's classificatory effort one doesn't want to invent superfluous categories which can be accounted for otherwise. Parsimony and Ockham's razor seem to be of relevance here unless one is able to come up with a good reason why another category is necessary in this case.

That the respective coarse brain diseases can cause depression and/or psychosis is something of which Swartz and Shorter are aware, for they (Swartz and Shorter 2007, p. 109) state that complex partial epilepsy can cause melancholia, psychosis, or psychotic depression, when the disease is untreated or undertreated. And there is no reason to think that what holds with regard to epilepsy might not also hold with regard to the other coarse brain diseases. Moreover, also in the case of epilepsy it seems reasonable to assume that if the symptoms of the disease are not completely reduced that one gets depressed about this state of affairs. Hence, it seems reasonable to conclude that it is actually not one disease (epilepsy) but rather two (epilepsy and depression).

In the following, Swartz and Shorter (2007, pp. 66-67) list the different kinds of delusions persons with psychotic depression can exhibit, the connection between emotions and delusions, and give evidence for the efficiency of electroconvulsive therapy (ECT) which Swartz and Shorter favor for psychotic depression as the proper treatment procedure:

"Delusional themes in psychotic depression are typically unpleasant (Parker et al., 1991a), meaning guilt, paranoia, sickness, worthlessness, or nihilism....In sickness delusions, the patient typically believes he is full of waste, poisoned, infested with parasites, or his body organs have quit working....Examples of less dramatic delusions are that the patient believes he is unwanted by family, deserves to be punished, or has committed a serious error that either was not committed or is not serious....Delusions can be rigid and systematized. Except in the catatonic type, the patient expresses emotions and concern about the delusions; there is no indifference. In the catatonic type, emotional expression can be diminished or absent....A patient's belief that he deserves to be punished can incite him into dangerous and even assaultive behavior. When the psychotic content consists solely of paranoid delusions, the response rate to ECT appears to be lower. In one small series, a mere 45 percent of twenty patients having only paranoid delusions in psychotic depression responded to ECT, but 100 percent of seven patients with nihilistic delusions responded (Solan et al., 1988)."

With regard to the diminished or missing emotions in the catatonic type, one might also want to consider the possibility that the person suffers from alexithymia. From the authors' description one cannot exclude such a possibility. If one considers the different success rates for patients with paranoid delusions and nihilistic delusions, one might think it to be justified to come up with two further subgroups of psychotic depression. Yet, the sample sizes were very small, so that one would have to await more confirming evidence for subdividing psychotic depression even further. However, Swartz and Shorter (2007, pp. 138-139) have also reported that three out of five statistical studies which compared different time periods have shown that there is a shift from sin to crime or at least away from sin in depressive delusional content. As the delusional content seems to depend on cultural changes and as it is possible that the persons involved in the previous study might have belonged to different subcultures, one might want to argue that further subdivisions don't seem to be justified on first sight and that further studies need to be conducted in order to obtain clearer results. However, one nevertheless might want to argue that the different success rates with the same treatment justify a categorical difference, for even if the delusional content might vary from culture to culture, it is not the relative arbitrariness of the acquisition of the delusions which counts but actually what can change the delusions to justify a categorical difference.

Swartz and Shorter (2007, p. 265) clarify further what kind of delusions patients with psychotic depression exhibit, namely that one finds nonbizarre delusions in psychotic depressions, where nonbizarre delusions might be for instance that the police is tracking me down, while bizarre delusions are unrelated to ordinary life, such as that green man will abduct me. Yet, how is one to determine with certainty whether such nonbizarre delusions are really given or not? After all, the patient also might speak the truth. Moreover, if one has such delusions and nobody believes the patient, but the patient him- or herself, it is understandable that the patient becomes depressed about that. Furthermore, one would consider it reasonable that delusions if they are not believed by others and if they are frightening, in the sense that one doesn't have any kind of control over what is happening to oneself, might lead to a feeling of helplessness in the patient à la Seligman (1992) and therefore cause a depression in the patient.

So far I have not seen any studies which state something about the development of psychotic depression on a time scale with the exception of cases where certain medication or hormonal changes lead to psychotic depression. Yet, in order to evaluate properly whether one has one disease or several diseases present, it would be helpful to have a time scale of the development of the disorder, such as in the case of syphilis. For if there are different stages of the disorder where one also knows which causes lead to the next stage, one could be sure to just deduce one disorder. However, if there is more than one distinctive temporal pattern to the disorder, it seems more likely to be confronted with more than one disorder.

Statistics of psychotic depression. Swartz and Shorter (2007, p. 6) report that half of hospitalized patients with endogenous depression are psychotic. Moreover, Swartz and Shorter (2007, p. 16) state that fifteen to thirty percent of endogenous depressions are accompanied by delusions. On first sight these two figures seem contradictory. However, in the first reference Swartz and Shorter speak of hospitalized patients, whereas in the second reference nothing is said about hospitalization. Moreover, while in the first reference Swartz and Shorter talk about psychotic depression, in the second reference they refer to endogenous depressions with a delusional component, leaving out endogenous depressions with hallucinations.

Other very valuable data and statistics with regard to psychotic depression are the following according to Swartz and Shorter (2007, pp. 72-73): Swartz and Shorter report that patients, which are admitted for depression to tertiary care hospitals, are fifteen to thirty percent psychotic. Swartz and Shorter cite studies which have observed that the prevalence of psychotic depression is higher in elderly patients with depression, namely thirty-five to forty-five percent. Moreover, Swartz and Shorter report that in the Epidemiologic Catchment Area study of past and present illness, it was discovered that fourteen percent of major depression episodes were psychotic. Furthermore, Swartz and Shorter cite a study which shows that less than one percent in the population suffers from psychotic depression. Swartz and Shorter report that one finds psychotic features more often in bipolar depression than in unipolar depression. Swartz and Shorter cite a study which observes that similar premorbid stressful life events and problems can be found in patients with psychotic depression and anxiety disorders. These findings suggest that the diseases are reactions to these events and problems. However, it is also possible that these events are a consequence of the diseases.

Swartz and Shorter (2007, p. 73) claim that one can find biological reasons for psychotic depression, such as genetic predisposition, bipolar disorder, childbirth, deteriorative brain disease, and jet lag. Swartz and Shorter cite a study which shows that one finds a six-fold prevalence of bipolar illness among relatives of delusionally depressed patients in comparison to relatives of other depressives and controls. This might suggest that either there is an overlap between bipolar disorder and delusional depressions or that bipolar disorder might provide the necessary background condition for delusional depressions to arise. According to Swartz and Shorter (2007, p. 73) other reasons for psychotic depression are exposure to substances that cause psychosis or depression or whose discontinuation can do so, such as hormones and drugs with hormonal effects (anabolic or androgenic steroids, high-potency corticosteroids, and thyroid hormones). Swartz and Shorter maintain that certain street drugs (amphetamines and phencyclidine) can cause psychotic depression and that antipsychotic tranquilizers can over the treatment course exacerbate or cause psychosis and depression.

Psychotic depression, cortisol, and the brain. While Swartz and Shorter already gave some evidence for tardive psychotic depression, for drug-induced and hormone-induced psychotic depression, and for coarse brain disease psychotic depression, here comes some further evidence that neurotransmitters, such as cortisol, and the brain are involved in cases of psychotic depression.

Swartz and Shorter (2007, pp. 49-50) report the following results of an experiment by Evans and Nemeroff where the level of cortisol was measured in patients with different kinds of depression: one hundred and sixty-six consecutive inpatients with depressive symptoms were looked at; one hundred and four of them suffered from major depression, and of these sixty-two had major depression without melancholia, twenty-three had major depression with melancholia, and nineteen had major depression with psychosis. Swartz and Shorter report that one mg of dexamethasone was administered orally at 11:00 PM and venous blood samples were taken the following day at 4:00 PM to determine serum cortisol. It was found with regard to patients with major depression that the following had high amounts of serum cortisol, Swartz and Shorter report: ninety-five percent of those with psychosis, seventy-eight percent of those with nonpsychotic melancholia, and forty-eight percent of those without melancholia. While these results are very interesting, although the sample sizes of twenty-three and nineteen are very small, it is not so obvious what these results really indicate. For high levels of cortisol are the cause of Cushing's syndrome. Yet, Cushing's syndrome has some features in common with major depressive disorder, namely weight gain and insomnia. Moreover, Cushing's syndrome can lead to heart disease and increased mortality, while psychotic depression and worse physical health are also correlated, as we will see later on.

Cortisol is a corticosteroid hormone which is produced by the adrenal gland. It is often called the stress hormone since it is involved in the organism's response to stress. Cortisol increases blood pressure and blood sugar mobilizing the body for action and reduces immune responses. If one looks at the different percentages from the study above, one can now understand why there are different cortisol levels in the blood in the different groups. For only forty-eight percent of the patients with the least strenuous disease, that is, major depression without melancholia, show high levels of cortisol. Then comes the group with moderate amounts of stress, namely patients with major depression with nonpsychotic melancholia, where seventy-eight percent of the patients have elevated levels of cortisol. Finally, comes the group with the highest amount of stress, namely patients with major depression and psychosis, where ninety-five percent have high levels of cortisol. Moreover, an increase in blood pressure and blood sugar is necessary if one looks at one of the symptoms of psychotic depression, namely psychomotor retardation.

Knowing what cortisol does makes it then obvious what it is good for, namely trying to reduce the amount of stress the body and mind is confronted with. Hence a higher level of cortisol is not an essential component of psychotic depression, but rather is a response of the body to the disease to become normal again by mobilizing the body with higher blood pressure and higher blood sugar to do something against the disease. There is also a connection of cortisol to catecholamines, namely that cortisol increases the effectiveness of catecholamines, which is an interesting connection if one thinks of the catecholamine hypothesis of affective disorders.

The inhibition of pain is also observed for cortisol, and as patients with endogenous depression consider pain and not sadness as the central component of the disease (Swartz and Shorter 2007, p. 131), even here one could say that higher levels of cortisol go together with higher levels of pain, explaining the high percentage of high cortisol in patients with major depression and psychosis. People might want to object that physiological pain is not the same as psychological pain. Yet, how can anyone be so sure of that? Psychological pain surely hurts as bad, if not worse. Just remember when people picked on you or your parents, sisters or brothers, or your boy- or girlfriend made a humiliating remark about your physique or mental abilities. One never forgets that, although one might forget instances of physical pain.

While Swartz and Shorter (2007, p. 29) report that Johann Fritsch claimed in 1882 that the frontal lobes are responsible for psychotic melancholia, Swartz and Shorter (2007, p. 74) provide the following update to this historical account: one finds psychotic depression more in people with worse physical health, more depression in the family, or atrophy in certain areas of the brain, such as the left frontotemporal region and the brainstem. Swartz and Shorter report a magnetic resonance imaging (MRI) study which shows that two-thirds of patients, whose psychotic depression had started after age forty-five and who had no clinical signs of neurological disease, had abnormalities, such as lesions in the subcortical (deep) white matter and cortical atrophy, while such abnormalities were only found in less than ten percent of a comparison group of nonpsychiatric elderly people. With regard to this data, it would have been helpful to know whether these patients with abnormalities in the brain had been already treated with psycho-pharmaceuticals or with electroconvulsive therapy in order to evaluate better whether these abnormalities in the brain were due to therapy or a result or a cause of psychotic depression. Without this further information a proper evaluation of the data seems impossible.

Psychotic depression, electroconvulsive therapy (ECT), and other treatments. There is convincing evidence that ECT is a very effective treatment protocol for psychotic depression. Starting with a study by Friedman, de Mowbray, and Hamilton (1961, p. 952), they give the following evidence for the effectiveness of ECT in the case of psychotic depression, although the sample size is very small:

"Of 8 patients whose illnesses were characterized by the presence of frank delusions of guilt or unworthiness and who were clearly the most severely ill in our series, none showed any significant response to Tofranil [imipramine], while 5 of them subsequently responded to E.C.T."

Swartz and Shorter (2007, p. 161) report the results of another study in favor of ECT, although the sample size is not given, where ninety-five percent of the patients with psychotic depression experienced a remission, in contrast to eighty-three percent of patients with nonpsychotic depression.

Besides these two studies in favor of ECT, Swartz and Shorter (2007, pp. 54-55) report the following experiment on the effectiveness of ECT in cases of psychotic depression in comparison with nondelusional patients: while only three of thirteen delusional patients had responded to imprimine hydrochloride at the end of a four-week active medication period, fourteen of twenty-one nondelusional patients had responded to the drug. Swartz and Shorter report that the psychotic nonresponders were given ECT and nine of them got better. Moreover, the plasma norepinephrine levels of the delusional depressives exceeded the levels of the nonpsychotic depressives by far, Swartz and Shorter report.

Norepinephrine is a catecholamine and therefore to find higher levels of norepinephrine in psychotic depressives speaks in favor of the catecholamine hypothesis of affective disorders. Moreover, although the sample sizes in the given study are not phenomenal, the study helps to further support the thesis that ECT is effective against psychotic depression. Furthermore, to see that ECT is mostly effective against psychotic depression, while nondelusional patients didn't respond to ECT so positively, justifies the distinction between psychotic and nonpsychotic depression.

If ECT still leads to some kind of improvement in nondelusional patients (see the second to last study), perhaps psychosis lies on a continuum and therefore the patients with slightly elevated psychosis-levels, but which are not yet classified as having a psychosis, might respond positively to ECT, too, so that the distinction between psychotic and nonpsychotic depression doesn't represent a categorical distinction. Here it is interesting to get some more detailed results with regard to the effectiveness of ECT in psychotic and nonpsychotic depression. In this regard, Swartz and Shorter (2007, p. 194) report two studies: while in the first ECT produced a larger response in psychotic depression (ninety-two percent) than in nonpsychotic depression (fifty-five percent), in the second study eighty-three percent of seventy-seven psychotic depression patients

240

achieved remission in comparison to seventy-one percent of one hundred and seventy-six nonpsychotic depression patients. These results quite clearly support the effectiveness of ECT in psychotic depression, but also speak in favor of a continuum between psychotic and nonpsychotic patients. Otherwise it is very hard to explain why ECT leads to quite some change in nonpsychotic depression, too.

Swartz and Shorter (2007, pp. 56-57) report the results of a study by Parker and co-workers with a sufficient high sample size of one hundred and thirty-seven consecutive patients on the effectiveness of various treatment protocols with regard to psychotic depression and nonpsychotic depression: this study revealed convincingly that psychotic melancholia differs from nonpsychotic melancholia, for the former responded badly to antidepressants, well to combo therapies of antidepressants and antipsychotics, and well to ECT.

While this study doesn't show that ECT is superior to a combo therapy of antidepressants and antipsychotics, it nevertheless proves that ECT is an effective treatment. What would have been interesting to see is whether antipsychotics alone would have an effect on psychotic depression. If psychotic depression were really an alloy of psychosis and depression, then antipsychotics alone shouldn't have an effect on psychotic depression. That antidepressants alone didn't lead to an improvement in the case of psychotic depression, while combo therapies of antidepressants and antipsychotics did work, would go well together with Swartz and Shorter's hypothesis that psychotic depression is an alloy of depression and psychosis. Yet, previously we have also seen that ECT has a positive effect on nonpsychotic depression which supports the view that although psychotic depression is an alloy of depression and psychosis, nonpsychotic depression differs only in degree from psychotic depression.

As some of the studies seen so far had relatively small sample sizes, it makes sense to take a look at meta-studies with regard to psychotic depression. In this regard, Swartz and Shorter (2007, p. 193) present the following support for the effectiveness of ECT and for the relative effectiveness of anti-psychotics in combination with tricyclic antidepressants (TCAs): a meta-analysis of forty-four treatment studies of psychotic depression has revealed that ECT seems to be superior to the anti-psychotic-TCA combination and is definitely superior to tricyclics alone. Moreover, Swartz and Shorter report another meta-study of seventeen studies were eighty-two percent of psychotic depression patients responded to ECT in contrast to seventy-seven percent with an antipsychotic-tricyclic combination.

Again what is particularly interesting is that in both of these meta-studies the effects of antipsychotics alone on psychotic depression are not investigated. Yet, Swartz and Shorter (2007, p. 214) also report a meta-study of seventeen studies which deals with this issue, where the response rate of psychotic depression to dopamine-blocking antipsychotic drugs was fifty-one percent and where the response rate in psychotic depression was nineteen percent with perphenazine alone. While these results are supporting the view that anti-psychotics alone are not effective in treating psychotic depression, a partial effectiveness is established. Moreover, in order to evaluate these results better it would have been helpful to have had two classes of patients: one consisting of patients with psychosis and one consisting of patients with psychotic depression to see whether there is a significant difference between the groups in effectiveness of anti-psychotics. After all, although anti-psychotics do work better for patients with psychosis, it is not obvious whether the difference to patients with psychotic depression is significant.

In order to evaluate properly the hypothesis that psychotic depression is an alloy of psychosis and depression one would like to know why ECT is actually effective in treating psychotic depression in most of the cases and is somewhat effective in treating nonpsychotic depression. For the fact that combinations of antipsychotics and antidepressants work in the case of psychotic depression doesn't necessarily support the hypothesis that psychotic depression is an alloy. From the effects of the combination of antipsychotics and antidepressants one could equally conclude that one is confronted with two different diseases which are co-present.

According to Swartz and Shorter (2007, p. 199) ECT works as follows: before the treatment begins, there exists a certain pretreatment pattern of neurotransmitters that mediates psychiatric illness. This neurotransmitter pattern of illness is the result of an interaction between the patient's genes and his environment. Because the ECT seizure depletes the neurotransmitters, the pretreatment patterns are disrupted, so that in the process of neurotransmitter replenishment, gene DNA is transcribed,

242

leading to the production of enzyme proteins and their catalysis of new production of neurotransmitters which don't reflect the environment, nor the interaction of the environment with the genes. With each ECT treatment, the pattern of illness is disrupted further, so that in the end the pattern is sufficiently erased to bring the psychiatric disease to a halt.

While Swartz and Shorter don't explain here why ECT works better in psychotic depressives than in nondelusional depressives, one could reason as follows: as was said before, the plasma norepinephrine level is much higher in psychotic depressives than in nonpsychotic depressives. However, if ECT has some effect on the level of plasma norepinephrine, it should have an effect on both cases—the psychotic depressives and the nondelusional depressives—explaining that ECT has also an effect on nondelusional depressives. It was also said before that a possible cause for psychotic depression is a certain kind of genetic predisposition for psychotic depression, which then makes it difficult to understand why ECT works in the way it is supposed to work in the case of psychotic depression. Yet, the genetic predisposition could be just of such a kind that, provided that one is exposed to certain substances or environments, psychotic depression arises. In this way, it still seems plausible to argue that ECT is very effective in treating psychotic depression in the way Swartz and Shorter claim. Moreover, if the environment doesn't change, it could become understandable why psychotic depression could recur over time given that one has that genetic predisposition.

Yet, based on how ECT works one cannot conclusively draw the inference that psychotic depression is an alloy of psychosis and depression. Especially if one considers all the different possible causes of psychotic depression, it seems very difficult to defend the view that psychotic depression is an alloy of psychosis and depression. That is to say, given the many possible causes of psychotic depression one would like to know much more about how psychotic depression arises with regard to each possible cause before one makes a thoroughly justified judgment that psychotic depression is an alloy of psychosis and depression.

Anxiety disorders and psychotic depression. Swartz and Shorter (2007, pp. 124-125) highlight the following connection between anxiety disorders and psychotic depression on the basis of several studies: there is an enormous co-morbidity of anxiety disorders among patients with mood disorders, which is higher than can be attributed to coincidence or genetics alone. Hence according to Swartz and Shorter one overlooks the psychological and physiological stresses patients with psychotic depression go through. Swartz and Shorter (2007, pp. 124-125), however, claim that the high incidence of anxiety disorders in patients with bipolar-I disorder who are not presently in an episode of mania or endogenous depression suggests that a separation between the mood disorder and the anxiety disorder seems reasonable to postulate. Swartz and Shorter maintain that if one considers the mood disorder as a threatening and potentially traumatic stress, one can recognize the anxiety disorder as PTSD.

Yet, one might wonder why Swartz and Shorter don't come to the conclusion as in the case of psychotic depression that there are such alloys as anxiety disorder psychotic depression, anxiety disorder nonpsychotic depression, etc. For if anxiety disorders go together with different forms of depression, as psychosis goes together with depression in some particular cases, why should one treat these cases differently? Perhaps the reason for the different treatment besides the temporal one (see previous paragraph) is that there is no specific treatment for anxiety disorder psychotic depression. Yet, on first sight one might wonder why shouldn't one be justified in reasoning that psychosis causes depression as it seems reasonable to suppose that depression and/or psychosis cause anxiety, so that there is no difference between the two cases given and we also have an alloy in the case of depression/psychosis and anxiety?

Swartz and Shorter (2007, p. 179) support their view further that psychotic depression might lead to an anxiety disorder by pointing out that it is at least one-third of patients with psychotic depression who have a concurrent anxiety disorder. Moreover, Swartz and Shorter claim that the anxiety disorder becomes more severe the longer and more intensely the patients suffer from serious depression, bipolar disorder, or medical illnesses. Furthermore, Swartz and Shorter highlight the fact that anxiety can make the depression appear worse, for anxiety disorders make patients unhappy, which raises scores on depression rating scales. Yet, by pointing out that unhappiness is common among patients with anxiety disorder and among patients with depression and that measurement devices don't distinguish between the source of the unhappiness with such items as "I am unhappy because I am anxious" vs. "I am unhappy because I am depressed", vagueness in the sense of underspecificity enters the diagnosis of the respective disorders.

Suicide and psychotic depression. Swartz and Shorter (2007) provide some evidence for the view that psychotic depression leads to more suicides than nonpsychotic depression and that one therefore has found more justification for the divide between psychotic depression and nonpsychotic depression. In particular, Swartz and Shorter (2007, p. 60) report the results of a particular study by Vythilingam and co-workers which shows that the death rate of patients with psychotic depression, which were admitted to Yale University Hospital, is higher (forty percent within fifteen years of admission) than that for patients with severe nonpsychotic depression (twenty percent within fifteen years of admission) even if one factors out age effects. Unfortunately, Swartz and Shorter don't say anything about the sample size here, so that it is difficult to evaluate these results properly. Yet, Swartz and Shorter (2007, p. 71) also report a study which provides a small sample size, namely twenty-two suicides of mood-disordered patients, where sixty-four percent had psychotic unipolar depression in contrast to twelve percent with nonpsychotic unipolar depression. As this study confirms the results of the previous study, there is little reason to doubt that these results can generalize to the overall population. However, this is just a quantitative difference between psychotic depression and non-psychotic depression and not a qualitative one, which might make it difficult to use it as a justification for a divide between the two categories.

Schizophrenia and psychotic depression. Swartz and Shorter (2007) provide some convincing evidence that there is a connection between schizophrenia and psychotic depression. While anxiety might be a side-effect of psychotic depression in some cases, Swartz and Shorter actually entertain the idea that schizophrenia is the progressive exemplification of the disease. In particular, Swartz and Shorter (2007, pp. 19-20) give the following historical account and clinical studies to motivate their point of view: in German psychiatry in the nineteenth century the idea that depressive psychosis and madness are related to each other was launched under the term Einheitspsychose or unitary psychosis. Whereas the mild form of the disease is perhaps affective disorder, the severe acute form is psychotic depression and the persistent form is schizophrenia, Swartz and

Shorter speculate. Swartz and Shorter report a study by Hill and colleagues, in which neurological dysfunction was investigated in patients having their first episode of unipolar psychotic depression and in which the deficit in motor skills and executive function of these patients differed from that of patients with nonpsychotic depression and was similar to that of schizophrenics. Swartz and Shorter report another study where they found that white matter deficits in schizophrenia and in psychotic forms of manic-depressive illness were likely to appear in the frontal and parietal lobes; however, with regard to grey matter, there were extensive deficits in schizophrenia and none in psychotic depression.

While the extreme loss of grey matter in schizophrenia and no loss of grey matter in psychotic depression speaks in favor of schizophrenia being the more extreme form of the disease, Swartz and Shorter (2007, p. 75) report some more evidence to support this view, namely that schizoaffective disorder carries the prognosis of unending psychosis, whereas the prognosis for patients with psychotic depression is better. Moreover, Swartz and Shorter (2007, p. 203) report a study which has argued that the nearly complete overlap in family occurrence of schizophrenia and mood disorders, including among identical twins, can be best explained if one assumes that schizophrenia is the extreme form of the disease. Given that becoming chronic is the main difference between schizophrenia and psychotic depression, and given that ECT was effective in the case of psychotic depression, it seems reasonable to assume that ECT would also be effective in the case of schizophrenia unless becoming chronic amounts to a qualitative difference and not only to a quantitative one. However, perhaps the difference in grey matter might make a reversal of schizophrenia impossible and therefore might amount to a qualitative difference between psychotic depression and schizophrenia.

Rationality and psychosis. On first sight one might think it absurd that any form of psychosis can be considered to be rational. Yet, sometimes it might be rational to fool oneself. If one, for instance, believes of oneself that one is healthy, although in reality one is not, under certain circumstances this might be the rational thing to do, especially if there is no cure for the disease now and in the foreseeable future and one is horribly suffering (cf. also Ledwig 2006, pp. 55-56). Also if delusions make life easier to endure or live, such as one thinks of oneself as being

246

Kant, and one therefore can live one's life in the security and care of a psychiatric institution, then it might be rational to prefer the delusions to one's real life. In this regard it might be interesting to note that during times of depression the movie industry is actually not suffering, but blooming, so people really need some kind of diversion from their real life in order to lead a better life, so that it seems rational to fool oneself under certain circumstances.

However, one would also like to think that if one is rational, one might be willing to change one's view given reasonable evidence and that other people are able to reason with the respective person about their rationality (cf. Ledwig 2006, p. 20). Yet, this doesn't seem to be the case in psychotic depression. For Swartz and Shorter's (2007, p. 68) have observed that psychosis cannot be changed by discussion, psychological training, logical reasoning, hypnotic suggestion, psychoanalysis, etc. That is to say, if one tries to reason with the patient, the result will be anger, agitation, suspicion, or resentment, even blunt assault or battery is possible. Yet, perhaps the only way to maintain an equilibrium in their life, patients with psychotic depression have to deny any kind of contrary evidence or questioning; otherwise they might become even more psychotic or even loose complete control over their life. That is to say, perhaps they have a good reason for behaving the way they do. Here further evidence is needed in order to evaluate the psychotic depressive's rationality more properly.

However, that the patient's reasoning faculty seems to have suffered in the case of psychotic depression has been supported by studies, Swartz and Shorter (2007, pp. 69-70) report; these show that patients with psychotic depression suffer from a diminished ability to solve problems, understand new complex situations, manage social interactions, and pay attention well, which are all associated with prefrontal lobe function and occur in mania, schizophrenia, and delirium. Hence psychotic depression goes together with a diminished form of rationality.

III. Major depressive disorder

Characteristics of depression. The most surprising insight into depression which I made is that according to Swartz and Shorter (2007, p. 131) one of the most important subjective symptoms of endogenous depression is pain and not sadness. Besides pain, the other major symptom which one would ordinarily consider as a symptom for depression would be crying. In this regard, Nelson (2008, p. 210) points out that:

"Excessive crying is believed to be associated with depression (though recent research by Rottenberg, Gross, Wilhelm, Najmi, & Gotlib [2002] has called this into question) as is the inability to cry in a person who normally cries (Steer, Beck, Brown, & Berchick, 1987)."

Furthermore, as crying and pain are both negative, one could expect other symptoms of depression also to exhibit negative connotations, as in the case of sadness.

In order to find out the respective characteristics of depression, one has to study people. As it is ethically problematical to induce a depressed mood in an experiment, one has to study depression in naturalistic settings besides observing depressed inpatients. Yet, naturalistic settings are even preferable to the artificial setting of a psychiatric hospital, so studies which are based on naturalistic settings are more believable and reliable, and this doesn't only hold for depression but also for other kinds of psychopathological diseases. After having gathered an enormous amount of studies as evidence, Rottenberg and Vaughan (2008, p. 130) state justifiedly that "depressed individuals evince more frequent displays of negative emotion in naturalistic settings." Moreover, Rottenberg and Vaughan (2008, p. 131) point out that: "Corroborating naturalistic studies, experimental findings largely indicate that depressed individuals express fewer positive emotions than their nondepressed counterparts."

Yet, Rottenberg and Vaughan (2008, p. 134) weigh the fewer positive and more negative emotions in a certain way:

"Though deficits in positive expression have received the bulk of the attention, depressed persons often exhibit a broad behavioral insensitivity that is independent of valence. We thus recommend the term *emotion context-insensitivity* as a parsimonious way to characterize depressed persons' expressive behavior (ECI; Rottenberg & Gotlib, 2004; Rottenberg, Gross, & Gotlib, 2005)."

While the idea of emotion context-insensitivity of depressives is an interesting one, one would like to know why the depressives show this kind of behavior. In the introduction to this book I already pointed out that depressives tend to pay attention to negative things instead of positive things, so that they don't get out of their loop of negativity (cf. Bach 1994;

Wenzlaff et al. 2002, p. 544). This might be one explanation for the emotion context-insensitivity of depressives. Yet, of course one would like to know why do they fix their attention in such a way? Perhaps because they have learned it so and have reinforced it ever since? Perhaps they have a genetic disposition for that? Perhaps a genetic disposition and a certain learning experience have been present? An answer to these questions doesn't seem obvious.

Statistics on depression. As depression is such a common phenomenon, there should be more than enough statistics on depression. In this regard, Swartz and Shorter (2007, p. 140) report the results of a study which has shown that whether one has been treated or not, every new depressive episode increases the risk of yet another episode. Yet, unfortunately no precise figures are given in this study, so that it is difficult to evaluate these results properly. Rottenberg and Vaughan (2008, p. 125), however, come up with some real figures:

"Depression, an often painful psychological disorder that is the leading cause of psychiatric hospitalization, and which affects nearly 20% of the population over the lifetime (Kessler, 2002), is an important place to apply the insights of basic emotion research. Depression is also a natural context to examine *interconnections* between emotion expression and social functioning, as it typically involves impairments in both of these domains (Rottenberg & Gotlib, 2004)."

That social functioning is impaired in depressives seems reasonable to assume, after all who can imagine a depressive reacting normally at a dinner party? Also that there is an impairment in emotion expression seems plausible, because one cannot expect the individual to express the whole range of emotional expressions, if he or she is depressed. In the chapter on the rational functions of emotions, I already pointed out the rational function of sadness. Something analogous seems to hold in the case of depression. For if depressives are unable to function socially and if their emotional expressions are impaired, they might focus more on the problems which have caused the disease similar to what was observed with regard to the rational function of sadness.

Depression and writing. It is interesting to note that not all therapies of depression include medication and that some of them might be really cheap, don't take so much of an effort, and are even effective. In this regard, Solano, Bonadies, and Di Trani (2008, p. 241) report that: "a lower incidence of postpartum depression (Bucci, Donati, & Solano, 2004) were found after asking study participants to focus their writing on the difficulties of their ongoing situation". Similarly, Smyth, Nazarian, and Arigo (2008, p. 220) point out the results of a study which showed that "expressive writing produced significant improvement on measures of sleep quality, anxiety, and depression." One might wonder, though, how expressive writing actually can accomplish these results. For writing about depression results in further focusing on depression and not getting out of that circle. However, when people start writing on the difficulties of their particular situations, they might also find solutions to problems which they have not thought about before.

Depression and health. On first sight one might wonder why depression should have an effect on one's physical health. After all it is only a mental disease. Yet, such an approach is to ignore the fact that in lots of cases the mental has an effect on one's physical being and that in many cases one's physical being also has an effect on one's mental being. Moreover, (1) as at least in some cases expressive behavior, that is, crying, is going together with depression and (2) as parts of the brain are involved in depression (see a later section), and (3) as neurotransmitters also play a part in depression (see a later section), it seems much more reasonable to suppose that depression also has an effect on one's physical well-being. In this regard, Bekker and Spoor (2008, p. 172) provide the following evidence:

"Much research indicates that expressing feelings, especially 'negative' ones accompanying traumatic experiences, such as fear, sadness, and depression, is related to better mental and physical health, including better immune functioning (Nyklíček, Vingerhoets, & Denollet, 2002). The long tradition of psychoanalytic theory and practice is even based on the idea that repressed emotions cause psychosomatic and neurotic problems and that awareness raising of and working through these repressed feelings are necessary conditions for recovery."

Yet, the mental might not only have an effect on the physical, it might be also possible that one part of the mental has an effect on another part of the mental. In this regard, van Heck and den Oudsten (2008, p. 114) report studies that higher emotional intelligence is associated with less depression, greater optimism, and greater life satisfaction. Although such an association might not guarantee a causal relation, at least the possibility exists that there might be some direct or indirect causal relation given. Further studies need to be done here.

Freud on depression. When one thinks of psychology, one's first association is Sigmund Freud. According to Swartz and Shorter (2007, p. 36) Freud considered depression to be entirely reactive, for in Freud's view depression was a response to the loss of a love-object. Freud's account of depression, however, has then problems with drug-induced, hormone-induced, medication-induced, and genetically caused cases of depression.

Depression and the brain. A summary of the findings gathered by Heilman (2000, pp. 334-335) indicate that so far there is little agreement among researchers with regard to which parts of the brain are involved in depression. On the basis of Heilman's summary, the only hypothesis that has got relatively good support seems to be that there is a difference between the hemispheres with regard to depression, so that (1) patients with left hemisphere disease have a higher mark on a depression scale than patients with right hemisphere disease, (2) there is a decrease of activation in the left frontal lobe and the left cingulate gyrus in depressives, (3) there is increased activity in the left prefrontal cortex, amygdala, basal ganglia, and thalamus in depressives, and (4) strokes in the right hemisphere are likely to increase serotonergic receptor binding and left hemisphere strokes tend to lower serotonergic binding, where the lower the serotonergic binding is, the more severe the depression is. Other findings in Heilman's summary are that there are abnormalities in the subgenual prefrontal cortex in depression and that the rostral anterior cingulate gyrus could have an important role in depression. However, going against point three above, Hermans and van Honk (2006, p. 316) report that depression is related to left prefrontal cortex hypoactivity. Consequently one has to await further studies to determine what kind of role the prefrontal cortex plays in depression.

Previous studies have shown that the amygdala is of relevance for emotion regulation, especially with regard to fear (see the chapter on the brain in this book). As depression in lots of cases goes together with anxiety (see the section on anxiety disorders and psychotic depression) and fear is very close to anxiety, one could reasonably assume that also in the case of depression one finds abnormalities in the amygdala, which is basically what Davidson (2000, p. 381) has found:

"We examined individual differences in glucose metabolic rate in the amygdala and its relation to dispositional negative affect in depressed subjects (Abercrombie et al., 1998)....We found that subjects with greater glucose metabolism in both the right and left amygdala report greater dispositional negative affect on the PANAS scale....These findings indicate that individual differences in resting glucose metabolism in the amygdala are present and that they predict dispositional negative affect among depressed subjects."

The following results basically confirm the previous findings that the amygdala is of relevance for depression, for Reiman, Lane, Ahern, Schwartz, and Davidson (2000, p. 399) state: "medial prefrontal activity was found to be inversely related to amygdala activity in patients with major depressive disorder (Davidson, 1996)".

Depression and schizophrenia. Not only is there a connection between psychotic depression and schizophrenia, but also between depression and schizophrenia. For Rottenberg and Vaughan (2008, p. 128) report the following results:

"In one such investigation, the frequency and duration of smiling, eyebrow movements, head movements, and gaze (a measure of interest) were examined among recently admitted depressed or schizophrenic inpatients and healthy nonpsychiatric controls (Jones & Pansa, 1979). Depressed and schizophrenic inpatients smiled less frequently and for a shorter period of time during the interview than the control group. Depressed inpatients also demonstrated abnormalities in gaze, exhibiting shorter gaze duration than the other two groups and less frequent gaze than healthy controls."

As in the case of the comparison between psychotic depression and schizophrenia, one not only finds similarities between depression and schizophrenia, but also finds a difference, namely shorter gaze duration in depressed inpatients. Yet, one has to be aware of the fact that the study was not done in a naturalistic setting but was performed with inpatients. Shorter gaze duration in depressed inpatients in contrast to schizophrenics could amount to a quantitative difference, which could lie on a continuum, in contradistinction to the differences in grey matter which we have already observed (see the previous section on schizophrenia and psychotic depression).

IV. Bipolar disorder

While there are different forms of bipolar disorder (BP for short) according to the *DSM*, the foremost question is whether major depressive disorder (MDD for short) can be quite easily distinguished and separated from bipolar disorder. In this regard, Angst et al. (2005, p. 218) provide the following evidence:

"The APA guidelines on the management of bipolar disorders (BP) state that bipolar-II disorder (BP-II) is frequently misdiagnosed as unipolar major depressive disorder (MDD) and as a result may receive inadequate or inappropriate treatment....This notion is compatible with recent work in the field suggesting several reasons for the under-diagnosis and under-treatment of BP....First, individuals who experience depression do not always perceive hypomania as pathological, and as such do not spontaneously report it to clinicians....Also, the latter do not always make relevant direct inquiries of patients presenting with MDD....The consequences are that the correct diagnosis and treatment may be delayed by 8—10 years....Furthermore, the recognition of hypomania may require more subtle inquiry than detailed in the currently available structured diagnostic interviews (SCID, CIDI) and the diagnostic criteria in DSM-IV and ICD-10 may be less reliable and valid than previously believed. An expert group recently concluded that the current diagnostic criteria have high specificity but might have too low a sensitivity and that a greater focus on certain symptoms (such as activation levels) or less emphasis on symptom duration may improve recognition of those at risk of BP episodes....Although not all researchers agree with these proposals, there is emerging evidence for a dimensional view of hypomania and mania....As found previously in studies of depressive disorders...Meyer and Keller's (2003) study failed to find evidence for latent classes for hypomania but did find evidence for a dimensional structure supporting the idea of an affective spectrum from 'normal' highs through to hypomania and mania".

A spectrum view of hypomania and mania might also explain the misdiagnosis of bipolar-II disorder, for if the individuals have only hypomania this doesn't differ so much from normal highs and would therefore just lead to the view that the individual has major depressive disorder.

Measurement devices of bipolar disorder. Angst et al. (2005, p. 227) report with regard to Italian and Swedish samples that their multi-lingual hypomania checklist (HCL-32) showed a two-factor structure of hypomania, namely an active/elated factor and a risk-taking/irritable factor: "The active/elated factor included mainly overactivity, mood elation and improved thinking. The risk-taking/irritable factor included symptoms of risk taking behavior, anger/irritability, and flight of ideas." Moreover, according to Angst et al. (2005, p. 217) "The HCL-32 distinguished between BP and MDD with a sensitivity of 80% and a specificity of 51%." The latter might indeed suggest that there is a more of a quantitative than a qualitative difference between BP and MDD.

With regard to the active/elated factor, overactivity is also something which could be present in the case of anxiety. Moreover, as we will see in a later section there is a connection between bipolarity and anxiety disorder. Hence this checklist might not properly distinguish hypomania from anxiety and might therefore lead to the impression that bipolar disorder and anxiety disorder are overlapping phenomena.

Statistics of bipolar disorder. As with depression also with bipolar disorder one would expect that enough statistics are available, for it is such a common phenomenon. In this regard, Phillips (2006, p. 233) provides the following information:

"Bipolar disorder affects up to 1.5% of the population (Kessler et al., 1994), with illness relapse rates estimated at between 37% and 44% per year (O'Connell, Mayo, Flatow, Cuthbertson, & O'Brien, 1991; Gitlin, Swendsen, Heller, & Hammen, 1995)".

Bipolar disorder and recognition deficits. Some of the more essential characteristics of bipolar disorder are recognition deficits. In this regard, Phillips (2006, p. 234) points out the following results:

"Previous studies of euthymic and remitted individuals with bipolar disorder indicate impaired fear (Yurgelun-Todd et al., 2000), and enhanced disgust recognition (Harmer, Grayson, & Goodwin, 2002) in facial expressions, or no specific deficits in recognizing emotion (Venn et al., 2004) in unfamiliar others. Studies in manic individuals with the disorder have indicated both specific impairments in the recognition of fear and disgust of unfamiliar others (Lembke & Ketter, 2002), and generalised deficits in the recognition of all emotional expressions (Getz, Shear, & Strakowski, 2003). Finally, a tendency to misinterpret the faces of peers as being angry has been reported in adolescent individuals with bipolar disorder (McClure, Pope, Hoberman, Pine, & Leibenluft, 2003)."

Similarly to Phillips, Kohler and Martin (2006, pp. 260-261) provide the following information:

"Over the last 15 years, a large body of literature has examined emotion recognition, as measured by the ability to identify the emotional quality of facial expression, in brain-related disorders and healthy people and documented impairment in…depression (Feinberg, Rifkin, Schaffer, & Walker 1096; Gur et al., 1992; Mikhailova, Vladimirova, Iznack, Tsusulkovskaya, & Sushko, 1996), bipolar disorder (Addington & Addington, 1998; Lembke & Ketter, 2002)".

Yet, how can one account for these recognition deficits? Do they have to do with the fact that depressives and perhaps also individuals who are bipolar are too much focused on their own problems, so that they can't identify the emotional quality of another person's facial expression properly? This open question still needs further research to be answered properly.

Bipolar disorder and the brain. As there is a connection between anxiety disorders and bipolar disorders (see a later section) and as the amygdala is activated especially when it comes to the emotion of fear, it is to be expected that also with regard to bipolar disorders there will be activity in the amygdala. In this regard, Phillips (2006, p. 236) has observed the following:

"our recent findings in remitted individuals with bipolar disorder…indicate increased activity within limbic and subcortical regions, predominantly to expressions of fear and happiness, in the absence of any deficits in facial expression recognition (Lawrence, et al., 2004;...). These findings support earlier reports of increased subcortical (amygdalar) activity to fearful expressions (Yurgelun-Todd et al., 2000) in remitted individuals. Interestingly, other recent findings indicate decreased amygdalar responses to sad, but not happy, facial expressions in individuals with mania (Lennox, Jacob, Calder, Lupson, & Bullmore, 2004). Our findings also indicate subsyndromal depression-related abnormalities, namely a positive correlation between depression severity and hippocampal response to sad expressions, in remitted individuals with bipolar disorder. We also demonstrated increased ventromedial prefrontal cortical responses in these individuals, particularly in response to expressions of mild happiness."

In the chapter on the brain, we saw that the prefrontal cortex is activated when emoting which goes together with the findings on bipolar disorder in the previous quote. Phillips (2006, p. 243) gives further evidence for the involvement of the amygdala and the prefrontal cortex in bipolar disorders: in remitted individuals with bipolar disorder one finds an increased activity within subcortical and limbic regions implicated in the initial appraisal of emotive stimuli (amygdala ventral striatum, anterior insula), resulting in increased activity in regions associated with mood generation and decision-making about emotional material (ventromedial and ventrolateral prefrontal cortices, ventral anterior cingulated gyrus), and reduced activity within regions implicated in the regulation of these responses and attentional processes (predominantly dorsomedial prefrontal cortices).

Phillips (2006, pp. 236-237) not only gives further evidence for prefrontal cortex activation in bipolar disorders, but also in major depressive disorder, for they have found increased activity within dorsomedial and ventromedial prefrontal cortex in individuals with major depressive disorder during happy mood induction and an absence of the normal increase in skin conductance, whereas Phillips reports with regard to other studies that they have found relative decreases in activity within these regions in depressed individuals with bipolar disorder during sad mood induction.

As we saw in the chapter on the brain and the emotions, skin conductance was involved with regard to the emotions. Moreover, it was hypothesized that as there is a connection between fear and the amygdala, there might be also a connection between electrodermal activity, skin conductance response, and the amygdala, for our skin quite clearly responds to situations of fear, such as sweating and hair standing on end because of fear. As depressive disorders in many cases are accompanied by anxiety disorders, one could also expect abnormal skin conductance responses in individuals with depressive disorders, as was confirmed by Phillips with regard to major depressive disorder.

Further support for abnormal prefrontal cortex activation not only for bipolar disorders but also for major depressive disorder have been reported by Phillips (2006, pp. 238-239), where manic individuals with bipolar disorder showed decreased ventromedial prefrontal cortical responses during semantic task versus orthographic go/no-go task performance, but increased ventrolateral prefrontal cortical responses to emotional versus neutral targets, and elevated ventral and medial prefrontal cortical responses to emotional distractors demonstrating increased attention to emotional distractors during attentional task performance; in individuals with major depressive disorder one found a similar pattern of increased response within ventral anterior cingulate gyrus to sad targets, and increased ventrolateral prefrontal cortical response to sad distractors.

Bipolar disorder and schizophrenia. As was already stated with regard to psychotic depression and schizophrenia, Kohler and Martin (2006, p. 258) point out that bipolar disorder (BPD) and schizophrenia (SZP) may have genes in common as shown by "epidemiologic characteristics, family studies, and overlap in confirmed linkages of BPD and/or SZP (Craddock, O'Donovan, & Owen, 2005; Murray et al., 2004)."

Bipolar disorder and anxiety disorder. As we have already seen with regard to psychotic depression and anxiety disorder, there is also a connection between bipolar disorder and anxiety disorder according to Swartz and Shorter (2007, p. 210), for in the U.S.A. one finds anxiety disorders in thirty-five percent of bipolar-I patients and in one hundred percent of bipolar-II patients. Swartz and Shorter maintain that one finds anxiety to such a huge percentage in bipolar-I patients, because the disease causes anxiety, whereas in the case of bipolar-II patients hypomania is identical with anxiety disorder in almost all of the cases.

Yet, if hypomania is identical with to anxiety disorder in bipolar-II, one might wonder why one doesn't call it depression with anxiety disorder instead of bipolar-II? Perhaps because depression with anxiety disorder wouldn't reflect the rapid cycling present in persons with bipolar-II disorder, where rapid cycling refers to patients who switch from manic episode to bipolar depression four or more times during the year. Swartz and Shorter (2007, p. 79) indirectly support this point of view by claiming that one can explain rapid cycling by means of anxiety disorder.

Conclusion

While Swartz and Shorter consider psychotic depression as an alloy, it is not obvious to me whether it is not merely a combination of two disorders where the depression turns out to be caused by the psychosis. The hypothesis that schizophrenia is the chronic form of the disease, whereas psychotic depression is the acute form of the disease can be supported by several factors which psychotic depression and schizophrenia have in common, where each can be measured on a continuum. However, the differences in grey matter might speak in favor of a qualitative difference between psychotic depression and schizophrenia. As psychotics are not open to reasoning about their disease and have problems in diverse reasoning tasks, it seems plausible to assume that psychotic depression doesn't turn out to be rational.

With regard to major depressive disorder, it might serve a rational function. However, as in the case of bipolar disorder, not enough evidence has been accumulated yet to draw final conclusions in that regard. In the case of bipolar disorder it might be particularly difficult to be open to logical reasoning, because individuals with that disorder have recognition deficits. With regard to major depressive disorder and bipolar disorder, a spectrum view of these disorders seems to establish itself, so that vagueness enters the picture.

Bibliography

Aggleton, J. P. and Young, A. W. (2000), "The Enigma of the Amygdala: On its Contribution to Human Emotion", in R. D. Lane and L. Nadel (eds.), *Cognitive Neuroscience of Emotion*, Oxford University Press, New York, Oxford, pp. 106-128.

Aleman, A., Medford, N., and David, A. S. (2006), "Dissecting the Cognitive and Neural Basis of Emotional Abnormalities", in A. Aleman, N. Medford, and A. S. David (eds.), *The Cognitive Neuropsychiatry of Emotion and Emotional Disorders*, Psychology Press, Hove, New York, pp. 193-197.

American Psychiatric Association (1994), *Diagnostic and Statistical Manual of Mental Disorders: DSM-IV*, Washington, DC.

American Psychiatric Association (2000), *Diagnostic and Statistical Manual of Mental Disorders: DSM-IV-TR*, Washington, DC.

Angst, J., Andolfsson, R., Benazzi, F., Gamma, A., Hantouche, E., Meyer, T. D., Skeppar, P., Vieta, E., and Scott, J. (2005), "The HCL-32: Towards a Self-Assessment Tool for Hypomanic Symptoms in Outpatients", *Journal of Affective Disorders* 88, pp. 217-233.

Arbib, M. A. (2005), "Beware the Passionate Robot", in J.-M. Fellous and M. A. Arbib (eds.), *Who Needs Emotions? The Brain Meets the Robot*, Oxford University Press, New York, pp. 333-383.

Auerbach, S. M., Kiesler, D. J., Strentz, T., and Schmidt, J. A. (1994), "Interpersonal Impacts and Adjustment to the Stress of Simulated Captivity: An Empirical Test of the *Stockholm Syndrome*", *Journal of Social and Clinical Psychology* 13, pp. 207-221.

Bach, K. (1994), "Emotional Disorder and Attention", in G. Graham and G. Stephens (eds.), *Philosophical Psychopathology*, MIT Press, Cambridge, pp. 51-72.

Barlow, D., Chorpita, B., and Turovsky, J. (1996), "Fear, Panic, Anxiety, and Disorders of Emotion", in D. Hope (ed.), *Perspectives on Anxiety, Panic, and Fear*, Nebraska University Press, Lincoln, pp. 251-328.

Bekker, M. and Spoor, S. (2008), "Emotional Inhibition, Health, Gender, and Eating Disorders: The Role of (Over) Sensitivity to Others", in A.

Vingerhoets, I. Nyklíček, and J. Denollet (eds.), *Emotion Regulation: Conceptual and Clinical Issues*, Springer, New York, pp. 170-183.

Ben-Ze'ev, A. (1993), "You Always Hurt the One You Love", *The Journal of Value Inquiry* 27, pp. 487-495.

Ben-Ze'ev, A. (2000), *The Subtlety of Emotions*, MIT Press, Cambridge.

Ben-Ze'ev , A. (2004), "Emotions Are Not Mere Judgments", *Philosophy and Phenomenological Research* LXVIII, pp. 450-457.

Bermond, B., Vorst, H. C. M., and Moormann, P. P. (2006), "Cognitive Neuropsychology of Alexithymia: Implications for Personality Typology", in A. Aleman, N. Medford, and A. S. David (eds.), *The Cognitive Neuropsychiatry of Emotion and Emotional Disorders*, Psychology Press, Hove, New York, pp. 332-360.

Blackburn, S. (1998), *Ruling Passions: A Theory of Practical Reasoning*, Clarendon Press, Oxford.

Bradley, M. M. and Lang, P. J. (2000), "Measuring Emotion: Behavior, Feeling, and Physiology", in R. D. Lane and L. Nadel (eds.), *Cognitive Neuroscience of Emotion*, Oxford University Press, New York, Oxford, pp. 242-276.

Breazeal, C. and Brooks, R. (2005), "Robot Emotion: A Functional Perspective", in J.-M. Fellous and M. A. Arbib (eds.), *Who Needs Emotions? The Brain Meets the Robot*, Oxford University Press, New York, pp. 271-310.

Braun, D. and Sider, T. (2007), "Vague, So Untrue", *Noûs* 41, pp. 133-156.

Cargile, J. (1999), "The Sorites Paradox", in R. Keefe and P. Smith (eds.), *Vagueness: A Reader*, MIT Press, Cambridge, London, pp. 89-98.

Carroll, N. (2003), "Art and Mood: Preliminary Notes and Conjectures", *The Monist* 86, pp. 521-555.

Changizi, M. A. (1999), "Vagueness, Rationality and Undecidability", *Synthese* 120, pp. 345-375.

Changizi, M. A. (2003), *The Brain from 25,000 Feet: High Level Explorations of Brain Complexity, Perception, Induction and Vagueness*, Kluwer, Dordrecht.

Clark, A. (2003), "Artificial Intelligence and the Many Faces of Reason", in S. Stich and T. Warfield (eds.), *The Blackwell Guide to Philosophy of Mind*, Blackwell, Malden, pp. 309-321.

Clore, G. L. and Ortony, A. (2000), "Cognition in Emotion: Always, Sometimes, or Never?", in R. D. Lane and L. Nadel (eds.), *Cognitive Neuroscience of Emotion*, Oxford University Press, New York, Oxford, pp. 24-61.

Coates, J. (1996), *The Claims of Common Sense*, Cambridge University Press, Cambridge.

Cotton, J. L. (1981), "A Review of Research on Schachter's Theory of Emotion and the Misattribution of Arousal", *European Journal of Social Psychology* 11, pp. 365-397.

Daly, M., Wilson, M., and Weghorst, S. J. (1982), "Male Sexual Jealousy", *Ethology and Sociobiology* 3, pp. 11-27.

Damasio, A. R. (1994), *Descartes' Error: Emotion, Reason, and the Human Brain*, G. P. Putnam's Sons, New York.

Damasio, A. R. (1999), *The Feeling of What Happens: Body and Emotion in the Making of Consciousness*, Harcourt Brace and Company, New York, San Diego, London.

Damasio, A. R. (2000), "A Second Chance for Emotion", in R. D. Lane and L. Nadel (eds.), *Cognitive Neuroscience of Emotion*, Oxford University Press, New York, Oxford, pp. 12-23.

Damasio, A. R. (2004), "William James and The Modern Neurobiology of Emotion", in D. Evans and P. Cruse (eds.), *Emotion, Evolution, and Rationality*, Oxford University Press, New York, pp. 3-14.

D'Arms, J. and Jacobson, D. (2003), "The Significance of Recalcitrant Emotion (or, Anti-Quasi-Judgmentalism)", in A. Hatzemoysis (ed.), *Philosophy and the Emotions*, Cambridge University Press, Cambridge, pp. 127-145.

Davidson, R. J. (2000), "The Functional Neuroanatomy of Affective Style", in R. D. Lane and L. Nadel (eds.), *Cognitive Neuroscience of Emotion*, Oxford University Press, New York, Oxford, pp. 371-388.

Denollet, J., Nyklíček, I., and Vingerhoets, A. (2008), "Introduction: Emotions, Emotion Regulation, and Health", in A. Vingerhoets, I. Nyklíček, and J. Denollet (eds.), *Emotion Regulation: Conceptual and Clinical Issues*, Springer, New York, pp. 3-11.

De Sousa, R. (1987), *The Rationality of Emotion*, MIT Press, Cambridge.

De Sousa, R. (2004), "Emotional Consistency", manuscript.

Dolan, R. J. and Morris, J. S. (2000), "The Functional Anatomy of Innate and Acquired Fear: Perspectives from Neuroimaging", in R. D. Lane and L. Nadel (eds.), *Cognitive Neuroscience of Emotion*, Oxford University Press, New York, Oxford, pp. 225-241.

Dretske, F. I. (1981), *Knowledge and the Flow of Information*, MIT Press, Cambridge.

Dummett, M. (1999), "Wang's Paradox", in R. Keefe and P. Smith (eds.), *Vagueness: A Reader*, MIT Press, Cambridge, London, pp. 99-118.

Ekman, P. (2003), "Darwin, Deception, and Facial Expression", *Annals New York Academy of Sciences* 1000, pp. 205-221.

Elster, J. (1999), *Alchemies of the Mind: Rationality and the Emotions*, Cambridge University Press, Cambridge, New York, Melbourne.

Essau, C., Conradt, J., and Petermann, F. (2000), "Frequency, Comorbidity, and Psychosocial Impairment of Specific Phobia in Adolescents", *Journal of Clinical Child Psychology* 29, pp. 221-231.

Evans, D. (2001), *Emotion: The Science of Sentiment*, Oxford University Press, Oxford.

Feagin, S. L. (1997), "Imagining Emotions and Appreciating Fiction", in M. Hjort and S. Laver (eds.), *Emotion and the Arts*, Oxford University Press, New York, Oxford, pp. 50-62.

Fellous, J.-M. and LeDoux, J. E. (2005), "Toward Basic Principles for Emotional Processing: What the Fearful Brain Tells the Robot", in J.-M. Fellous and M. A. Arbib (eds.), *Who Needs Emotions? The Brain Meets the Robot*, Oxford University Press, New York, pp. 79-115.

Fine, K. (1999), "Vagueness, Truth and Logic", in R. Keefe and P. Smith (eds.), *Vagueness: A Reader*, MIT Press, Cambridge, London, pp. 119-150.

Friedman, C., de Mowbray, M. S., and Hamilton, V. (1961), "Imipramine (Tofranil) in Depressive States: A Controlled Trial with In-Patients", *Journal of Mental Science* 107, pp. 948-953.

Ginsburg, G. and Walkup, J. (2004), "Specific Phobia", in T. Ollendick and J. March (eds.), *Phobic and Anxiety Disorders in Children and Adolescents*, Oxford University Press, New York, pp. 175-197.

Goldberg, D. and Huxley, P. (1980), *Mental Illness in the Community: The Pathway to Psychiatric Care*, Tavistock, London.

Goldie, P. (2000), *The Emotions: A Philosophical Exploration*, Clarendon Press, Oxford.

Graham, D. L. R., Rawlings, E. I., Ihms, K., Latimer, D., Foliano, J., Thompson, A., Suttman, K., Farrington, M., and Hacker, R. (2001), "A Scale for Identifying 'Stockholm Syndrome'—Reactions in Young Dating Women: Factor Structure, Reliability, and Validity", in K. D. O'Leary and R. D. Maiuro (eds.), *Psychological Abuse in Violent Domestic Relations*, Springer, New York, pp. 77-100.

Graham, D. L. R., Rawlings, E., and Rimini, N. (1988), "Survivors of Terror: Battered Women, Hostages, and the Stockholm Syndrome", in K. Yllö and M. Bograd (eds.), *Feminist Perspectives on Wife Abuse,* Sage Publications, Newbury Park, London, New Delhi, pp. 217-233.

Greenspan, P. (1980), "A Case of Mixed Feelings", in A. Rorty (ed.), *Explaining Emotions*, University of California Press, Berkeley, pp. 223-250.

Greenspan, P. (1981), "Emotions as Evaluations", *Pacific Philosophical Quarterly* 62, pp. 158-169.

Greenspan, P. (2001), "Good Evolutionary Reasons", *Philosophical Psychology* 14, pp. 327-338.

Griffiths, P. (1997), *What Emotions Really Are*, University of Chicago Press, Chicago.

Griffiths, P. (2003), "Basic Emotions, Complex Emotions, Machiavellian Emotions", in A. Hatzemoysis (ed.), *Philosophy and the Emotions*, Cambridge University Press, Cambridge, pp. 39-67.

Gruber, M.-C. (2008), "Social Emotions and Brain Research: From Neurophilosophy to a Neurosociology of Law", in N. C. Karafyllis and G. Ulshoefer (eds.), *Sexualized Brains: Scientific Modeling of Emotional Intelligence from a Cultural Perspective*, MIT Press, Cambridge, pp. 317-328.

Heilman, K. M. (2000), "Emotional Experience: A Neurological Model", in R. D. Lane and L. Nadel (eds.), *Cognitive Neuroscience of Emotion*, Oxford University Press, New York, Oxford, pp. 328-344.

Hendriks, M., Nelson, J., Cornelius, R., and Vingerhoets, A. (2008), "Why Crying Improves Our Well-being: An Attachment-Theory Perspective on the Functions of Adult Crying", in A. Vingerhoets, I. Nyklíček, and

J. Denollet (eds.), *Emotion Regulation: Conceptual and Clinical Issues*, Springer, New York, pp. 87-96.

Hermans, E. J. and van Honk, J. (2006), "Toward a Framework for Defective Emotion Processing in Social Phobia", in A. Aleman, N. Medford, and A. S. David (eds.), *The Cognitive Neuropsychiatry of Emotion and Emotional Disorders*, Psychology Press, Hove, New York, pp. 307-331.

Huddleston-Mattai, B. A. and Mattai, P. R. (1993), "The Sambo Mentality and the Stockholm Syndrome Revisited: Another Dimension to an Examination of the Plight of the African-American", *Journal of Black Studies* 23, pp. 344-357.

Huesing, B. (2008), "Technology Assessment of Neuroimaging: Sex and Gender Perspectives", in N. C. Karafyllis and G. Ulshoefer (eds.), *Sexualized Brains: Scientific Modeling of Emotional Intelligence from a Cultural Perspective*, MIT Press, Cambridge, pp. 103-116.

Hyde, D. (1994), "Why Higher-Order Vagueness is a Pseudo-Problem", *Mind* 103, pp. 35-41.

Isen, A. (1999), "Positive Affect and Creativity", in S. Russ (ed.), *Affect, Creative Experience, and Psychological Adjustment*, Brunner-Mazel, Philadelphia, pp. 3-7.

Izard, C. (1993), "Four Systems for Emotion Activation: Cognitive and Noncognitive Processes", *Psychological Review* 100, pp. 68-90.

James, W. (1967), "The Emotions", in C. G. Lange and W. James (eds.), *The Emotions*, Hafner Publishing Company, New York, pp. 93-135.

Johnson-Laird, P. N. and Oatley, K. (1992), "Basic Emotions, Rationality, and Folk Theory", *Cognition and Emotion* 6, pp. 201-223.

Jones, K. (2003), "Emotion, Weakness of Will, and the Normative Conception of Agency", in A. Hatzimoysis (ed.), *Philosophy and the Emotions*, Cambridge University Press, Cambridge, pp. 181-200.

Kahneman, D., Wakker, P., and Sarin, R. (1997), "Back to Bentham? Explorations of Experienced Utility", *The Quarterly Journal of Economics* 112, pp. 375-405.

Keefe, R. (2006), *Theories of Vagueness*, Cambridge University Press, Cambridge, New York.

Keefe, R. and Smith, P. (1999), "Introduction: Theories of Vagueness", in R. Keefe and P. Smith (eds.), *Vagueness: A Reader*, MIT Press, Cambridge, London, pp. 1-57.

Kendall, P., Pimentel, S., Rynn, M., Angelosante, A., and Webb, A. (2004), "Generalized Anxiety Disorder", in T. Ollendick and J. March (eds.), *Phobic and Anxiety Disorders in Children and Adolescents*, Oxford University Press, New York, pp. 334-380.

Kohler, C. G. and Martin, E. A. (2006), "Emotional Processing in Schizophrenia", in A. Aleman, N. Medford, and A. S. David (eds.), *The Cognitive Neuropsychiatry of Emotion and Emotional Disorders*, Psychology Press, Hove, New York, pp. 250-271.

Kolb, B. and Taylor, L. (2000), "Facial Expression, Emotion, and Hemispheric Organization", in R. D. Lane and L. Nadel (eds.), *Cognitive Neuroscience of Emotion*, Oxford University Press, New York, Oxford, pp. 62-83.

Kuleshnyk, I. (1984), "The Stockholm Syndrome: Toward an Understanding", *Social Action and the Law* 10, pp. 37-42.

Lane, R. D. (2000), "Neural Correlates of Conscious Emotional Experience", in R. D. Lane and L. Nadel (eds.), *Cognitive Neuroscience of Emotion*, Oxford University Press, New York, Oxford, pp. 345-370.

Lane, R. D., Nadel, L., Allen, J. J. B., and Kaszniak, A. W. (2000), "The Study of Emotion from the Perspective of Cognitive Neuroscience", in R. D. Lane and L. Nadel (eds.), *Cognitive Neuroscience of Emotion*, Oxford University Press, New York, Oxford, pp. 3-11.

Langton, C. G. (1996), "Artificial Life", in M. A. Boden (ed.), *The Philosophy of Artificial Life*, Oxford University Press, New York, pp. 39-94.

Lazarus, R. S. (1991). *Emotion and Adaptation*, Oxford University Press, New York.

LeDoux, J. (2000), "Cognitive-Emotional Interactions: Listen to the Brain", in R. D. Lane and L. Nadel (eds.), *Cognitive Neuroscience of Emotion*, Oxford University Press, New York, Oxford, pp. 129-155.

Ledwig, M. (2000), *Newcomb's Problem*, University of Konstanz, on-line at http://www.ub.uni-konstanz.de/kops/volltexte/2000/524.

Ledwig, M. (2001), *Ueberraschung und Handlung unter Beruecksichtigung des Schemakonzeptes*, Logos, Berlin.

Ledwig, M. (2005), *Reid's Philosophy of Psychology*, University Press of America, Lanham.

Ledwig, M. (2006), *Emotions: their Rationality and Consistency*, Peter Lang, New York.

Ledwig, M. (2007), *Common Sense: its History, Method, and Applicability*, Peter Lang, New York.

Ledwig, M. (2008), *Vagueness in Context*, by S. Shapiro, Clarendon Press, Oxford (2006), in *Philosophy in Review* 28, pp. 163-165.

Lorenz, K. (1943), "Die angeborenen Formen moeglicher Erfahrung", *Zeitschrift fuer Tierpsychologie* 5, pp. 235-409.

Lumley, M., Beyer, J., and Radcliffe, A. (2008), "Alexithymia and Physical Health Problems: A Critique of Potential Pathways and a Research Agenda", in A. Vingerhoets, I. Nyklíček, and J. Denollet (eds.), *Emotion Regulation: Conceptual and Clinical Issues*, Springer, New York, pp. 43-68.

Machina, K. F. (1999), "Truth, Belief and Vagueness", in R. Keefe and P. Smith (eds.), *Vagueness: A Reader*, MIT Press, Cambridge, London, pp. 174-203.

Mahtani, A. (2004), "The Instability of Vague Terms", *Philosophical Quarterly* 54, pp. 570-576.

Matravers, D. (1998), *Art and Emotion*, Clarendon Press, Oxford.

Matthews, G., Zeidner, M., and Roberts, R. (2003), *Emotional Intelligence*, MIT Press, Cambridge.

Mehlberg, H. (1999), "Truth and Vagueness", in R. Keefe and P. Smith (eds.), *Vagueness: A Reader*, MIT Press, Cambridge, London, pp. 85-88.

Merriam-Webster's On-line Dictionary (11/26/2004a), "Ambivalent", on-line at http://www.britannica.com/dictionary?book=Dictionary&va=ambivalent&query=ambivalent.

Merriam-Webster's On-line Dictionary (11/26/2004b), "Contrast", on-line at http://www.britannica.com/dictionary?book=Dictionary&va=contrast&query=contrast.

Meyer, S. (2005), *Twilight*, Little, Brown and Company, New York, Boston.

Meyer, T. D. and Keller, F. (2003), "Is there Evidence for a Latent Class Called 'Hypomanic Temperament'?", *Journal of Affective Disorders* 75, pp. 259-267.

Mezzacappa, E. S., Katkin, E. S., and Palmer, S. N. (1999), "Epinephrine, Arousal, and Emotion: A New Look at Two-Factor Theory", *Cognition and Emotion* 13, pp. 181-199.

Moore, B., Underwood, B., and Rosenhan, D. (1984), "Emotion, Self, and Others", in C. Izard, J. Kagen, and R. Zajonc (eds.) *Emotions, Cognition, and Behavior*, Cambridge University Press, New York, pp. 464-483.

Moormann, P., Bermond, B., Vorst, H., Bloemendaal, A., Tejn, S., and Rood, L. (2008), "New Avenues in Alexithymia Research: The Creation of Alexithymia Types", in A. Vingerhoets, I. Nyklíček, and J. Denollet (eds.), *Emotion Regulation: Conceptual and Clinical Issues*, Springer, New York, pp. 27-42.

Nelson, J. (2008), "Crying in Psychotherapy: Its Meaning, Assessment, and Management Based on Attachment Theory", in A. Vingerhoets, I. Nyklíček, and J. Denollet (eds.), *Emotion Regulation: Conceptual and Clinical Issues*, Springer, New York, pp. 202-214.

Neu, J. (1977), *Emotion, Thought and Therapy*, Routledge and Kegan Paul, London and Henley.

Neu, J. (2000), *A Tear Is an Intellectual Thing: The Meanings of Emotion*, Oxford University Press, New York, Oxford.

Newman, D., Moffitt, T., Caspi, A., Magdol, L., Silva, P., and Stanton, W. (1996), "Psychiatric Disorder in a Birth Cohort of Young Adults", *Journal of Consulting and Clinical Psychology* 64, pp. 552-562.

Nussbaum, M. C. (2001), *Upheavals of Thought*, Cambridge University Press, Cambridge.

Oatley, K. and Johnson-Laird, P. N. (1987), "Towards a Cognitive Theory of Emotions", *Cognition and Emotion* 1, pp. 29-50.

Öhman, A., Flykt, A., and Lundqvist, D. (2000), "Unconscious Emotion: Evolutionary Perspectives, Psychophysiological Data, and Neuropsychological Mechanisms", in R. D. Lane and L. Nadel (eds.), *Cognitive Neuroscience of Emotion*, Oxford University Press, New York, Oxford, pp. 296-327.

268

Ortony, A. Norman, D. A., and Revelle, W. (2005), "Affect and Proto-Affect in Effective Functioning", in J.-M. Fellous and M. A. Arbib (eds.), *Who Needs Emotions? The Brain Meets the Robot*, Oxford University Press, New York, pp. 173-202.

Panksepp, J. (1998), *Affective Neuroscience*, Oxford University Press, New York, Oxford.

Peirce, C. S. (1902), "Vague", in J. M. Baldwin (ed.), *Dictionary of Philosophy and Psychology*, Macmillan, New York, p. 748.

Perwien, A. and Bernstein, G. (2004), "Separation Anxiety Disorder", in T. Ollendick and J. March (eds.), *Phobic and Anxiety Disorders in Children and Adolescents*, Oxford University Press, New York, pp. 272-305.

Phillips, M. J. (2006), "The Neural Basis of Mood Dysregulation in Bipolar Disorder", in A. Aleman, N. Medford, and A. S. David (eds.), *The Cognitive Neuropsychiatry of Emotion and Emotional Disorders*, Psychology Press, Hove, New York, pp. 233-249.

Pizarro, D. (2000), "Nothing More than Feelings? The Role of Emotions in Moral Judgment", *Journal for the Theory of Social Behaviour* 30, pp. 355-375.

Plutchik, R. (1984), "Emotions: A General Psychoevolutionary Theory", in K. R. Scherer and P. Ekman (eds.), *Approaches to Emotion*, Erlbaum, Hillsdale, pp. 197-219.

Plutchik, R. and Ax, A. F. (1967), "A Critique of 'Determinants of Emotional State' by Schachter and Singer (1962)", *Psychophysiology* 4, pp. 79-82.

Priest, G. and Tanaka, K. (Winter 2004), "Paraconsistent Logic", in E. N. Zalta (ed.), *The Stanford Encyclopedia of Philosophy*, on-line at http://plato.stanford.edu/archives/win2004/entries/logicparaconsistent.

Prinz, J. J. (2004), *Gut Reactions: A Perceptual Theory of Emotion*, Oxford University Press, New York.

Prinz, J. J. (2007), *The Emotional Construction of Morals*, Oxford University Press, New York.

Pugmire, D. (1996), "Conflicting Emotions and the Indivisible Heart", *Philosophy* 71, pp. 27-40.

Rawlings, E. I., Allen, P. G., Graham, D. L. R., and Peters, J. (1994), "Chinks in the Prison Wall: Applying Graham's Stockholm Syndrome

Theory to the Treatment of Battered Women", in L. Vandecreek, S. Knapp, and T. L. Jackson (eds.), *Innovations in Clinical Practice: A Source Book* vol. 13, Professional Resource Press, Sarasota, pp. 401-417.

Ray, T. S. (1995), "An Evolutionary Approach to Synthetic Biology: Zen and the Art of Creating Life", in C. G. Langton (ed.), *Artificial Life: An Overview*, MIT Press, Cambridge, London, pp. 179-209.

Reddy, W. M. (2008), "Emotional Styles and Modern Forms of Life", in N. C. Karafyllis and G. Ulshoefer (eds.), *Sexualized Brains: Scientific Modeling of Emotional Intelligence from a Cultural Perspective*, MIT Press, Cambridge, pp. 81-100.

Reid, T. (1994), *The Works of Thomas Reid*, W. Hamilton (ed.), Thoemmes Press, Bristol.

Reiman, E. M., Lane, R. D., Ahern, G. L., Schwartz, G. E., and Davidson, R. J. (2000), "Positron Emission Tomography in the Study of Emotion, Anxiety, and Anxiety Disorders", in R. D. Lane and L. Nadel (eds.), *Cognitive Neuroscience of Emotion*, Oxford University Press, New York, Oxford, pp. 389-406.

Rescher, N. (2008), "Vagueness: A Variant Approach", manuscript.

Rieffe, C., Terwogt, M., and Jellesma, F. (2008), "Emotional Competence and Health in Children", in A. Vingerhoets, I. Nyklíček, and J. Denollet (eds.), *Emotion Regulation: Conceptual and Clinical Issues*, Springer, New York, pp. 184-201.

Rodebaugh, T. and Heimberg, R. (2008), "Emotion Regulation and the Anxiety Disorders: Adopting a Self-Regulation Perspective", in A. Vingerhoets, I. Nyklíček, and J. Denollet (eds.), *Emotion Regulation: Conceptual and Clinical Issues*, Springer, New York, pp. 140-149.

Rolls, E. T. (2005), "What Are Emotions, Why Do We Have Emotions, and What Is Their Computational Basis in the Brain?", in J.-M. Fellous and M. A. Arbib (eds.), *Who Needs Emotions? The Brain Meets the Robot*, Oxford University Press, New York, pp. 117-146.

Rottenberg, J. and Vaughan, C. (2008), "Emotion Expression in Depression: Emerging Evidence for Emotion Context-Insensitivity", in A. Vingerhoets, I. Nyklíček, and J. Denollet (eds.), *Emotion Regulation: Conceptual and Clinical Issues*, Springer, New York, pp. 125-139.

270

Rozin, P., Lowery, L., Imada, S., and Haidt, J. (1999), "The CAD Triad Hypothesis: A Mapping between Three Moral Emotions (Contempt, Anger, Disgust) and Three Moral Codes (Community, Autonomy, Divinity)", *Journal of Personality and Social Psychology* 76, pp. 574-586.

Sainsbury, R. M. (1999), "Concepts without Boundaries", in R. Keefe and P. Smith (eds.), *Vagueness: A Reader*, MIT Press, Cambridge, London, pp. 251-264.

Salmon, M. (2007), *Introduction to Logic and Critical Thinking*, Thomson Wadsworth, Belmont, fifth edition.

Sartre, J.-P. (1957), *Existentialism and Human Emotions*, The Wisdom Library, New York.

Schachter, S. and Singer, J. (1962), "Cognitive, Social and Physiological Determinants of Emotional States", *Psychological Review* 69, pp. 379-399.

Schuetzwohl, A. (2008), "The Intentional Object of Romantic Jealousy", *Evolution and Human Behavior* 29, pp. 92-99.

Shapiro, S. (2006), *Vagueness in Context*, Clarendon Press, Oxford.

Seligman, M. E. P. (1992), *Helplessness: On Depression, Development, and Death*, W. H. Freeman, New York.

Sizer, L. (2000), "Towards a Computational Theory of Mood", *British Journal for the Philosophy of Science* 51, pp. 743-769.

Sloman, A. (2002), "How Many Separately Evolved Emotional Beasties Live within Us?", in R. Trappl, P. Petta, and S. Payr (eds.), *Emotions in Humans and Artifacts*, MIT Press, Cambridge, pp. 35-114.

Sloman, A., Chrisley, R., and Scheutz, M. (2005), "The Architectural Basis of Affective States and Processes", in J.-M. Fellous and M. A. Arbib (eds.), *Who Needs Emotions? The Brain Meets the Robot*, Oxford University Press, New York, pp. 203-244.

Smyth, J., Nazarian, D., and Arigo, D. (2008), "Expressive Writing in the Clinical Context", in A. Vingerhoets, I. Nyklíček, and J. Denollet (eds.), *Emotion Regulation: Conceptual and Clinical Issues*, Springer, New York, pp. 215-233.

Solano, L., Bonadies, M., and di Trani, M. (2008), "Writing for All, for Some, or for No One? Some Thoughts on the Applications and Evaluations of the Writing Technique", in A. Vingerhoets, I.

Nyklíček, and J. Denollet (eds.), *Emotion Regulation: Conceptual and Clinical Issues*, Springer, New York, pp. 234-246.

Solomon, R. (1979), "Paul Ricoeur on Passion and Emotion", in C. E. Reagan (ed.), *Studies in the Philosophy of Paul Ricoeur*, Ohio University Press, Athens, pp. 2-20.

Solomon, R. (1993), *The Passions*, Hackett, Indianapolis.

Solomon, R. (2007), *True to our Feelings: What our Emotions Are Really Telling Us*, Oxford University Press, New York.

Sorensen, R. (1985), "An Argument for the Vagueness of 'Vague'", *Analysis* 27, pp. 134-137.

Sorensen, R. A. (1998), "Self-Strengthening Empathy", *Philosophy and Phenomenological Research* 58, pp. 75-98.

Sorensen, R. (2001), *Vagueness and Contradiction*, Clarendon Press, Oxford.

Spitzer, R. (1974), *Task Force on Nomenclature and Statistics*, meeting of September 4, 5, 1974 in New York, APA Archives, Professional Affairs, box 17, folder 188.

Strange, B. A. and Dolan, R. J. (2006), "Anterior Medial Temporal Lobe in Human Cognition: Memory for Fear and the Unexpected", in A. Aleman, N. Medford, and A. S. David (eds.), *The Cognitive Neuropsychiatry of Emotion and Emotional Disorders*, Psychology Press, Hove, New York, pp. 198-218.

Stricker, G. (1967), "A Pre-Experimental Inquiry Concerning Cognitive Determinants of Emotional State", *Journal of General Psychology* 76, pp. 73-79.

Swartz, C. M. and Shorter, E. (2007), *Psychotic Depression*, Cambridge University Press, New York.

Tomkins, S. (1963), *Affect, Imagery, Consciousness: The Negative Affects*, vol. 2, New York, Springer.

Tranel, D. (2000), "Electrodermal Activity in Cognitive Neuroscience: Neuroanatomical and Neuropsychological Correlates", in R. D. Lane and L. Nadel (eds.), *Cognitive Neuroscience of Emotion*, Oxford University Press, New York, Oxford, pp. 192-224.

Tranel, D., Gullickson, G., Koch, M. and Adolphs, R. (2006), "Altered Experience of Emotion Following Bilateral Amygdala Damage", in A. Aleman, N. Medford, and A. S. David (eds.), *The Cognitive*

272

Neuropsychiatry of Emotion and Emotional Disorders, Psychology Press, Hove, New York, pp. 219-232.

Tree of Life Web Project (1995), "Arachnida: Spiders, Mites, Scorpions, Whipscorpions, Pseudoscorpions", Version 01 January 1995 (temporary), on-line at http://tolweb.org/Arachnida/2536/1995.01.01, in *The Tree of Life Web Project*, on-line at http://tolweb.org/.

Tree of Life Web Project (2007), "Eudyptula Minor: Fairy Penguin, Little Penguin", Version 21 March 2007 (temporary), on-line at http://tolweb.org/Eudyptula_minor/57252/2007.03.21, in *The Tree of Life Web Project*, on-line at http://tolweb.org/.

Truax, S. R. (1984), "Determinants of Emotion Attributions: A Unifying View", *Motivation and Emotion* 8, pp. 33-54.

Tucker, A. (2004), *Our Knowledge of the Past: A Philosophy of Historiography*, Cambridge University Press, Cambridge.

Tversky, A. and Kahneman, D. (1983), "Extension versus Intuitive Reasoning: The Conjunction Fallacy in Probability Judgment", *Psychological Review* 90, pp. 293-315.

Van Dijke, A. (2008), "The Clinical Assessment and Treatment of Trauma-Related Self and Affect Dysregulation", in A. Vingerhoets, I. Nyklíček, and J. Denollet (eds.), *Emotion Regulation: Conceptual and Clinical Issues*, Springer, New York, pp. 150-169.

Van Heck, G. and den Oudsten, B. (2008), "Emotional Intelligence: Relationships to Stress, Health, and Well-being", in A. Vingerhoets, I. Nyklíček, and J. Denollet (eds.), *Emotion Regulation: Conceptual and Clinical Issues*, Springer, New York, pp. 97-121.

Van Honk, J. and Schutter, D. J. L. G. (2006), "Unmasking Feigned Sanity: A Neurobiological Model of Emotion Processing in Primary Psychopathy", in A. Aleman, N. Medford, and A. S. David (eds.), *The Cognitive Neuropsychiatry of Emotion and Emotional Disorders*, Psychology Press, Hove, New York, pp. 285-306.

Varzi, A. (2003), "Higher-Order Vagueness and the Vagueness of 'Vague'", *Mind* 112, pp. 295-298.

Wenzlaff, R., Rude, S., and West, L. (2002), "Cognitive Vulnerability to Depression", *Cognition and Emotion* 16, pp. 533-548.

Wesselius, C. L. and de Sarno, J. V. (1983), "The Anatomy of a Hostage Situation", *Behavioral Sciences and the Law* 1, pp. 33-45.

Williamson, T. (1994), *Vagueness*, Routledge, London, New York.

Williamson, T. (1999), "Vagueness and Ignorance", in R. Keefe and P. Smith (eds.), *Vagueness: A Reader*, MIT Press, Cambridge, London, pp. 265-280.

Marion Ledwig

God's Rational Warriors
The Rationality of Faith Considered

This book stands in the tradition of philosophers who advance the rationality of faith. Yet this book goes beyond their accounts, for it not only defends the view that faith can be termed rational, but it also considers the different senses in which faith can be termed rational. While this book advances the idea that faith as a general category can be termed rational, it does not investigate in a detailed way whether there are arguments for the rationality of particular faiths which would go beyond the arguments for the rationality of faith as a general category. Besides discussing whether betting on God in Pascal's wager and believing in miracles are forms of the rationality of faith, I will provide unique solutions to the problem of evil and the paradoxes of omnipotence and omniscience.

About the author

Marion Ledwig is currently visiting assistant professor at the University of Nevada, Las Vegas. She has studied psychology and philosophy at the University of Bielefeld, Germany, and received her Ph.D. in philosophy from the University of Konstanz, Germany. Her main interests are the philosophy of Thomas Reid, decision theory, emotion theory, philosophy of religion, and aesthetics. She is the author of "Reid's Philosophy of Psychology" (2005), "Emotions: Their Rationality and Consistency" (2006), and "Common Sense: Its History, Method, and Applicability" (2007).

ontos verlag

Frankfurt • Paris • Lancaster • New Brunswick

2008. 239pp.
Format 14,8 x 21 cm
Hardcover **EUR 79,00**
ISBN 13: 978-3-938793-87-9

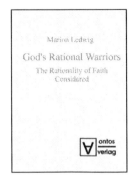

 ontos P.O. Box 1541 • D-63133 Heusenstamm bei Frankfurt
verlag www.ontosverlag.com • info@ontosverlag.com
Tel. ++49-6104-66 57 33 • Fax ++49-6104-66 57 34